INTEGRATIVE PROCESSES AND SOCIALIZATION
Early to Middle Childhood

CHILD PSYCHOLOGY

A series of books edited by **David S. Palermo**

INTEGRATIVE PROCESSES AND SOCIALIZATION:
Early to Middle Childhood

Edited by
Thomas D. Yawkey
James E. Johnson
The Pennsylvania State University

LEA LAWRENCE ERLBAUM ASSOCIATES, PUBLISHERS
1988 Hillsdale, New Jersey   Hove and London

Lawrence Erlbaum Associates, Inc., Publishers
365 Broadway
Hillsdale, New Jersey 07642

Library of Congress Cataloging-in-Publication Data

Integrative processes and socialization: early to middle childhood/
  edited by Thomas D. Yawkey, James E. Johnson.
     p. cm.
  Bibliography: p.
  Includes index.
  ISBN 0-89859-604-1
  1. Socialization. 2. Social integration. 3. Child psychology.
I. Yawkey, Thomas D. II. Johnson, James E. (James Ewald), 1947–
BF723.S62I57 1987
155.4'18—dc19   87–11879
                                             CIP

Printed in the United States of America
10 9 8 7 6 5 4 3 2 1

To professionals, from allied disciplines in the varied fields of human development, who are seeking additional understanding and insight into the developing child from an integrated processes and intersystems approach— this volume is herein dedicated.

Contents

6

7

8

List of Contributors

Elliott Asp   *School District 23, Colorado Springs, CO 80901*

Victor A. Christopherson   *Division of Child Development and Family Relations, University of Arizona, Tuscon, AZ 85721*

Debra Cochran   *Ninsonger Center, The Ohio State University, Columbus, OH 43210*

Walter Emmerich   *Senior Psychologist, Research Division, Educational Testing Service, Princeton, NJ 08541*

James Garbarino   *Erikson Institute, Chicago, IL 60610*

Jane Goldman   *Department of Child Development and Family Relations, University of Connecticut, Storrs, CT 06268*

Susan Harter   *Dept. of Psychology, University of Denver, Denver, CO 80208*

James E. Johnson   *College of Education, The Pennsylvania State University, University Park, PA 16802*

Linda Rose-Krasnor   *Department of Psychology, Brock University, Saint Catherine, Ontario, CANADA L25 3A4*

Karen Levine   *Department of Psychology, Boston University, 64 Cummington St., Boston, MA 02215*

Nina Mounts   *Child and Family Studies, University of Wisconsin, Madison, WI 53706*

Edward Mueller   *Department of Psychology, Boston University, 64 Cummington St., Boston, MA 02215*

Sherri Oden   *High/Scope Educational Research Foundation, Ypsilanti, MI 48198*

Jaipaul L. Roopnerine   *Child and Family Studies, Syracuse University, 200 Slocum Hall, Syracuse, NY 13210*

Myrna Shure   *Department of Mental Health Sciences, Hahnemann Medical College and Hospital, Philadelphia, PA 19102*

Thomas D. Yawkey   *Division of Curriculum and Instruction, Early Childhood Education, The Pennsylvania State University, University Park, PA 16802*

Preface

The social world of the developing child is an intriguing one—a world filled with challenges, discoveries, and barriers. In the past, we tended for the most part to view this social world partly through rather independent, separate windows. Traditional theories of personality and socialization processes focused largely on the role of the parent, particularly the mother. Social learning theories also focused on the roles of parents and significant others with personality development seen as outcomes of differential age- and gender-appropriate reinforcement. In contrast, cognitive theories emphasized representational capacities mediating social transactions between the child and caregivers.

In recent years many psychologists are employing constructs derived from cognitive developmental theories in viewing the social development during early and middle childhood. At present there is growing realization of the complexities of the developing child's social life and greater consideration of the multifaced set of influences that impact the child's social world.

This volume assumes that social integration takes place within interdependent and highly complex sets of systems—social, cognitive, biological, and technological. These define the developing child's social world with the child and the environment forming a reciprocal relation. The contributing authors focus on intrapersonal and interpersonal integration and socialization at early and middle childhood levels.

The volume is sectioned into four parts—all of which deal with integration. Each section has an overview that pulls together salient concepts and related ideas identified and discussed in its respective chapters. Section I provides the foundation for understanding intrapersonal and interpersonal processes and socialization. The need and rationale for focusing on integrative processes are discussed. The value of traditional theories are reconsidered in light of inter-system's approaches deemed central to a contemporary view of socialization processes. Sections II and III explore intrapersonal and interpersonal integrations, respectively. The development of self concept, social cognition, and play are viewed as forming intrapersonal integration. Socialization and integrative processes as the child moves from family to the peer group and into the school and community highlight interpersonal integrations. Finally, section IV stresses the integration of intrapersonal and interpersonal processes of the developing child in differing, related social contexts. Biological and social-behavioral phenomena, social and affective elements, communication, and individual differences in socialization are discussed.

The editors, authors, and publishers hope that this volume provides a greater insight into the complex nature of socialization and development in early and middle childhood.

Thomas D. Yawkey
James E. Johnson

Acknowledgments

The editors wish to express gratitude to a number of individuals who helped make this text possible.

Thomas D. Yawkey gratefully acknowledges the fertive ideas and insights of colleagues, Dr. Rimmert van der Kooij, Professor of Special Education, The University of Groningen, The Netherlands; and Dr. Detlef H. Rost, Professor of Experimental Psychology, the University of Marburg, West Germany; generated from our discussions on socialization and children held in Marburg during the Summer of 1982. These interactive, productive dialogues resulted in the concept of an international textbook aimed at exploring institutions and processes through which children become socialized (e.g., communication, play, school, family). Unfortunately, the concept of such an international treatment of the subject did not grow into a published text. This author, however, owes them much gratitude for these group discussions and their insightful ideas that provided the impetus for this volume. In turn, he wishes to thank sincerely James E. Johnson for his conceptualizations on anchoring this text within evolving human ecological systems and insightful social context perspectives for viewing the complex world of the developing child and for his diligent and numerous thoughtful contributions that helped shape this entire text.

James E. Johnson wishes to acknowledge Carolyn U. Shantz, his former dissertation advisor, for her lasting influence on his thinking about complex and controversial topics and for her encouragement to continue to seek greater understanding of the same. He also wishes to thank Anthony Pellegrini of the University of Georgia and James Christie of the University of Kansas for their reading of an earlier draft of the chapter "Play and Integration." Thomas D. Yawkey and James E. Johnson together extend their gratitude to Cecil R. Trueblood,

Head of the Division of Curriculum and Instruction, for his commitment to support early education projects such as the one represented here. In addition, they wish to express their sincere appreciation to the contributors of the chapters of this book for their excellent work and patience in seeing this volume come to fruition.

Foreword

In natural science . . . there is nothing petty to the mind that has a large vision of relations, and to which every single object suggests a vast sum of conditions. It is surely the same with the observations of human life.
—George Eliot
The Mill on the Floss (1860)

In this book, authors explore topics as diverse as play, diet, social cognition, self-concept, friendship, family, and school. It is evident to the reader that the "large vision of relations" and the "vast sum of conditions" that we observe in human life cannot be reduced to simple equations. Rather, the task at hand is to examine the interdependence of the various conditions and relations in the hope of gaining a more authentic understanding of integration and socialization.

Although the study of integrative processes and socialization has been important to child psychologists for many decades, the questions addressed and the methods employed have changed over time. Guided by the notion that development was something that happened *to* children as a result of biology or socializing agents, the earliest researchers examined antecedent-consequent conditions and temporal patterns. The correlation between certain maternal behaviors and child competencies was a popular focus of study. When the 1970s ushered in a concern for the father as a socializer, the same dyadic models were applied to paternal behaviors. Another approach was to examine deviant behaviors and try to determine how the socializing agent failed.

A separate group of researchers focused on the role of biology and maturation, carefully mapping out developmental stages and suggesting individual differences that might be attributed to genotype. This approach helped explain how development proceeded in a normative fashion even in the face of less than optimal environmental conditions.

After years of assuming that the mechanism of developmental change was unidirectional (i.e., from adult to child), children's influence on others and their environments was finally recognized. Related to this current emphasis was growing interest in the child's cognitive processes. Viewing children as active participants in their own integration and socialization was an important breakthrough, but it was not until a human ecological model was put forward that the complexity of interdependence of developmental systems was considered. While this emphasis on the multiple contexts of human development was intuitively appealing, the methods of inquiry appeared overwhelming. How can the researcher take into account all of the factors directly and indirectly affecting development? Obviously, a single study or theoretical approach cannot accomplish this task. Rather, it is the sharing of information gleaned from many studies on different aspects of the human experience that will help us understand overlapping developmental systems.

The book indicates that many of the false divisions of the past are being erased. The psychologists, sociologists, ethologists, and biologists are talking to each other and are paying attention to what is said. There is now a recognition that there is not one correct way to study child development and that information from multiple perspectives is necessary. Heredity, learning, imitation, cognitive structures—none of these mechanisms by itself is *the* necessary and sufficient condition that explains socialization and integration.

In the past, there have also been false divisions drawn between developmental domains. Those who studied social development were not interested in cognitive or physical development. Those who studied schools were not interested in the family. Those who studied innate predispositions were not interested in how these factors interacted with the environment. These divisions ignored the interrelatedness of human experience and neglected the interdependent of developmental domains. Similarly, the relationship between socialization and other integrative processes has been considered only in recent times. We are finally recognizing the possibility that the multiple mechanisms involved in development act in relation to one another.

It is refreshing that this volume deals with integrative processes from birth through middle childhood. Earlier studies neglected the continuity of behaviors across the life span by looking too closely at what an individual was doing at a particular point in time. Our knowledge of the preschool child's social and cognitive world is certainly enhanced by an understanding of the integrative products and processes previously experienced by the child. Similarly, if we look forward to the developmental issues that lie ahead in middle childhood, we find clues about what the preschool child is currently experiencing. It is reasonable to assume that where one is going bears some relation to where one is now.

This book indicates that a community of scholars has accepted the challenge of hammering out new paradigms. Past practices of examining a limited domain with microscopic precision provided detail that could have been obscured by a more panoramic view, but it also ignored developmental continuity and social interrelatedness. In contrast, today's study of integrative processes and socialization is viewing human experience with wide-angle lens in the hope of understanding the multiple sources of influence in the child's life.

Carole Martin
Somerset, New Jersey

Development and Context

Thomas D. Yawkey
The Pennsylvania State University

The chapters in this section overview human development and social context and provide an orientation to research issues and evaluation in applied social developmental programs. As such, the overview becomes a foundation for integrative processes of the developing child at early and middle childhood levels. Of major interest is the examination of multiple, interdependent sources and conceptual theories from traditional and more contemporary cognitive traditions that provide a necessary set of understandings underlying integrative processes. Growth of interest about the developing child's integrative processes is emerging because of the concern that the child's social world is more complex and expansive than originally perceived. Also, researchers are currently recognizing cognitive theories that have attempted to explore socialization in early to middle childhood in rather theory-specific ways.

Roopnarine, Cochran, and Mounts view traditional psychological theories and orientations to socialization as fertile ground for reconceptualizing the socialization of the child. They begin by surveying major and pertinent conceptual frameworks on cognitive and social development in early to middle childhood. Then, through reconceptualization they include factors and discuss integrative issues that add to further understanding and insight into socialization based on previous frameworks.

Roopnarine, Cochran, and Mounts, in discussing several key elements in socialization processes in order to extend understand-

1

ings regarding developmental change, reconsider the ethological approach to cognitive-social functioning. They recommend coupling the ethological approach in examining relations between intelligence and social behavior with perspectives suggesting that cognitive skills and social behaviors are reciprocally related through the life span. Hence, they propose an interrelated and interactive approach that takes into account covariation between cognitive, social and biological functioning in order to provide a more comprehensive understanding of socialization processes in the developing child.

Also, and at another level of recommendation, they examine whether concordance exists among socialization systems. Although little information currently exists on the relationships among various agents of socialization in the developing child, they propose an intersystem's approach in which consideration is given to multiple, interdependent sources influencing children's lives. Here, developmental consequences of social competence in one socialization system become predicators of behavioral adaptation in other systems. They propose a model that includes complex environmental factors both internal and external to the child which is set within interactive forces of cognitive, social, and biological development. This becomes a workable referent in attempting to explicate interactive processes of socialization among simultaneously changing systems.

Finally, Roopnarine, Cochran, and Mounts consider factors of stability and predictability in socialization. Based on the increasing need to examine interrelatedness of and reciprocal influences within major socialization systems, different methodological approaches are needed to examine stability of behavioral changes within and across childhood. To this end, they propose the use of several structural models to assess behavioral change using the time-lag behavior-environment and synchronous behavior-environment series. Both take into account organism-environment interactions. They note that these models address themselves to consistency and stability in behavioral observations and to the relationship between proximal and distal factors. For empirical purposes these structural models lend themselves well to path-analyses. Examining stability and predictability in behavioral adaptation using complex and interactive systems would, they feel, enhance understanding of integrative processes in socialization during early and middle childhood.

Shure addresses interrelated issues focusing on prevention research, evaluation and program application of interest in applied developmental psychology. She begins the chapter by noting that if we assume prevention of emotional/behavioral problems of atypical children are pertinent goals then the means for reaching these goals must be more clearly mapped. Shure identifies three main issues fundamental to prevention research: choice of research and intervention, subtleties of scientific and practical aspects of evaluation, and research as a service to applied programs and their clients—before, during, and after program implementation. In addressing these issues, Shure uses her own research on Interpersonal Cognitive Problem Solving (ICPS) skills as pertinent examples and as a vehicle for those interested in socialization processes and prevention research.

In addressing the issue of choice of research and intervention strategies in prevention research, Shure notes that researchers can design studies that contribute to identifying and reducing behavioral/emotional risks at early and middle childhood by building them on theory and methodology while at the same time recognizing their limitations. For example, in initial development of research studies, Shure and her associates found that mutually ICPS skills of alternative solution, consequential and casual thinking appeared to be mediators of impulsivity, inhibition and prosocial behaviors and that ultimately and after continued investigation two were substantiated. The next level of prevention research she notes is actually testing the validity of the theory of prevention research through experimental manipulation (e.g., ICPS intervention strategies). Further, prevention research should also address choice of intervention strategies and practical considerations such as whether the program could be implemented in schools/agencies.

In addressing the second issue concerning subleties of evaluation, she views evaluation of program impacts as critical as valid theory and methodology in identifying and treating "at risk" children with social problems. By carefully considering data interpretations, evaluation methodology, replication, and implementation, programs have the potential for wider applicability and more effective utilization. For example, in developing and implementing the ICPS skills program, Shure acknowledges that theory should guide evaluations and interpretations of program outcomes and further examination and reexamination of the data. The outcomes of the linkages between theory, evaluation and theory based reassessment of data provide for greater validity of the program by checking on conclusions.

Program methodology plays a vital role in identifying and controlling potential spurious factors that create confounds in data interpretation. Providing for built-in validity checks such as the use of independent raters in the ICPS skills program are imperative for program validity. Also, she notes that evaluation methodology is guided by practical considerations of replication and implementation. These considerations focus on intervention as research and include interpretation of procedures by the replicator/implementor for example, the length and intensity of the training.

Finally, the third issue addressed in the chapter is that of research as a service—before, during, and after intervention. Research as a service before program development should account for the needs of different groups connected in varying degrees with the intervention program. As examples from the ICPS skills program, research services were used to meet the needs of administrators who desired staff training, the teachers who were most concerned about classroom management and variety in daily teaching and the children about "feeling good" and "being smart." During the research phase and from the ICPS skills services' perspective, attention was given to further refinement of techniques, supervision of training-agents, and continued contact with the teachers' supervisors. After the effect of intervention program is evaluated and potential validity is assessed and cross-checked, providing feedback relevant to the needs of different groups connected with the intervention, according to Shure, is the most important immediate post research consideration. Within intervention research, this is regarded as pure research service delivery. Using the ICPS program as an example, training workshops were given and print materials about the program addressing preresearch concerns were distributed to administrators, teachers, and parents.

Lastly, Shure argues that for intervention research, additional steps are in order to insure answers to program validity and solve related questions. For example, these questions might include: "Who did the program intervention really help?" "How did it help?" "How long would it take to help still more clients?", and "How long does the impact last?"

Traditional Psychological Theories and Socialization During Middle and Early Childhood: An Attempt at Reconceptualization

1

Jaipaul L. Roopnarine
Syracuse University

Debbie Cochran
Ohio State University

Nina S. Mounts
University of Wisconsin

If one were to attempt to group the major theories that have considered the processes of socialization during childhood, one would find two basic categories: those that have specifically dealt with parent–child (mother–child for the most part) relationships (e.g., psychoanalytic, attachment, social learning, and reciprocal role) and those that have espoused behavioral changes from a cognitive-developmental perspective (e.g., Piaget, and Charlesworth). Our goal is to present brief overviews of the theories in accord with these two global categories. *The focus is on the stages or phases that deal with socialization during early and middle childhood.*

We begin with the very traditional perspectives, because they have laid the foundations for the development of other theories of socialization. We then examine how the cognitive theorists have explained behavioral change. Note that contemporary cognitive psychologists (e.g., Shantz, 1983) have embarked on the study of social–cognitive processes. We then present some alternative perspectives on socialization in early and middle childhood.

PARENT–CHILD PERSPECTIVES

Psychoanalytic Approach

The earliest and perhaps the most comprehensive theory of psychosexual development was formulated by Freud (1905, 1962). The psychoanalytic theory, rooted in biology, proposed a developmental sequence of stages that all individuals pass through during early and middle childhood. The developmental

5

stages—oral, anal, phallic–urethral, latency, and genital—are marked by their specific reference to particular erogenous zones of the body. During the first two stages, the oral and the anal, children form attachments to and identify primarily with their mothers. The mother is viewed as the primary love object and the source of warmth and nurturance.

Although "mother love" was emphasized during the first few years of life, Freud (1905, 1962) placed a good deal of importance on the resolution of the Oedipal and Electra complexes during the late preschool years. At about age 6, the beginning of the phallic stage, boys and girls notice the anatomical differences between the sexes. Freud suggested that when boys discover that girls do not have penises, they reason that girls once possessed them but that they were cut off. Boys interpret this as proof of what might happen to them. Because the boy's primary love object is the mother, he perceives the father as a competitor for the mother's love and fears that his father, viewing him as a rival, may castrate him. Realizing that he cannot conquer the father to win the mother, however, the young boy represses his sexual desires for the mother and identifies with the strength and authority of the father. Through identification with the father, the aggressive parent, the boy acquires masculine behaviors.

By comparison, when the little girl discovers that boys have a penis and she does not, she feels cheated and disappointed. Consequently, she turns away from the mother blaming her for the lack of a penis. Because the mother is perceived as the one responsible for sending her ill equipped into the world, the young girl transfers her love to the father. Despite this, she realizes that her desires for the father cannot be fulfilled and once again identifies with the mother whose love she cannot afford to lose (Freud, 1905, 1962). The wish for a penis is replaced by the desire to have children.

During the latency stage, that spans from roughly 5 years to puberty, the sexual drives and fantasies are repressed, and the child through play and school-related activities learns about the cultural mores of its society. Cognitive growth quickens, and social relationships with extrafamilial agents such as peers and teachers become important.

Freud's (1905, 1962) emphasis on psychosexual development during the early and middle childhood periods and the processes through which children achieve identification with same-sex parents have been criticized by several social scientists (Lamb, 1978). First, many aspects of Freud's theory cannot be tested empirically because the exact nature of the processes that children engage in to switch affiliation and identification from one parent to the next is not very clear. This very ambiguous state of affairs would obscure attempts to operationally define personality constructs associated with the resolution of the Electra and Oedipal complexes. Second, recent investigations have demonstrated that children form attachments to both mothers and fathers during the first year of life (Lamb, 1976, 1977, 1978). This evidence seriously challenges the validity of the psychoanalytic perspective because Freud proposed that both boys and girls are initially and primarily attached to their mother. Moreover, Lamb's (1982a,b) findings suggest that children are attached to fathers far sooner than Freud predicted, and that fathers are active participants in socialization during infancy. Finally, as Lamb (1978) and others have noted, Freud's theory is blatantly sexist. Historically, Freud's propositions have been used to justify the differing statuses of men and women in society and to confirm traditional division of parental roles (Millett, 1970). Thus, whereas his propositions were innovative, they assumed the appropriateness of the status quo.

In view of the problems associated with psychoanalytic theory, the tremendous impact it had in explaining social and personality development has waned immensely. Today, few social scientists believe that the psychoanalytic perspective adequately accounts for the process of psychosocial development during the early and middle childhood periods. Nonetheless, the theory served as a springboard for the development of some aspects of feminist thinking (see Chodorow, 1978).

The Eriksonian Approach

The Eriksonian approach added tremendously to and in some respects modified Freud's psychosexual notion of personality development during early and middle childhood. Unlike Freud, however, Erikson (1950) concentrated on the development of identity. This life-span theory of psychosocial development espoused that the individual strives for continuity in its personal character and attempts to achieve and maintain an "inner solidarity" based on certain cultural ideals. Identity is transformed as the individual moves from one stage to the next, and earlier forms of identity lay the foundation for and influence later personality developments.

Erikson's early stages of development are quite similar to those outlined by Freud. Thus, Erikson focused on the development of trust with the mother during infancy. Through sensitive care given by the mother, the child develops a sense of personal trustworthiness. Mistrust is viewed as necessary in order to detect honest from dishonest persons. Generally, if the child is mistrustful of others, this can lead to feelings of frustration, withdrawal, suspicion, and lack of self-confidence later on. During toddlerhood, the development of autonomy is paramount. The sense of autonomy is shaped by the cultural mores of one's society as expressed through parents. It is assumed that parents who provide a supportive social environment will enable their children to develop self-control without hampering their self-esteem.

During the early and middle childhood periods, the child "finds out what kind of person he or she is going to be." First, from about 4 to 5 years, Erikson placed primary emphasis on identification with parents. He believed that the processes involved in the resolution of the Oedipal complex, as outlined by Freud, can also lead to the development of a conscience, new interests and attitudes, and sex-stereotypic behaviors. Initiatives to explore the social roles and objects in the immediate environment are aided by increasing competence in language and cognition, mobility, and the ability to engage in fantasy. However, because development during the stage can range from successful initiative to overwhelming guilt, children face the danger of getting into modes of functioning that involve constantly proving one's worth as an individual.

Between age 6 and puberty, the child enters the industrious stage. The child acquires knowledge through schooling and interactions with friends. Meaningful experiences that lead to mastery of particular skills give the child a sense of industry, whereas failure in achieving competence can lead to feelings of inadequacy and inferiority. This stage is marked by relative calm. The sense of trust, autonomy, and initiative prepares the child for entry into a complex society.

Like the Freudian perspective regarding development during early and middle childhood, it is often difficult to empirically test Erikson's abstract ideas. It is often difficult to ascertain continuity in development between stages. How do children move from one stage to the next? Finally, the primary importance placed on the mother–child relationship minimizes the contributions of fathers.

Reciprocal-Role Theory

As in the psychoanalytic perspective, reciprocal-role theory stresses the acquisition of social skills and gender-role identification through parental socialization. Reciprocal-role theory is attributed to the work of Parsons (Parsons & Bales, 1955). According to Parsons, socialization of children occurs through the internalization of the cultural norms within which the individual is born. Such socialization takes place within a markedly sex-delineated system—the nuclear family. The nuclear family, a microcosm of the larger society, contains a husband–wife dyad and two children. Within the nuclear family, Parsons proposed that the husband is expected to assume the instrumental, task-oriented roles, whereas the wife is expected to assume the emotional, sensitive, expressive roles. The woman's sensitivity is best suited for child rearing, whereas the man, the supposed link between the family system and the larger social system, is responsible for teaching his family the mores, values, and customs of the general social structure. Children learn behaviors and roles through observation and interactions with members of each sex. Girls, for example, learn female roles— sensitivity and nurturance—by observing and interacting with their mothers. Interactions with the father, meanwhile, provide the young girl with opportunities to practice the behavioral skills she leaned from her mother. In this context, her behaviors are scrutinized and corrected.

Presumably, the process of socialization and the acquisition of male-oriented behaviors are less routine and more difficult for boys than girls, because girls need only to continue their identification with their mothers whereas boys must renounce their initial identification with their mothers and identify with their fathers. This switch is motivated by parental insistence that the boy relinquish his strong reliance on the mother (Parsons & Bales, 1955). During the transition period, the father gradually becomes the new instrumental figure and, through his role as disciplinarian, increases his demands for achievement-oriented goals in his son. The mother is now seen as the primary source of emotional sensitivity. As the boy internalizes these roles, he becomes less "mother-centered" and more "family-centered" (Rosenberg & Sutton-Smith, 1972).

Reciprocal-role theory shares some of the same drawbacks that were noted for the psychoanalytic perspective. In addition to minimizing the father's role in the development of boys before the preschool years, reciprocal-role theory obviously cannot deal with the changing social structure of families. The political, social, and economic changes that have occured within the last two decades have witnessed dramatic increases in single parenthood and dual-career families. These family structures often contain female breadwinners and heads of households. Thus, both boys and girls are exposed to authoritative models that are quite different from the traditional ones outlined by Parsons and Bales (1955). It is likely, and indeed highly probable, that these structural changes would exert different types of influences on the social development of young children. Researchers (e.g., Hetherington, 1979; Rapoport & Rapoport, 1971) have begun the massive task of delineating the influence of structural changes on socialization practices, and we are close to providing concrete evidence for major reconceptualizations of theories in general.

Social-Learning Theory

Due to the difficulty encountered in proving or disproving Freud's theory, observational learning theorists maintain that the psychoanalytic approach to psychosocial development is inadequate in explaining the process of social and personality development. Some learning theorists (Maccoby & Jacklin, 1974; Mischel, 1966) believe that parents and significant other adults in children's lives shape social development by rewarding or praising behaviors tha are considered appropriate for a given sex, while punishing o discouraging behaviors that are inappropriate for a given sex. These theorists suggest that parents might reward assertive, aggressive behaviors and ignore submissive types of behaviors in sons. Similarly, they might encourage and reward submissive, nurturant, and dependent behaviors and punish aggressive behaviors in their daughters.

Although the evidence regarding the differential treatment of boys and girls is inconclusive, we know that parents have sex-typed expectations regarding the socialization of boys and girls. Such differential socialization seems to begin at birth. For instance, fathers describe their newborn girls as being smaller, softer, and more delicate than do fathers of newborn boys. Fathers of newborn boys, meanwhile, describe them as being larger and more active than do fathers of newborn girls (Rubin, Provenzano, & Luria, 1974). Parents, furthermore, dress boys and girls differently and provide them with different toys (see Rheingold & Cook, 1975). Other evidence indicates that fathers are more likely to initiate physical and idiosyncratic games with their infants than mothers do (Lamb,

1977). These patterns of socialization become more accentuated as children confront societal values within the family and in the peer group during the early and middle childhood periods (see Langlois & Down, 1980; Roopnarine, 1984).

One other method whereby children acquire important social behaviors is through the process of imitation or identification with a model (Bandura & Walters, 1963; Sears, Rau, & Alpert, 1965). Both psychoanalytic and observational learning theorists propose that boys and girls initially imitate their mothers because they are the primary caretakers in the early years. Girls continue to model their mother's behaviors whereas boys shift to identification with their fathers. To the observational learning theorists, the switch is motivated by the young boy's appraisal of the father's power and control over familial resources. This theory suggests that girls acquire behaviors that are appropriate for their own sex by modeling the behaviors of their mothers, whereas boys renounce their primary attachment figures and identify with the behaviors of their fathers. The processes, though, are influenced by several important factors.

First, Bandura, Ross, and Ross (1963) have demonstrated that children tend to imitate the behaviors of models who are more powerful and have control over resources. Second, the warmth and nurturance of models affect the degree to which they will be imitated (Bandura, 1977). Evidence regarding the importance of power, warmth, and nurturance of models on imitative behaviors has been presented (Hetherington, 1965, 1967; Mussen, 1961).

Despite the fact that social-learning theory has had a significant impact on research and theorizing about social development during early childhood, it suffers from one major limitation. The theory does not explain why girls choose not to imitate their fathers like boys do (Lamb, 1978). It is possible that mothers make themselves more available as models to daughters than to sons than fathers do and, therefore, encourage their daughters to identify with them. By contrast, fathers might make themselves more available to sons than to daughters than mothers do (cf. Lamb, 1977). Of course, this will depend on the traditionality of the parents.

Social-learning theory, however, underwent a major revision concerning the role of mental processes in social functioning (see Bandura, 1977). Despite the reformulation of social-learning theory to include internal rather than purely external approaches to the acquisition of social behaviors, the role of cognitive functioning still assumes an ancillary role in social development. To social-learning theorists, behaviors are still largely shaped by the environment. The specific role that cognition assumes in socialization remains largely undefined in the mechanistic school of thought.

Attachment Theory

Attachment theorists and researchers (Ainsworth, 1969; Bowlby, 1969) agree that it is the quality and consistency of parent–child relationships in the first few months of life that are crucially important for the formation of parent–child attachments. The predictability and reliability of the attachment figure(s) will largely determine the nature of the parent–child attachment relationships and perhaps thereby affect later relationships as well. Infants whose parents provide adequate care, warmth, and reassurance in their everyday interactions will develop secure relationships with parents. They can depend on their parents to be able and willing to respond to their signals when help is warranted (Lamb, 1978). These infants are more willing to explore and investigate various aspects of their surroundings and, as a result, may benefit from the extensive social interactions. By contrast, infants who cannot rely on their attachment figures lack "faith in the reliability and predictability" of their attachment figures (Lamb, 1978). They are often concerned about their parents' whereabouts, and their anxious behavioral patterns can interfere with other adaptive behavior (Ainsworth, Bell, & Stayton, 1974). Insecurely attached infants may become so engaged in assuring the presence of and proximity of their attachment figures that their exploration and social interactions may be negatively affected (Lamb, 1978).

Whereas attachment theory has been largely substantiated by observations of infants and toddlers, some evidence exists for its importance for the development of social competence during the preschool years. A number of researchers (Lieberman, 1977; Sroufe, 1983) have reported that security of attachment can predict social competence in preschool. Children who were securely attached as infants were ranked as having more friends and were nominated as being more popular in preschool. They were also more empathic toward peer distress. On the other hand, children who were insecurely attached as infants were less responsive to peer distress in preschool (Sroufe, 1983). Likewise, Lieberman (1977) has shown that peer competence was related to the mother–child relationship at home.

Attachment theory, though, has for the most part been concerned with infant development. Attempts to extend the theory to predict stability in the acquisition of early social skills have been rare (Bretherton & Waters, 1985; see volume by Parkes & Stevenson-Hinde, 1982). Moreover, the classification of infants into securely and insecurely attached groups has been controversial at best, and the validity of the "strange situation" procedure has been questioned for use with older children. For this theory to maintain its vigor as a viable tool for explaining the acquisition of social processes, especially during the preschool and school years, will require systematic observations of covariation of parent–child and peer relationships over long periods of time.

THE COGNITIVE PERSPECTIVES

Few theories have influenced the study of social cognition during early and middle childhood more than Piaget's (1970) theory of mental development. In Piaget's theory, development proceeds in a stage-like sequence and involves the transformations of cognitive structures. The transformation of structures is not a direct outcome of learning or maturation but rather a result of an individual's interaction with its environment. The organization of these structures will depend largely on how the individual perceives and learns from its experiences with others. The goal here is not to describe Piaget's theory in general, but an attempt is made to discuss how cognitive perspectives have influenced the study of role-taking skills, sex-stereotyped behaviors, and aspects of prosocial development.

A comprehensive model of role-taking perspective has been formulated by Selman (1976). His work was derived from children's responses to hypothetical stories and dilemmas in which different perspectives are presented via various characters. Selman (1976) found that five levels of role-taking abilities existed from about age 3 to 15 that are intimately tied to the developmental processes that occur during Piaget's preoperational and concrete operational stages of intellectual development. The acquisition of perspective-taking ability proceeds from egocentric notions of others' and one's own actions in early childhood toward coordinated perspectives in middle childhood. Perhaps as the child begins to develop an understanding of logical thought patterns, social awareness of others' intentions and the meaning of one's own behaviors become increasingly sophisticated.

A second example of an area of social development that has relied on cognitive-developmental theory to assist in the explanation of the emergence of social behaviors has been sex typing. Developmentalists such as Kohlberg (1966) and Emmerich (1973) believe that sex-role patterning during middle and early childhood is fundamentally due to the child's cognitive awareness of social-role concepts. The learning of these concepts is based on internally organized schemes of the child's perceptions of the social environment. It is argued that during the concrete operational thought period, children have a firm concept of gender constancy (Slaby & Frey, 1975; Thompson, 1975); that is, the child, through cognitive self-categorization, realizes that he or she is a boy or a girl and that such a categorization is irreversible. The judgments are made on the basis of physical properties that are like the self. Thus, little girls will categorize themselves and their mothers as females and will model the things females do. Likewise, boys will classify themselves as males and will identify with the things males do. Subsequently, children learn roles by imitating or identifying with the attitudes and behaviors that are characteristic of the models they have chosen (Mischel, 1970).

There is considerable impact of cognitive-developmental theory on the study of social constructs. Given the reciprocal relationship between cognitive and social functioning, theories of development should attempt to discuss the intermeshing of cognitive and social change temporally.

A Reconceptualization

As noted earlier, a number of the major theories of social development have been narrow in focus, some have ignored considerations of key agents of socialization in children's lives, whereas others have simply failed to acknowledge that cognitive functioning is intertwined with social development. The goal in this section is to discuss key elements in the socialization process during early and middle childhood that should serve as extensions of earlier notions regarding developmental change. As such, the notions presented can be viewed as a "re-conceptualization" of some well-established ideas that should better explain integrative processes during childhood.

The Ethological Approach to Cognitive-Social Functioning

Perhaps one of the most appealing perspectives on the acquisition of behavioral phenomenon has been presented by Charlesworth (1976). It is our contention that this approach is a viable one for conceptualizing behavioral change and adaptation. Although few studies have actually examined the acquisition of social processes from the ethological approach, this conceptual framework states that intelligence is acquired through learning that results as individuals interact with their environment. According to Charlesworth (1976), the acquisition of intelligence that is largely responsible for intelligent behavior "takes place during *phylogenesis,* when the nervous system mechanisms responsible for intelligent behavior of a particular species are 'shaped' by the forces of natural and sexual selection that take place during the species' interaction with the environment" (p. 149). Intelligent behavior from Charlesworth's perspective has two major components: First, it is behavior that helps individuals to adapt to everyday problems that might result from imbalances in their social commerce with the environment. Adaptation from this approach would be reflected in the qualitative aspects of an individual's personal, social, material, and reproductive success. Thus, the ability of an individual to successfully reach a state of equilibration when problems in its environment threaten its physiological, physical, and social needs and perhaps its long-term survival would be highly indicative of intelligent behavior. The second component of intelligent behavior is that cognitive processes belie its organization. This essential link between cognition and intelligent behavior presumes that (a) "there are operations involved, such as comparing, recalling, separating, combining, analyzing, conceptualizing, and counting" (p. 150); (b) "there is the raw material such as long- and short-term memory traces, immediate perceptions or sensations, and other kinds of information upon which cognitive operations operate" (p. 150); (c) "there is an element of goal consciousness to intelligent behavior that sets it off from fortuitous behavior such as reflexes, fixed action patterns, and other instinctual acts which appear 'blind' and 'compelled'" (p. 150).

Thus, intelligent behavior is seen as being propelled by cognition that is used in the solution of environmental problems that pose a threat to the general welfare and long-range survival of the individual.

The study of the relationship between intelligence and social behavior within this framework is advantageous for two reasons. It could provide a more complete picture of how individuals, depending on their level of intellectual development, use social behaviors to confront problems within their everyday environment; it could provide an index of what behaviors might facilitate adaptation in terms of young children's interpersonal relationships. For example, high levels of derogation might not be consistent with high levels of thought and therefore, could affect the psychological well-being of the child. In a way, derogation is unintelligent behavior and could affect interpersonal adaptation.

The ethological perspective, coupled with the perspective presented by others, that cognitive skills and social behaviors are reciprocally related as development progresses through the life-span (see Emmerich, Cocking, & Sigel, 1979; Hoffman, 1975), could lead to a broader model that incorporates cognitive and biological factors in the study of socialization. Researchers have begun the task of conceptualizing individual differences in terms of how cognitive functioning unfolds over time as the impact of environmental factors is mediated within the realm of intra and extrafamilial influences (see Wohlwill, 1979). Thus, future attempts to *revise* traditional theories will have to develop a conceptual framework that considers covariation between cognitive and social functioning. Gradients of behavioral change could be magnified in the acquisition of cognitive structures. It is often assumed that cognitive and biological changes are givens, and that the processes of socialization during childhood occur in harmony or disharmony by themselves. The simple model presented in Fig. 1.1 demonstrates the possible interrelatedness of the three factors that are key elements in the process of growth and development. Perhaps an anecdote would serve to drive

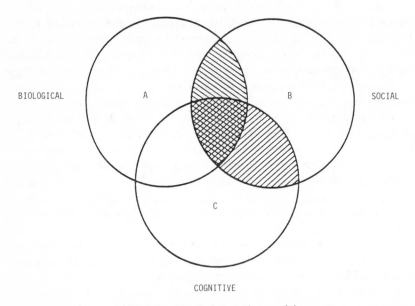

FIG. 1.1. Simple interactive model.

our point home. When presented with the various theories of sex-role development (biological, social, and cognitive), it is obvious to students of developmental psychology that each theory has something valid to offer, and that if the major
points of each theory were to be presented in concert, we would achieve a very
comprehensive understanding of sex-role development. As simplistic as this
approach may seem, it makes good sense.

Does Concordance Exist Among Socialization Systems?

Research and theorizing on socialization during early childhood have primarily
focused on parental or peer influences. Few attempts have been made to determine the relationship among the various agents of socialization in children's
lives. The dearth of information in this area is rather surprising because there is
reason to believe that concordance might exist among socialization systems
(Hartup, 1979). More importantly, the processes of socialization might be more
easily validated if we consider the multiple yet interdependent sources of influences in children's lives, and the developmental consequences of social competence in one socialization system might be a good predictor of the continuity or
discontinuity in behavioral adaptation in other systems (see Lamb & Roopnarine,
1979; Waters, Wippman, & Sroufe, 1979).

A growing body of research suggests that interdependencies exist among
socialization systems. For example, popularity in the peer group has been shown
to be related to child-rearing practices (Elkind, 1958; Peery, Jensen, & Adams,
1985; Winder & Rau, 1962; see Hartup, 1979, and Roopnarine & Honig, 1985
for reviews) and children's prosocial behaviors have been linked to parental
styles of functioning (Baumrind, 1967). Yet, the interrelated systems approach
toward understanding socialization during childhood is still largely ignored. For
instance, we know very little about the impact of marital relations, job satisfaction, and social-support networks on family functioning and children's interper-

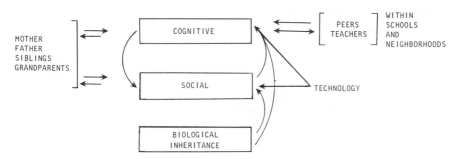

FIG. 1.2. Complex interactive model of major agents of socialization.

sonal relationships. Belsky (1984) has proposed a model in which all these factors are linked to a family's psychological well-being. The intersystem approach must be taken seriously if we are to tease out factors that are central to healthy personality development and to develop a more comprehensive understanding of social development. Our attempt at reconceptualization in terms of intersystems dynamics is presented in Fig. 1.2. The model is an extension of the one presented earlier. Thus, as stated before, we believe that a workable model should involve the exploration of complex environmental factors, internal and external to the child, within the interactive forces of cognitive, social, and physiological development. The goal facing developmental psychologists, then, is the description and explication of the interactive processes of socialization among simultaneously changing systems.

Stability and Predictability in Behavioral Adaptation

In any chapter on the consideration of theories of development, a discussion of stability and predictability of any phenomenon, in our case socialization, would almost always involve the treatment of how we optimize the estimation and prediction of theoretical claims. The major theories in general were initially grounded in the notion that adults shaped children's behaviors. Later (see Bell, 1968, see volume by Lewis & Rosenblum, 1974), we debated whether developmental change should be viewed in terms of unidirectionality as opposed to reciprocity. Although some theoretical conceptualizations have more recently acknowledged the need to examine the interrelatedness of major socialization systems and their reciprocal influences, efforts to examine the stability of behavioral change during early and middle childhood have been severely hampered by the lack of sound methodological approaches. As Labouvie (1974) pointed out and our own examinations of the current literature reveals, the experimental methods for the most part have been based on the static, unidirectional analysis of the variance model. Moreover, while correlational analyses have been appropriate for the assessment of change at a macroscopic level (see Wohlwill, 1973), it has proven to be inadequate for determining the causal structure among various indices of socialization (Labouvie, 1974).

In his methical explanation of structural models to assess behavioral change, Labouvie (1974) suggested two approaches that take into account organism–environment interactions—the asynchronous or time-lagged behavior–environment series and the synchronous behavior–environment series. We briefly describe his proposed models here because they could aid us tremendously in reshaping existing theoretical conceptualizations. In the asynchronous model, observations or assessments of behavioral and environmental variables are made alternatingly at different points in time over equally spaced periods. Figure 1.3, taken from Labouvie, demonstrates different configurations of the asynchronous model. All between-domain relationships are recursive. In Fig. 1.3a, only prox-

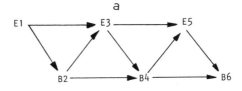

a

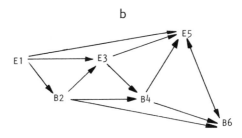

b

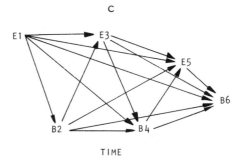

c

FIG. 1.3. Time lagged series of Behavioral (B) and Environmental (E) measures: within–between proximal (a), within–distal between proximal (b), and within–between distal (c). *Note.* From "Developmental causal structures of organism-environment interactions" by E. W. Labouvie, 1974, *Human Development, 17,* p. 444–452.

TIME

imal relationships are shown both between and within domains. Thus, the nature of the behavior and environment at time *1* would determine subsequent behavior–environment relationships. Figure 1.3b describes the between-domain proximal-within-domain distal model that assumes that antecedent–subsequent relationships are determined within domain, whereas 3c represents a between-domain distal-within-domain distal model.

Lastly, Fig. 1.4 shows the nonrecursive types that are similar to those in Fig. 1.3. These approaches allow simultaneous observations of both behavioral and environmental factors (Labouvie, 1974).

These models can allow us to determine consistency and stability in behavioral observations and the relationship between proximal and distal relationships over time. Furthermore, for empirical approaches concerned with multiple sets of influences, a path-analytical approach lends itself to concurrent and historical approaches to assessing behavioral change.

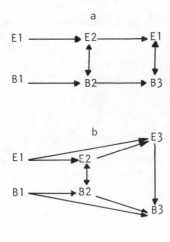

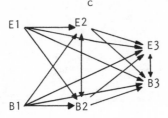

FIG. 1.4. Recursive-nonrecursive, simultaneous series of behavioral (B) and environmental (E) measure: within-between proximal (a), within distal-between proximal (b), and within-between distal (c).

Our attempt to examine the stability of behavioral development via complex interactive models can only enhance our understanding of integrative processes in socialization during middle and early childhood. We do realize that there are researchers who conduct systematic and painstaking investigations. Our research questions, however, have been guided by conceptual frameworks that are too narrowly focused.

A Word of Warning

The theories described herein and our attempt at reconceptualization generally refer to processes rather than to agents of socialization. The structures of families have changed tremendously during the last decade. (See Christopherson, this volume.) Single parent and dual-earner families have increased dramatically. But changes in the structural elements of families would eventually lead to changes in functions as well. Thus, contexts of stress and support will invariably affect socialization processes regardless of the structure of families. Theoretical orientations and conceptual models will undoubtedly be framed and reframed as the social and economic ecologies of families undergo various metamorphoses.

Traditional theories also do not appear to adequately explain the processes of development within atypical children. Nevertheless, it is our contention that some of the issues discussed earlier do bear on the development of atypical children. We discuss these issues in our other work (Roopnarine & Gregory, in preparation).

Summary

When we were asked to review the major theories and their views on social development during early and middle childhood, we felt somewhat uncomfortable in restating conceptual frameworks that have been expressed many times. As we studied our task, we hoped we would state those elements of the theories discussed earlier that were pertinent to socialization processes during early and middle childhood. We realized, however, that the theories that have served us so well in explaining developmental change in the past needed to expand with a changing field of study. Our criticisms and suggestions are by no means new. We have attempted to include factors and to discuss issues in the process of socialization that would *add,* via the substantiation mode, validity to notions that have already been studied. We hope we have achieved these goals.

To conclude, we have a few suggestions:

1. Existing theories must consider cognitive, social, and biological factors in concert. Thus, substantiation efforts would be soundly guided if patterns of covariation among these three domains are included in research thrusts.
2. Socialization occurs within a complex set of systems that include intrafamilial and extrafamilial members and technological gadgets. An attempt to look at the interrelatedness of biological, social, and cognitive factors as the child moves from one socialization system to the next would bring us closer to developing a truly integrative understanding of development in general.
3. Finally, predicting the stability of behavioral adaptation would be greatly enhanced if we were to look at development from a multifaceted interdependent approach.

ACKNOWLEDGMENTS

The first author acknowledges the support he received from the College for Human Development at Syracuse University and the W144 Project at Utah State University during the preparation of this chapter.

REFERENCES

Ainsworth, M. D. (1969). Object relations, dependency and attachment: A theoretical review of the infant-mother relationship. *Child Development, 40,* 969–1025.

Ainsworth, M. D. S., Bell, S., & Stayton, D. (1974). Infant–mother attachment and social development: "Socialisation" as a product of reciprocal responsiveness to signals. In M. P. M. Richards (Ed.), *The integration of the child into a social world* (pp. 99–135). Cambridge, England: Cambridge University Press.

Bandura, A. (1977). *Social learning theory.* Englewood Cliffs, NJ: Prentice–Hall.

Bandura, A., Ross, D., & Ross, S. (1963). Imitation of film-mediated aggressive models. *Journal of Abnormal and Social Psychology, 66,* 3–11.

Bandura, A., & Walters, R. H. (1963). *Social learning and personality development.* New York: Holt, Rinehart, & Winston.

Baumrind, D. (1967). Child care practices anteceding three patterns of preschool behavior. *Genetic Psychology Monographs, 75,* 43–88.

Bell, R. Q. (1968). A reinterpretation of the direction of effects in studies of socialization. *Psychological Review, 75,* 81–95.

Belsky, J. (1984). The determinants of parenting: A process model. *Child Development, 55,* 83–96.

Bowlby, J. (1969). *Attachment and loss. Vol 1: Attachment.* New York: Basic Books.

Bretherton, I. & Waters, E. (1985). Attachment theory: Retrospect and prospect. In I. Bretherton & E. Waters (Eds.), Growing points in attachment theory and research. *Monographs of the Society for Research in Child Development, 50,* (209, Nos. 1–2) 3–36.

Charlesworth, W. R. (1976). Human intelligence as adaptation: An ethological approach. In L. B. Resnick (Ed.), *The nature of intelligence* (pp. 147–168). Hillsdale, NJ: Lawrence Erlbaum Associates.

Chodorow, N. (1978). *The reproduction of mothering: Psychoanalysis and the sociology of gender.* Berkeley: University of California Press.

Elkind, D. (1958). Some factors related to the choice status of 90 eighth-grade children in a school society. *Genetic Psychology Monographs, 58,* 207–272.

Emmerich, W. (1973). Socialization and sex-role development. In P. B. Baltes & K. W. Schaie (Eds.), *Life-span developmental psychology: Personality and socialization* (pp. 124–143). New York: Academic Press.

Emmerich, W., Cocking, R., & Sigel, I. (1979). Relationships between cognitive and social functioning in preschool children. *Developmental Psychology, 15,* 494–504.

Freud, S. (1905, 1962). *Three essays on the theory of sexuality.* New York: Avon.

Hartup, W. W. (1979). The social worlds of childhood. *American Psychologist, 34,* 944–950.

Hetherington, E. M. (1965). A developmental study of the effects of sex of the dominant parent on sex-role preference, identification, and imitation in children. *Journal of Personality and Social Psychology, 2,* 188–194.

Hetherington, E. M. (1967). The effects of familial variables on sex-typing, on parent–child similarity, and on imitation in children. In J. P. Hill (Ed.), *Minnesota symposium on child psychology* (Vol. 1, pp. 82–107).

Hetherington, E. M. (1979). Divorce: A child's perspective. *American Psychologist, 34,* 851–858.

Hoffman, M. (1975). Developmental synthesis of affect and cognition and its implications for altruistic motivation. *Developmental Psychology, 11,* 607–622.

Kohlberg, L. (1966). A cognitive-developmental analysis of children's sex-role concepts and attitudes. In E. E. Maccoby (Ed.), *The development of sex differences* (pp. 82–173). Stanford: Stanford University Press.

Labouvie, E. W. (1974). Developmental causal structures of organism–environment interactions. *Human Development, 17,* 444–452.

Lamb, M. E. (1976). Effects of stress and cohort on mother- and father-infant interaction. *Developmental Psychology, 12,* 435–443.

Lamb, M. E. (1977). The development of parental preferences in the first two years of life. *Sex Roles, 3,* 495–497.

Lamb, M. E. (1978). Social interaction in infancy and the development of personality. In M. E. Lamb (Ed.), *Social and personality development* (pp. 26–49). New York: Holt, Rinehart, & Winston.

Lamb, M. E. (1982a). Early contact and maternal–infant bonding: One decade later. *Pediatrics, 70,* 763–768.

Lamb, M. E. (1982b). *The role of the father in child development.* New York: Wiley.

Lamb, M. E., & Roopnarine, J. L. (1979). Peer influences on sex-role development in preschoolers. *Child Development, 50,* 1219–1222.

Langlois, J. H., & Down, A. C. (1980). Mothers, fathers, and peers as socialization agents of sex-typed behaviors in young children. *Child Development, 51,* 1237–1247.

Lewis, M., & Rosenblum, L. A. (1974). *The effect of the infant on its caregiver.* New York: Wiley.

Lieberman, A. F. (1977). Preschoolers' competence with a peer: Relationship with attachment and peer experience. *Child Development, 48,* 1277–1287.

Maccoby, E. E., & Jacklin, C. N. (1974). The psychology of sex differences. Stanford, CA: Stanford University Press.

Millett, K. (1970). *Social politics.* New York: Doubleday.

Mischel, W. (1966). A social learning view of sex differences in behavior. In E. E. Maccoby (Ed.), *The development of sex differences* (pp. 56–81). Stanford, CA: Stanford University Press.

Mischel, W. (1970). Sex-typing and socialization. In P. H. Mussen (Ed.), *Carmichael's manual of child psychology* (3rd ed., Vol. 2, pp. 3–72). New York: Wiley.

Mussen, P. H. (1961). Some antecedents and consequences of masculine sex-typing in adolescent boys. *Psychological Monographs, 75*(506).

Parsons, T., & Bales, R. F. (1955). *Family socialization and interaction process.* Glencoe, IL: The Free Press.

Peery, D., Jensen, L., & Adams, G. (1985).Relationships between parent's attitudes regarding child rearing and the sociometric status of their preschool children. *Journal of Psychology, 119,* 567–574.

Piaget, J. (1970). Piaget's theory. In P. H. Mussen (Ed.), *Carmichael's manual of child development* (Vol. 2, pp. 703–732). New York: Wiley.

Rapoport, R., & Rapoport, R. N. (1971). *Dual career families.* Harmondsworth, England: Penguin Books.

Rheingold, H. L., & Cook, K. O. (1975). The contents of boys' and girls' rooms as an index of parents' behavior. *Child Development, 46,* 459–463.

Roopnarine, J. L. (1984). Sex-typed socialization in mixed-age preschool classrooms. *Child Development, 55,* 1078–1084.

Roopnarine, J. L., & Honig, A. S. (1985). Review of research: The unpopular child. *Young Children,* 56–64.

Roopnarine, J. & Gregory, S. (in prep.). Intervention and its effects: A major reconceptualization.

Rosenberg, B. G., & Sutton-Smith, B. (1972). *Sex and identity.* New York: Holt, Rinehart, & Winston.

Rubin, J. Z., Provenzano, F. J., & Luria, Z. (1974). The eye of the beholder: Parents' views of sex of newborns. *American Journal of Orthopsychiatry, 44,* 512–519.

Sears, R. R., Rau, L., & Alpert, R. (1965). *Identification and child rearing.* Stanford, CA: Stanford University Press.

Shantz, C. (1983). The development of social cognition. In J. Falvell & E. Markman (Eds.), *Handbook of child psychology* (pp. 495–555). New York: Wiley.

Slaby, R. G., & Frey, K. S. (1975). Development of gender constancy and selective attention to same-sex models. *Child Development, 46,* 849–856.

Sroufe, L. A. (1983). Individual patterns of adaptation from infancy to preschool. In M. Perlmutter (Ed.), *Minnesota symposium on child psychology* (pp. 41–81). Hillsdale, NJ: Lawrence Erlbaum Associates.

Thompson, S. (1975). Gender labels and early sex role development. *Child Development, 46,* 339–347.

Waters, E., Wippman, J., & Sroufe, L. A. (1979). Attachment, positive affect, and competence in the peer group: Two studies in construct validation. *Child Development, 50,* 821–829.

Winder, C. L., & Rau, L. (1962). Parental attitudes associated with social deviance in preadolescent boys. *Journal of Abnormal and Social Psychology, 64,* 418–424.

Wohlwill, J. (1973). *The study of behavioral development.* New York: Academic Press.

Wohlwill, J. (1979). Stability and change in cognitive development in childhood. In O. Brim, Jr., & J. Kagan (Eds.), *Constancy and change in human development* (pp. 359–444). Cambridge, MA: Harvard University Press.

Prevention Research, Evaluation, and Application: Reflections on a Cognitive Approach

2

Myrna B. Shure, Ph.D.
Hahnemann University

When John F. Kennedy called for a "bold new approach" to mental health as early as 1963, he was speaking of prevention, an approach that is "far more economical and . . . far more likely to be successful" (quoted by Price, Bader, & Ketterer, 1980, p. 9). In 1979 his brother, Edward M. Kennedy, chaired a subcommittee on Health and Scientific Research, to which Gary VandenBos, Administrative Officer of Mental Health Policy of the APA, submitted, "By failing to be responsive to the emotional/behavioral problems of children and youth, later problems and cost of dealing with the mental health problems of an older population are compounded" (letter dated June 21, 1979, p. 9). If this kind of testimony, the 1978 recommendations of the task force on prevention to the President's Commission on Mental Health, and the numerous recent state and local conferences reflect a heightened acceptance of prevention as a goal, then, as Price et al. suggest, the routes to that goal need to be more clearly mapped. In fact, Price et al. (1980) said, "the field of prevention is presently struggling with a number of critical issues; some are conceptual, others political, some are organizational, and still others are operational" (p. 10).

This chapter addresses issues critical to promoting that "bold new approach," issues of research, evaluation, and application in one field of interest to applied developmental psychologists—the field of primary prevention in mental health. It is always important to think about how to upgrade the quality of our work. It is especially important now. Given the austere climate of the 1980s, and the demands to reduce government spending, professionals who are actively engaged in promoting quality mental health activities must pause, reflect on issues germaine to those activities, and then educate and convince the public and powers-that-be that we know what we are doing, we care about what we are doing, but that we cannot continue to do it alone. Using our own research in competence building as the primary example, three of these issues are: (1) choice of research and intervention strategies, (2) subtleties of evaluation (both scientific and practical aspects), and (3) when research is also a service—before, during, after. Thought to these (overlapping) issues may help us appreciate some of the complexities and subtleties of an applied approach that has a beginning, a middle, but hopefully, not an end.

ISSUE 1:
CHOICE OF RESEARCH AND INTERVENTION STRATEGIES

When research includes examining the impact of some specific activity, such as intervention to prevent something from happening, the critical question is how we know, over time, that it was really that intervention that prevented that something, or whether the recipients were really at risk at all (Iscoe, 1980; Price, 1982). Maybe we can never know for sure, and maybe that is why prevention activities are hard to sell. But we, as researchers, can design the best possible studies to demonstrate that by doing what we do, we *probably* can contribute to identifying and reducing that risk. How? By guidance from both theory and methodology, recognizing their limits, and then setting out to improve them.

In research with my colleague, George Spivack, we have learned that as early as age 4 children can or can *learn* to solve typical interpersonal problems with peers and adults, and those who can do that are likely to be less impulsive, less inhibited, and display more positive prosocial behaviors than those who cannot (Shure & Spivack, 1978; Spivack & Shure, 1974). Guided by earlier research with adolescents (Spivack & Levine, 1963), later confirmed by Platt, Spivack, Altman, Altman, and Peizer (1974), and further validated in 9- to 12-year-olds (Shure & Spivack, 1972), Spivack theorized that regardless of IQ interpersonal cognitive problem-solving (ICPS) skills mediate social adjustment and interpersonal competence (Spivack, Platt, & Shure, 1976).

Because our goal was to design intervention to enhance adjustment by training people how to problem solve, we reasoned that the earliest feasible age should be optimal to enhance mental health and support cognitive growth. To this end, our first research strategy was to identify, through correlational analyses, which ICPS skills could distinguish good from poor problem solvers, at how early an age, and with which (if any) behaviors those cognitive skills would be associated. Testing both middle-and lower SES groups, the earliest common testable age was 4, and three distinguishing ICPS skills emerged: (1) alternative solution, (2) consequential, and (3) causal thinking skills (Shure, Newman & Silver, 1973; Spivack & Shure, 1974). These ICPS abilities, especially alternative solution skills, related to specific indices of impulsivity and inhibition as well as to positive prosocial behaviors. Specifically, poor problem solvers were likely to display impatience, overemotionality in the face of frustration, physical and/or verbal agression, *or,* overinhibition, shyness, timidity in the classroom. They were also more likely to have difficulties in developing satisfactory peer relations and were likely to be unconcerned about the feelings of others.

If ICPS skills are mediators of these behaviors, our next step was to test that theory by experimental manipulation (intervention). By enhancing these *cognitive* skills, the question was whether those who would most improve in the trained ICPS skills would also most improve in behavior—not by direct modification of behavior itself, but by altering the child's interpersonal problem-solving style of thinking.

Thus, initially our intervention strategy was guided by a theory, an ICPS/behavioral mediation theory. If educators and clinicians have assumed that relieving emotional tension paves the way for one to think straight, our research would test the reverse idea—that ability to think straight can pave the way for emotional relief.

The next question was *who* the recipients should be. As a group, innercity black 4-year-olds were more ICPS deficient and displayed more ICPS-relevant behavior difficulties than their middle-class counterparts. However, in choosing to target our intervention on the innercity black groups, we also recognized that *some* children did not appear to be "at risk." Their ICPS and social adjustment, as measured at age 4, was at a par with the most competent middle-SES youngsters. We had to decide whether to include all tested children, or focus only on ICPS-deficient, generally more poorly adjusted ones. For children trained in school by their teachers, our decision to include all the tested children was prompted by (a) our research goals, (b) our choice of intervention stratgies, and (c) practical considerations.

Our *research* goals were to test not only the validity of our theory, but also the preventive effects of ICPS intervention. To do this, the design required follow-up of *all* children. If children who were considered to be adjusted in nursery school should *begin* to show behavior problems later, and if they should show up more among the nontrained than the trained, then it could be argued that more children were really "at risk" than at first appeared to be, and that the intervention could, indeed, contribute to incidence reduction from that risk. In addition to enhancing ICPS skills and behavior of youngsters already displaying behavior problems (Shure & Spivack 1973, 1980; Spivack & Shure, 1974), the preventive influence is precisely what we found. Youngsters who began the program as behaviorally adjusted were less likely than controls to begin showing signs of impulsivity or social inhibition as measured 1 and 2 years later (Shure & Spivack, 1979a, 1982). If, as Spivack and Swift (1977) have discovered, a significantly greater percentage of innercity children begin to show behavior problems as they move through the early grades, perhaps ICPS intervention can help to reverse that trend.

Our *choice of intervention* strategies also required training of all tested children. From our correlational research, we learned that even the best adjusted youngsters could *think* of forceful ways to obtain a toy from a peer, but they could also think of more nonforceful ways than could more poorly adjusted ones. We also learned that some of the more poorly adjusted children repeatedly suggested "say please" (especially more inhibited ones) but could think of little else to say or do (when asked, in the test situation). Thus, our training strategy would focus on a process-not-content approach (discussed in Shure, 1982). We would not discourage cognitive solutions a child already knew but rather would add to their repertoire and then help them consider more than one way to solve a problem. We would not focus only on helping children to get what they want, but also to better cope with the frustration when they could not have what they want (by helping children to think of how they can wait, or change their goal, if need be). Placing the decision on the child is much more likely to lead to positive action than demands or even suggestions of what he or she could do. Given that high-ICPS children *told us* solutions, consequences, and causes, our approach focused on encouraging children to think for themselves, and our program script (Shure & Spivack, 1971; in Spivack & Shure, 1974) included skills to help them learn to do that.

The *process*—not-content approach of ICPS intervention—not only accepted all offered relevant solutions (the child would subsequently evaluate them in light of potential consequences), but this approach also stimulated a style of thought that would focus on the notion that, if the first way is not successful, it is possible to try a different way. And thus, the child simultaneously learns to decide when it is too soon to give up, and when it is in fact time to let this problem go (to save face, to save interpersonal relationships in the long run). Because of the child-responding nature of the program, it was important to have competent children together (based on pretest scores) in order to avoid group silence. To maintain interest in early games, designed for the most ICPS-deficient child, the more competent children were encouraged to help "teach" the early concepts.

Practical considerations also necessitated inclusion of all tested children. After our pilot (Shure, Spivack, & Gordon, 1972), the next step was to learn whether teachers could implement the program, a critical step for utility wider than our own direct-child training. In Philadelphia Get-Set day care, classes ranged from 12 to 18 children each. Divided into groups of 6 to 9 children (for maximum response potential), whole classes (10 of them) were included because children excluded from the formal lesson-games could feel left out and unhappy; those included could feel "special" (creating a potential "Hawthorne Effect"). And teachers would have children responding differentially to informal problem-solving communication techniques when real problems arise outside of the formal lesson-games (an essential part of the program; see Issue 2, following), creating potential frustration for the teacher learning to use those techniques.

Thus, it was theoretical, empirical, and practical considerations that led us to our choice of research and intervention strategies and priorities in the nursery year, the details of which may differ from project to project but are considerations that can guide the strategies and priorities of any prevention activity. If one defines prevention as "primary" by considering that none of the children in our research were as yet diagnosed as disturbed, and the goal is to prevent behavioral aberrance from turning to more severe maladjustment, then practical (sometimes cost-effective) considerations, style of the particular program, of profession of the training agent may favor not training the whole group. Or, if one were working with interventions to meet specific and very individualized needs such as Rolf and Fischer (1984), who worked with youngsters of disordered or abusing parents, and who may themselves have accrued developmental, cognitive, or behavioral deficits—or with interventions designed to coach specific social-skill deficits (e.g., Oden & Asher, 1977; Gottman, Gonso, & Schuler, 1976)—then it would also not be logical or cost-effective to train whole groups.

If, as we did in our teacher-training research, one wished to include both preventing behavioral aberrance from getting worse and/or improving it, *as well as* prevention of aberrance from first occurring, then training not already identified "at-risk" recipients as defined by the theory and empirical data is not only preferable, but required.

ISSUE 2: SUBTLETIES OF EVALUATION

If theory and methodology can help us to identify "at-risk" recipients, either immediately or a later time, they become even more critical in the evaluation of program impact. Such evaluation can begin with the researcher/creator who has developed a sense of the subtleties involved.

Crossing paths with Issue 1 (strategies choice), and with Issue 3 following (research as a service), evaluation of any intervention must include both scientific research and practical program considerations. Without appreciating the finer points of research methodology and interpretation of outcome, erroneous conclusions about program impact can result. Without considering practical subtleties of implementation, training agents can misuse, or misinterpret, the critical features of what the intervention is supposed to convey. It is the consideration of both that gives a program the potential for wider applicability and effective utilization (Shure & Spivack, 1981).

Research Considerations: Data Interpretation

Not only can a theory serve as a springboard to the style and approach of an intervention, but, as Morell (1981) noted, it can also guide the evaluation of program impact and interpretation of outcome. Based on outcome, questions as how a program should increase, decrease, or maintain its' activities, and to what extent restructuring a program may be necessary cannot, suggests Morell, be answered without a theory that attempts to explain the relationship among key variables. In our case, 50% of the nursery-trained youngsters who displayed impulsive behaviors before training were judged by their teacher to have shown marked reduction in observed impatience, overemotionality in the face of frustration, and/or physical and/or verbal aggression after the 10-week intervention program. Such behavioral improvement in only 21% of the initially impulsive controls (a percent difference significant at the .01 level) was indeed an outcome predicted by the ICPS framework. Similarly, among the initially inhibited, 75% of the ICPS-trained became dramatically less timid, fearful, and shy, compared to only 35% of the controls, a percent difference significant at the .01 level. If, given the difficulty of the problem, we believe that sufficient percentages of trained children improved in their behavior from ratings defined on the scale to be more than the "average" child the same age and sex (impulsive), *or*, as *less* than the "average" child (inhibited), to ratings defined to be within the "average" range, then we can conclude that the program did reasonably well.

But, as Morell further notes, the same pattern of results can lead to different recommendations because different theories might guide data interpretation. Thus, that same theory that guided our intervention strategies also led us to further examine the data. To more stringently test the ICPS/behavior mediation theory—that behavior gains could really be attributed to ICPS gains (and if so, which ones), an ICPS skill would be viewed a mediator only if increased scores on its measures would correlate significantly with change in adjustment (independent of IQ and test verbosity). In combination with pretraining correlations, such a relationship of change scores would suggest evidence of a direct link between ICPS and adjustment.

The mediational analyses revealed the strongest linkage for alternative solution skills, consequential skills borderline, and causal thinking showed no linkage at all (Shure & Spivack, 1980). Because all three of these cognitive skills did improve significantly in ICPS- trained youngsters, lack of causal skills as a significant mediator suggests an important consideration when interpreting training effects. Any training program that enhances a hypothesized mediating skill (ICPS) as well as a criterion skill (e.g., social adjustment) must at least demonstrate a relationship between change in the two before it is assumed that change in adjustment is a function of change in thinking. Had this not been done in our research, it might have been incorrectly concluded that increase in the trained causal thinking skills of nursery youngsters played a significant mediating role in their improved behavioral adjustment.

Assessing outcome, we considered the solution/behavior linkages to be sufficiently successful, attributed the consequential behavior linkages to developmental phenomena (later confirmed by its stronger linkage in kindergarten groups; Shure & Spivack, 1982), and attributed the absence of causal/behavior linkage to lack of sufficient training of that concept, lack of sensitive enough measures to detect that linkage and/or lack of causal thinking as an ICPS/behavioral mediator. The latter is possible because unlike solution and consequential skills, initial correlations of causal thinking and behavior were not significantly independent of IQ.

Research Considerations: Methodology

However difficult it may be to identify and control for all the most critical potential spurious factors in the laboratory, those difficulties probably triple in the field. In applied research, can sufficient controls be incorporated for us to learn enough about what we want to know? Acutely aware that our own methodology lacked certain controls, improvements have been designed, but we did have some built-in validity checks that might suitably fit other prevention designs.

In our teacher-training research, teachers who did the training also did the behavior ratings, creating potential bias in the results. In addition to the ICPS/behavior mediation analyses (teachers were not informed of the ICPS test scores), follow-up kindergarten and first-grade teachers, unaware of the children's earlier training experience, rated them remarkably similar to that of the nursery teachers (Shure, 1979; Shure & Spivack, 1979a). Although these data suggest the nursery teachers did rate the children honestly and objectively, further validation was provided in another leg of our research. Children trained by their mothers at home were rated by their teachers in school as showing significant pre–post behavior gains (Shure & Spivack, 1978; 1979b). Not only did these independent raters support the validity of our approach; they also showed that gains can last over time, and that ICPS skills learned in one environment (the home) can be applied in another (the school).

One could still question whether the improved school behavior of home-trained children could be attributed to extra attention their mothers gave to them. In this regard, two groups of mothers learned to help their child problem solve, but one of these groups were also taught ICPS skills of their own. All mother-trained children improved more than nontrained controls, but those children whose mothers were also trained to think improved still more. Had child gains been due to mere attention, then the parent–child ICPS interactions (requiring the same amount of time in both groups) would likely result in the same amount of child gains. Perhaps the ICPS-trained parents gained more insight into the concepts they taught to their child, and a greater sensitivity to the sensations their child experienced as he or she learned those concepts. That attention was not the critical factor was also supported in our earlier mentioned (1972) pilot, in which ICPS skills and behavior gains of attention–placebo groups were significantly less than those of the ICPS.

If doubts about *child* attention can be allayed (or at least reduced), and real child gains assumed, can those gains instead be attributed to the *trainers'* ego involvement because of participation in a special program (a Hawthorne-Effect)? If that were the case, would not children in both parent-trained groups have improved the same? Further, N. Wowkanech (personal communication, August, 1978) trained two groups of nursery teachers, one who administered the ICPS, the other a modeling, reinforcement program. As judged by independent raters, ICPS and behavior gains of the ICPS far surpassed that of the modeling group. Any Hawthorne-Effect on children's outcome that might have emerged from one program would likely have occurred in the other. Both would have been perceived as equally "special."

The aforementioned notwithstanding, all controls were not implemented simultaneously in any one of our projects. Our present research in schools (with 10- to 12-year-olds), though more costly, is strengthened by inclusion of a teacher-led placebo group (our pilot groups were researcher-led). Independent observers (also more costly) have unquestionably improved the design. That option was, at least for our program, superior to researchers training the children outside of the classroom, an option that would have allowed the teachers to remain unaware of who would and would not be trained and could therefore have rated the children "blind." The reason the *teacher* implementation of the ICPS intervention is more effective than researcher implementation (in addition to creating ease in training the entire class) is that, for maximum behavioral impact, it appears that at all age levels the trainer must apply the ICPS approach when real problems arise (and the researcher may not be on the scene when that occurs). ICPS-application, called "dialoguing," guides the child to explore solutions, consequences, etc., just as it does in the formal lesson-games. For example, instead of telling children who have just hit another someone that "you shouldn't hit, you should ask for that truck," an ICPS-trained teacher may ask the children to describe the problem as they see it, to think through how they and the others felt about having been hit, to talk about what happened next (the consequences of the act), and to think of something different to do (alternative solutions) so the other(s), for example, wouldn't "be mad," and wouldn't "hit back."

As Sigel (1982) has explained, ICPS dialoguing techniques are a form of what he calls "distancing strategies" because they consist of an open-ended inquiry that creates a tension, a discrepancy that creates cognitive strain and conflict. By asking the child "what happened?" followed by guiding the child to think of alternative solutions paired with anticipation of outcome (consequences), the child is, as Sigel (1970) has described, forced to distance him or herself in time and place from the present, re-present previous experience or construct an anticipated one, using previous experience as his or her guide (see also Sigel & Cocking, 1977). In addition to fostering representational competence, perhaps these techniques have impact because, as Sigel (1979) has also noted, "children become aware that they are finding the answer, that they are thinkers, and finally, that they are in control; they have become conscious that they are the thinkers who must come to grips with the task at hand'' (p. 89). In our case, that task is to think through and solve problems that are interpersonal.

Whereas our preschool pilot did show greater behavior gains in ICPS groups than in placebo controls, the gains of teacher- and parent-trained groups improved still more. The importance of dialoguing is supported by N. Wowkanech (personal communication, August, 1978), and by Allen (1978), who, in using that technique in combination with the formal lessons, found greater behavioral gains than investigators who used the formal lessons alone (e.g., Durlak & Sherman, 1979; Sharp, 1981). Although the Durlak and Sharp children, trained outside the classroom, did improve their ICPS skills, and other factors may account for lack of parallel behavior gains, dialoguing appears to introduce an in vivo quality by encouraging children to exercise their newly acquired thinking skills in the context of real problems—leading to a more effective use of ICPS skills when faced with real problems of their own.

Use of independent raters allows teachers to train the children, while instituting tight research design. Continued training by teachers in school research is essential not only for maximum impact of our program, but for wider use of any (school) program. Teachers can potentially affect far more children (an entire classroom each year) than can the researcher (who will eventually leave the scene). For that reason, it is essential during the research phase to learn the extent to which teachers can be effective training agents.

Practical Considerations: Replication and Implementation

If theory and methodology guide evaluation of a program's validity, so too can practical considerations. Still focusing on intervention as *research,* these considerations include: (a) interpretation of procedures by the replicator/implementor; (b) orientation of the training agent to the program; (c) logistical issues in different age groups and settings; and (d) length and intensity of the training.

Interpretation of Procedures. As Irving Sigel (personal communication, April, 1980) has asked, ''Is a new study really a replication or an application, and if the same results are not obtained, why is the original researcher so often blamed?'' In the interest of methodology, researchers might focus on different elements of evaluation. If the previously described concern about teacher-rating validity precludes dialoguing because researchers train children outside the classroom, then the ICPS program as designed is more application than replication (even though instituted as research). In older children, Weissberg and his colleagues (1981) designed their own teacher- training problem-solving intervention. They attribute greater increased behavior in their later studies, at least in part, to more closely monitored training and consultation efforts, to an expanded curriculum, and to a more *systematic incorporation of dialoguing* during the day.

In fact, Weissburg and Gesten (1982) noted that teachers of school-aged children report that dialoguing may be the key to independent problem-solving thought.

Whereas evaluation of program impact must consider its application of critical features (or lack of that application), awareness of other considerations are also crucial. For example, during our pilot research with teachers of innercity fifth graders (Shure, 1984), we learned that some aspects of implementation can be quite subtle and can vary by age group and setting. Several practical issues follow.

Orientation of the Training Agent.   Any intervention is only as effective as the agent who conducts it. We discovered that some of our fifth-grade teachers initially viewed interpersonal conflicts as annoyances or disturbances to be dealt with quickly and be rid of, rather than as problems to be solved. If teachers of younger children are, from the start, more oriented toward helping children adapt behaviorally than those of older children (due, perhaps, to fewer pressures of curriculum demands), then before-training orientation to new perceptions of child conflict can help.

Logistical Considerations.   At least in school interventions, issues as class size, other teacher responsibilities, and how many different teachers a child has can differentially affect the ease of implementation. Unlike nursery and kinder-garten, children have multiple teachers by fifth grade, giving less time to the homeroom (training) teacher. Also, it is clearly more difficult to dialogue a real problem in a class of 30 children than in a (nursery) class of 15. Although kindergarten teachers also have 30 children, they also have more consistent aides to help, and more total time with the class. Also, unlike teachers of younger children, homeroom teachers are less likely to accompany the class to the play-ground at recess, when so many typical problems arise. Because dialoguing is most effective when applied during or shortly after the conflict, it can lose its potency when reported and worked through later. At the suggestion of one of our creative fifth-grade teachers, children role played problems that came up, a technique that, learned in the formal lessons, was possible and relatively suc-cessful. Another alternative is to train all school personnel who come in contact with the children, a procedure more costly but met with success by Elardo and Caldwell (1975, 1979).

Length and Intensity of Intervention.   If curriculum demands and other logis-tical differences affect the style of training, they also affect the intensity of it. Teachers of younger children could implement the formal 20–30 minute lesson-games daily for 12 weeks (allowing for pre–post testing time and holidays within the constraints of the school year). In the grades, three times a week over the same 12 training weeks was fortunate.

Some ICPS and some behavior change does occur in single-agent (teacher) trained school-aged children. Regarding our theoretical position that links ICPS gains with behavior gains, our first study with low-SES black fifth graders (Shure, 1980, 1984) showed the most consistent ICPS/behavioral linkages to occur with positive, prosocial behaviors. In both sexes, it was improvement in the number and range of solutions that best related to these behavior gains, most consistently to teacher ratings of concern for others, peer sociability, and the degree to which the child is liked by peers. In boys, though not girls, gains in consequential thinking, and in sequenced step-by-step means–ends thinking also related to these prosocial changes. We also learned something theoretically logical and extremely interesting about academic skills vis-a-vis ICPS intervention. Whereas ICPS gains did not link with academic gains (functional reading and math grade-book levels and California Achievement Test scores), prosocial behavior gains did. Nothing should suggest that training interpersonal cognitive skills should improve impersonal cognitive ones. But, if behavior gains can improve academic ability, and if ICPS can improve behavior, then we have an additional potential for the ICPS approach.

The mediational linkages for ICPS and adjustment gains for negative impulsive and inhibited behaviors in our fifth graders were less clear than were those for positive, prosocial indicators; and research to date suggests that these linkages are, indeed, weaker in older children than in younger ones (e.g., Elias, 1980; Weissberg et al., 1981). Because ICPS skills and these negative behaviors are correlated phenomena in older children (e.g., Asarnow & Callan, 1985; McKim, Weissberg, Cowen, Gesten & Rapkin, 1982; Pellegrini, 1985; Richard & Dodge, 1982; Shure, 1980), perhaps it just takes more than thrice-weekly intervention within a 3-to 4-month time frame before these children associate newly acquired ICPS skills directly with some overt negative behaviors displayed with teachers and with peers.

Before concluding that any intervention that has less than immediate maximum impact may not be suitable, or that after a given age it may be too late to impact negative behaviors, longer and/or more intense training may do the trick. In our case, that would further clarify which specific indices of social adjustment in school-aged children are (and are not) alterable by the ICPS approach. Given this, one other important possibility does exist. Perhaps, as Wienckowski[1] has suggested, early training bolstered by intermittent "booster shots" throughout the elementary school years might maximize the impact of ICPS intervention on older children. This, in combination with the Elardo and Caldwell procedure of training all school personnel to at least "dialogue" when real problems arise, would likely produce an optimal ecological environment as well as the most methodologically sound approach for continued ICPS and behavioral development.

---

[1]At Research Planning Mini Conference on Primary Prevention. Sponsored by the Office of Prevention and the Center for Prevention Research at NIMH, and the Community Psychology Training Program, University of Texas at Austin, February 24–26, 1982.

ISSUE 3:
WHEN RESEARCH IS ALSO A SERVICE: BEFORE, DURING, AFTER

While researchers are investigating the validity of new intervention, its' consumers are simultaneously receiving a service. The administrator (e.g., a school principal), the training agent (e.g., a teacher), and the direct recipients (e.g., the children) may, however, have very different needs. How can differences be made to work for the benefit of all? When, and with whom, is it appropriate to consult before finalizing the research design and contents of the program, and how much can be told about the study before and during the research phase (ethics considered)? How can researchers maximize potential for continued application after the research phase is over? Finally, how flexible can and should evaluation be when a program is applied differently than how it was originally designed?

Before. If the researcher is concerned about theory testing, program validity, measurement reliability and validity, etc., administrators may be most concerned about staff development, teachers about classroom management, improving their teaching skill, and/or adding variety to their day, and children about "feeling good" or "being smart." As described in Shure (1979), it took inquiring about and recognizing of these different needs to pave the way for initiating, planning, and staging the research phase of our program.

"Selling" the ICPS program was easy. Administrators, teachers, and later parents were all interested in children learning to problem solve, and once it got to the children, they were motivated and wanted more. But initial entrance into kindergarten was not as easy as in nursery. Even after clearance from the Director of Research and the Director of Early Childhood Programs and from all district supervisors, some principals still expressed suspicion of researchers who test the children, leave, and use the schools for their own ends. Assuring continued feedback, I explained the cognitive and behavioral goals and our previous efforts at achieving them. I particularly stressed the service focus (especially staff training), with minimum discussion of the theory testing or methodological subtleties that were of little interest to them. In both nursery and kindergarten, supervisors and principals of control (nontraining) schools had to be convinced of the ultimate benefits—a service we ultimately delivered to some of them (see following).

Although administrators could be told all the goals, participating research teachers could not. Because it was they who would rate behavior of the children, they were told only of the cognitive goals. What initially concerned teachers the most was that the program would not counter their own teaching values, and that it would not interfere with their ongoing activities. To teachers, we stressed the style of intervention—that in handling a real problem, at no time would we

34

"tell" them what to do, and also that they would play a key role in developing the techniques (though not the concepts) of the program itself. In nursery and kindergarten, the program could easily be incorporated into story time, a time normally set aside for group activity.

When we turned our research to parents, clearance was obtained from the Policy Advisory Committee (PAC), parent groups who provided input on all aspects of the day-care activities, operations, policies, and procedures related to service delivery of parents and children. What interested this group and the eventual training parents was essentially the same as what motivated teachers: that the program is flexible and does not tell people what to do; rather, it helps parents and children learn to think so they can solve problems important to them in ways that are relevant to them.

As for the children, our major concern was to obtain and maintain their enthusiasm, especially those who would be trained 2 years (see Shure & Spivack, 1974, 1979a). To this end, several rounds of prepiloting and piloting the lesson-games were conducted, with revisions based on children's reactions and responses.

During.   During the research phase, attention is generally focused on further refinement of techniques, supervision of the training agents, and continued contact with their superiors. It was during our first teacher-training year that we discovered the value of dialoguing, as on-site observations revealed teachers asking children for *their* ideas during the formal lesson-games, then creating confusion by telling them what to do when a real problem came up. During that year, we also discovered the value of including teacher aides, who not only maintained consistency of communciation, but whose participation made them feel important, leading to work attendance becoming dramatically more regular. This potential "Hawthorne-Effect" did not, we believe, affect the results any more than it did for the teachers. In fact, the aides provided us with behavior-rating reliability, ratings that were almost as discriminating as those of the teachers.

Teachers' freedom to create procedural techniques (e.g., the format of a game) made them feel part of a team to develop ways to teach the concepts. Their ideas, and some created by the children themselves, were later incorporated into the script. Although we now disseminate a "final" product, the program script is never final because it emphasizes that flexibility of content (again, not concepts) is not only allowed, but encouraged.

After.   Providing feedback relevant to the recipients' preresearch concerns may well be the most important immediate postresearch step of all. Focusing on what was important to them, not on what was important to us, eased the next step, which was expansion to pure service delivery.

The transition from research to wider use may be more difficult than the research itself. First, our participant (Get Set) research teachers, under my supervision, trained new teachers in geographically convenient centers. Parenthetically, it turned out that we probably did not have to worry about telling research teachers the behavioral goals. A remarkably similar percentage of children were rated as improved by service teachers (informed of *all* goals), suggesting that such knowledge, or inference about it, would not have changed the results. Having completed that step, I held large group workshops the following year, with all now-trained teachers working closely with still newer groups (see Shure, 1979). Also, the director of curriculum development attended those workshops, the goal being city-wide implementation (at the time, in 1974, over 5,000 children attended Get Set, across 106 different centers). Unfortunately, just as that person was ready to go with it, funds became too scarce to maintain her position, and she was never replaced. Even more unfortunately, only 66 centers serving slightly over 3,000 children exist today, and the prognosis is even worse.

Because our scripts are available for wider use, they were written as clearly as possible; they include subtleties of implementation learned during the research phase and explain the flexibility of content. Without any personal contact with me or on-site supervision by anyone already trained, many mental health workers and teachers have written and expressed success.

Given that some *researchers* have changed the program, we do not know how much those mental health workers and teachers really replicated it. If, as Morell (1981) suggests, "it is axiomatic that programs as implemented are never the same as programs as designed" (p. 29), modifications are no doubt magnified by practitioners whose needs and priorities may differ. Whereas the original researcher may have spent years developing and perfecting *one* program (in one or more locations), mental health practitioners may simultaneously implement different ones, their priorities, if not mandate, being more diverse community outreach. In that case, time restraints may alter the length and/or intensity of any one program, reduce any needed on-site supervision, and even eliminate critical elements of the intervention itself. But, as Kelly, Munoz, and Snowden (1979) pointed out:

> Even here, however, one wonders whether the apparent acceptance and obvious modification of such programs by community agencies may not be positive signs of psychological ownership over them. Although a total distortion of well-planned interventions could defeat their purpose, it is possible that modifications may increase their practical utility without radically reducing their effectiveness. (p. 346)

Perhaps the real question is how much modification a program can stand. For ours, we know that sharply curtailed training (e.g., 10 total hours, however spread over time) does not produce the desired effects (Dick, 1981). We also know that over the designed 12 weeks of daily 20–30 minutes training, ICPS gains in younger innercity children are greater when both prerequisite and problem-solving skills are trained than when either is trained alone (Egan, 1979; Sharp, 1981). Even in a different setting, a clinic (E. Kellogg, personal communication, July, 1981) could implement the formal games, then set up free-play activities and dialogue during conflict. Although impractical in schools (children would be out of class too long), that was an extremely creative way to adapt all the key and critical components of ICPS intervention in a nonschool setting.

Once the creator is out of the picture, he or she can only hope the program is used. What happens may be, in large part, due to how the research was done: before, during, and after.

CONCLUSION

Our choice of research and intervention strategies and priorities as described in this chapter epitomize an integrative applied approach in social, community, and developmental psychology. I have tried to show how they can reflect the implications of how basic research can serve as a springboard to develop feasible interventions with testable research questions, with a sound theoretical and conceptual base and methodological validity—and at the same time develop and maintain a "constituent validity," or the extent to which recipients assess the work as meeting their needs, aspirations, and values.

ACKNOWLEDGMENTS

ICPS research on 4- and 5-year-olds described in this chapter was supported by Grant #20372, National Institute of Mental Health, 1971–1975, and on fifth graders by Grant #27741, National Institute of Mental Health, 1978–1979.

REFERENCES

Allen, R. J. (1978). An investigatory study of the effects of a cognitive approach to interpersonal problem solving on the behavior of emotionally upset psychosocially deprived preschool children. Unpublished doctoral dissertation, Center for Minority Studies, Brookings Institute, Union Graduate School, Washington, DC.

Asarnow, J. R., & Callan, J. W. (1985). Boys with peer adjustment problems. *Journal of Consulting and Clinical Psychology, 53*, 80–87.

Dick, A. (1981). *The effects of training in social problem solving and verbal self-instruction on behavioral adjustment, social problem-solving cognition, and cognitive tempo in socially impulsive kindergarten children.* Unpublished doctoral disseration, New York University.

Durlak, J. A., & Sherman, D. (1979, September). Primary prevention of school maladjustmnt. In J. A. Durlak (Chair.), *Behavioral approaches to primary prevention: Programs, outcomes and issues*. Symposium conducted at the meeting of the American Psychological Association, New York.

Egan, F. B. (1979). *A components analysis of interpersonal problem solving skills training*. Unpublished doctoral dissertation, Hofstra University, New York.

Elardo, P. T., & Caldwell, B. M. (1975). *Project AWARE: A school program to facilitate the social development of kindergarten-elementary children*. Unpublished manuscript. University of Arkansas, College of Education, Little Rock.

Elardo, P. T., & Caldwell, B. M. (1979). The effects of an experimental social development program on children in the middle childhood period. *Psychology in the Schools, 16*, 93–100.

Elias, M. J. (1980). *Developing instructional strategies for television-based preventive mental health curricula in elementary school settings*. Unpublished doctoral dissertation, University of Connecticut, Storrs.

Gottman, J., Gonso , J. & Schuler, P. (1976). Teaching social skills to isolated children. *Journal of Abnormal Child Psychology, 4*, 179–197.

Iscoe, I. (1980). Conceptual barriers to training for the primary prevention of psychopathology. In J. M. Joffee & G. W. Albee (Eds.), *Prevention through political action and social change*. Hanover, NH: University Press of New England.

Kelly, J. G., Munoz, R. F., & Snowden, L. R. (1979). Characteristics of community research projects and the implementation process. In R. E. Munoz, L. R. Snowden, & J. G. Kelly (Eds.), *Social and psychological research in community settings* (pp. 343–363). San Francisco: Jossey–Bass.

Kennedy, J. F. (1963). Message from the President of the United States relative to mental illness and mental retardation. 88th Congress, First Session, U.S. House of Representatives Document No. 58. Washington, DC, U.S. Government Printing Office.

McKim, B. J., Weissberg, R. P., Cowen, E. L., Gesten, E. L., & Rapkin, B. 1982). A comparison of the problem-solving ability and adjustment of suburban and urban third-grade children. *American Journal of Community Psychology, 10*, 155–169.

Morell, J. (1981). Evaluation in prevention: Implications from a general model. *Prevention in Human Services, 1*, 7–40.

Oden, S. L., & Asher, S. R. (1977). Coaching children in social skills for friendship making. *Child Development, 48*, 495–506.

Pellegrini, D. S. (1985). Social cognition and competence in middle childhood. *Child Development, 56*, 253–264.

Platt, J. J., Spivack, G., Altman, N., Altman, D., & Peizer, S. B. (1974). Adolescent problem-solving thinking. *Journal of Consulting and Clinical Psychology, 42*, 787–793.

Price, R. H. (1982, February) *Four domains of prevention research*. Paper presented at the Conference on Research on Primary Prevention, Austin, TX.

Price, R. H., Bader, B. C., & Ketterer, R. F. (1980). Prevention in community mental health. In R. H. Price, R. F. Ketterer, B. C. Bader, & J. Monahan (Eds.), *Prevention in mental health: Research, policy, and practice* (Vol. 1, pp. 9–20). Beverly Hills, CA: Sage.

Richard, B. A., & Dodge, K. A. (1982). Social maladjustment and problem solving in school-aged children. *Journal of Consulting and Clinical Psychology, 50*, 226–233.

Rolf, J., & Fischer, M. (1984, August). Intervention and follow up stability in developmental risk. In M. B. Shure (Chair.), *Ecological and developmental issues in prevention research*. Invited symposium conducted at the meeting of the American Psychological Association, Toronto.

Sharp, K. C. (1981). Impact of interpersonal problem-solving training on preschoolers' social competency. *Journal of Applied Developmental Psychology, 2*, 129–143.

Shure, M. B. (1979). Training children to solve interpersonal problems: A preventive mental health program. In R. E. Munoz, L. R. Snowden, & J. G. Kelly (Eds.), *Social and psychological research in community settings* (pp. 30–68). San Francisco: Jossey-Bass.

Shure, M. B. (1980). *Interpersonal problem solving in ten-year-olds*. Final Report No. MH-27741, Washington, DC: National Institute of Mental Health.

Shure, M. B. (1982). Interpersonal problem solving: A cog in the wheel of social cognition. In F. Serafica (Ed.), *Social cognition and social development in context* (pp. 133–166). New York: Guilford Press.

Shure, M. B. (1984). Building social competence in fifth-graders: Is it too late? In K. H. Rubin & J. R. Asarnow (Cochairs.). *Social skills in preadolescents: Assessment and training.* Symposium conducted at the meeting of the American Psychological Association, Toronto.

Shure, M. B., Newman, S., & Silver, S. (1973, May). *Problem solving thinking among adjusted, impulsive and inhibited Head Start children.* Paper presented at the meeting of the Eastern Psychological Association, Washington, DC.

Shure, M. B., & Spivack, G. (1971).*Interpersonal cognitive problem solving (ICPS): A mental health program for four-year-old nursery school children:* Training script. Philadelphia: Hahnemann University, Department of Mental Health Sciences.

Shure, M. B., & Spivack, G. (1972). Means–ends thinking, adjustment and social class among elementary school-aged children. *Journal of Consulting and Clinical Psychology, 38,* 348–353.

Shure, M. B., & Spivack, G. (1973, March). *A preventive mental health program for four-year-old Head Start children.* Paper presented at the meeting of the Society for Research in Child Development, Philadelphia.

Shure, M. B., & Spivack, G. (1974). *Interpersonal cognitive problem solving (ICPS): A mental health program for kindergarten and first-grade children: Training script.* Philadelphia: Hahnemann University, Department of Mental Health Sciences.

Shure, M. B., & Spivack, G. (1978). *Problem solving techniques in childrearing.* San Francisco: Jossey-Bass.

Shure, M. B., & Spivack, G. (1979a). Interpersonal cognitive problem solving and primary prevention: Programming for preschool and kindergarten children. *Journal of Clinical Child Psychology, 2,* 89–94.

Shure, M. B., & Spivack, G. (1979b). Interpersonal problem solving thinking and adjustment in the mother–child dyad. In M. W. Kent & J. E. Rolf (Eds.), *The Primary Prevention of Psychopathology* (Vol. 3), *Social Competence in Children* (pp 201–219). Hanover, NH: University Press of New England.

Shure, M. B., & Spivack, G. (1980). Interpersonal problem solving as a mediator of behavioral adjustment in preschool and kindergarten children. *Journal of Applied Developmental Psychology, 1,* 29–43.

Shure, M. B., & Spivack, G. (1981). The problem-solving approach to adjustment: A competency-building model of primary prevention. *Prevention in Human Services, 1,* 87–103.

Shure, M. B., & Spivack, G. (1982). Interpersonal problem solving in young children: A cognitive approach to prevention. *American Journal of Community Psychology, 10,* 341–356.

Shure, M. B., Spivack, G., & Gordon, R. (1972). Problem-solving thinking: A preventive mental health program for preschool children. *Reading World, 11,* 259–273.

Sigel, I. E. (1970). The distancing hypothesis: A causal hypothesis for the acquisition of representational thought. In M. R. Jones (Ed.), *The effects of early experience.* Miami: University of Miami Press.

Sigel, I. E. (1979). Consciousness raising of individual competence in problem solving. In M. W. Kent & J. E. Rolf (Eds.), *The primary prevention of psychopathology: Social competence in children* (Vol. 3, pp. 75–96). Hanover, NH: University Press of New England.

Sigel, I. E. (1982, September). *A conceptual analysis of ICPS.* Paper presented at the Research Planning Workshop, cosponsored by the Center for Prevention Research and the Prevention Research Branch, NIMH, Rockville, MD.

Sigel, I. E., & Cocking, R. R. (1977). *Cognitive development childhood to adolescence: A constructivist perspective.* New York: Holt, Rinehart, & Winston.

Spivack, G., & Levine, M. (1963). *Self-regulation in acting-out and normal adolescents* (Report M-4531). Washington, DC: National Institute of Health.

Spivack, G., Platt, J. J., & Shure, M. B. (1976). *The problem solving approach to adjustment*. San Francisco: Jossey-Bass.

Spivack, G., & Shure, M. B. (1974). *Social adjustment of young children*. San Francisco: Jossey-Bass.

Spivack, G., & Swift, M. (1977). 'High risk'' classroom behaviors in kindergarten and first grade. *American Journal of Community Psychology, 5,* 385–397.

Weissberg, R. P., & Gesten, E. L. (1982). Considerations for developing effective school-based social problem-solving (SPS) training programs. *School Psychology Review, 11,* 56–63.

Weissberg, R. P., Gesten, E. L., Carnrike, C. L., Toro, P. A., Rapkin, B. D., Davidson, E., & Cowen, E. L. (1981). Social problem solving skills training: A competence-building intervention with second- to fourth-grade children. *American Journal of Community Psychology, 9,* 411–423.

Intraindividual Integration: An Introduction

James E. Johnson
The Pennsylvania State University

Processes internal to the developing child are the focus of the chapters in this section. The anchoring point is the individual person, centered in the microsystem of the home and family but gradually seen to be moving out into the realm of the neighborhood and school with its peers and teachers. Of particular interest to developmental theory is how the child comes to construct meaning regarding self, others, objects, and events.

The three topics covered in this section are the self concept, social cognition, and play. The chapters' commonality resides primarily in the fact that the material covered demonstrates in general a theoretical allegiance to a cognitive-interactionist model of intellectual development, specifically Piaget's. Each chapter concerns itself with "warm-blooded" as opposed to "cold-blooded" cognitions, or the individual's cognizing with regard to social phenomenon. Thinking about the self, thinking about others in relation to the self, and social and nonsocial play behavior developments are discussed in these pages, with special reference to the construct of integration.

Definitions of integration vary. Harter employs integration to describe how the preschool child begins to interrelate experiences and observations, how the person in middle childhood conceptually integrates trait labels, and how the adolescent continues this trend by combining traits to build a psychological interior using abstract concepts. In middle childhood, self-portraits become more coherent as children begin to connect separate experiences in forming a generalized concept of self. Developmental changes are dramatic and are dependent on the emergence of new cognitive abilities. Krasnor analyzes the developmental literature for how social cognitive components are coordinated within individuals—intraindividual integration. She defines the process-versus product-orientated studies and distinguishes horizontal, stage-like forms of integration (product integration) from vertical, sequential forms of integration (process integration). The definition of integration as the ability to combine separate elements is used in the next chapter, which traces developmental trends in integrative abilities seen within play behaviors of children from late infancy to middle childhood. Motor behavior and symbolization, language and communication, and narrative text are the areas examined. The role of play in development is also discussed in terms of its integrative functions (as opposed to its divergent functions) in cognitive, affective, and social areas. Together, then, play is seen to both reflect and promote integration.

Harter's chapter discussed how the self concept is gradually constructed. She describes characteristics and changes in self-awareness and self-evaluations during infancy and early childhood through middle childhood and adolescence. These changes in the construction of self over time are related to features of preoperational, concrete operational, and formal operational thought. They are also linked to the child's relationships with peers and other significant persons in the child's social environment. Harter further discusses methodological problems in research attempts at quantifying self-esteem and pits a domain-specific approach against a global approach in one of her own cross-sectional studies of children's self-concepts, a study inspired in part by the contrasts between Charles Horton Cooley's general self-worth notions and William James' theorizing on the importance of achievement in certain areas as being relevant to appraisals of self. Her data provided strong support for Cooley's position that positive regard from significant others is needed for the developing child's feelings of worth as a person. However, support also was indicated for James' position, in that the 10–13-year-olds in her study seemed able to discount areas in which they did not excel as being less important to them compared to areas in which they were doing better. Furthermore, children with the highest self-esteem scores evidently felt both an overall sense of worth and felt competent in specific domains deemed important to them.

Krasnor, in her chapter, discussed the nature and uses of social cognition and dealt with how components are coordinated within individuals. The research literature is seen by her as having been dominated to date by product-oriented studies of social cognition in contrast to process-oriented studies. Product-oriented studies of social cognition seek to establish developmental levels in social cognizing and attempt to identify quantitative and qualitative measures of the child's emerging abilities. Such investigations are much more numerous to date than are process-oriented empirical research, which are in contrast directed towards uncovering the sequences and dimensions of social cognizing in real time.

Krasnor elaborates on this distinction using the extant developmental literature on product integration and process integration. For the product-oriented studies, she evaluates the three alternative positions: That horizontal, stage-like integration (1) increases (2), decreases, or (3) shows a nonmonotonic change with age. Next, she spotlights one of her own studies that employed both factor analytic and ANOVA procedures to ascertain the extent of overlap in the number of problem-solving strategies that children exhibited across different task content areas (an example of product integration research). Finally, process integration is discussed, but with more reference to theory than to research as a limited empirical base exists. An analysis of the area supports her recommendations for needed research.

"Play and Integration" completes this section on intraindividual integration. This chapter first briefly discusses the difficulties of defining play and presents several current perspectives. The chapter then seeks to show the ways in which play has been studied in relation to integration within the extant developmental literature. General theoretical and specific empirical approaches are reviewed concerning research on integrative processes occurring when the child is playing, and in research on the developmental significance of play with reference to how playing helps the child integrate internal and external events. The place and value of play for children's education and socialization is discussed in conclusion.

The three chapters in this section, then, all concern themselves with research derived mainly from the cognitive developmental framework, with each chapter leading to the next. How children seek, organize, and use information about the self and others is associated with social and play behaviors. Each is about "warm-blooded" as opposed to "cold-blooded" cognitions. The developments of self concept, social cognition, and play behavior all have as their back-drop the unfolding of the child's intellectual capacities. However, an appreciation of the role of affective and social processes are also seen to be critical to understanding intrapersonal integration in the child as the child matures within expanding interpersonal contexts during the period from early to middle childhood.

Developmental Processes in the Construction of the Self

Susan Harter
University of Denver

INTRODUCTION

Who am I? Ask this question of yourself and you will discover that there are many answers, many dimensions of self-description. You are a student, a man or woman, you have a particular career goal, you are a family member, you consider yourself a member of a certain political party, you are a lover, a tennis player, a movie-goer, a musician, a member of a sorority or fraternity, etc. Your self-concept is based in part on the various roles and membership categories that define who you are.

In addition, you have the ability to reflect on these characteristics and to *evaluate* the self; that is, you are not merely a student but a *good* student. You are very able althletically. On the other hand, your social skills could use improvement, and you could be more tolerant of your parents. These are all evaluative judgments concerning the worth of the self. Moreover, these self-evaluations often provoke an emotional reaction: I am proud of myself for getting an A. I am ashamed of myself for the way I treated my parents during the holidays.

We take these dimensions of self-description for granted, as adults. Rarely do we reflect on their origins. As infants, however, we had none of these capacities; we had absolutely no concept of self. The ability to appreciate the fact that we were a boy or a girl, a son or a daughter, emerged gradually during the first years of our lives, as did the capacity for evaluating these characteristics. Initially, we had no notion of the worth of the self, no awareness that our propensities could be evaluated. The belief that one is a *bad* boy, a *good* sister, a *poor* reader, or a *fast* runner must also emerge with development, as does the ability to experience such affeciive reactions as pride or shame.

In this chapter we trace the origins and development of the self, demonstrating how the self is a concept that is gradually constructed. This process represents a complex interaction between one's developing cognitive capacities and one's socialization experiences. We demonstrate how one's level of cognitive development and one's relationships with parents, peers, and other significant people in one's life allow the child to construct, literally, a portrait of the self. Specifically, we examine the developmental stages of self-knowledge, self-awareness, and self-evaluation. How is the self-concept constructed, and what leads the child to hold the self in high esteem, or conversely to conclude that one has little worth as a person?

The Development of Self-Knowledge

Origins in Infancy. The focus of this chapter is the development of self during early and middle childhood. However, we must first briefly review the initial stages in this developmental process. Consider the fact that when the infant comes into the world, he or she not only has no concept of self, but no concept of the significant others in his or her life. The infant does not even have the most rudimentary notion that he or she is separate from the mother. Gradually, the infant advances through a series of stages of self-knowledge and self-awareness (see Harter, 1983).

The beginning awareness of self appears to emerge in the first year with the appreciation that one's body is separate from the mother's, and that one is an active, causal agent in space. Some clever experiments in which infants are placed in front of mirrors have provided this evidence (see Bertenthal & Fischer, 1978; Lewis & Brooks-Gunn, 1979). The infant playfully waves its arms, bounces, and engages in other rhymthic activities before the mirror, as if it appreciated the fact that "the image moves when I move"; that is, the infant appears to have some rudimentary awareness of the cause and effect relationship between one's own body movements and the moving visual image in the mirror. The infant also comes to realize that the self is an active agent independent of other people who can cause their own movements in space. Thus, movement of the self is separate from the movement of the mother. This is a major advance that occurs toward the end of the first year. However, there are still major limitations. For example, the infant does not yet know what he or she looks like in the sense that the infant cannot recognize its own face.

To become accustomed to one's face requires considerable experience with reflective surfaces such as mirrors. The experiments have demonstrated that it is not until the second year of life that infants can recognize their own facial features (Amsterdam, 1972; Bertenthal & Fischer, 1978; Lewis & Brooks-Gunn, 1979). In these studies, the experimenter takes some rouge and places a red mark on the infant's nose and then puts the infant in front of a mirror. Prior to about 15 months of age, the infant displays no reaction to the rouge on its nose, whereas from 15 months on the infant will touch its nose or point to the rouge. In touching one's nose, the infant appears to recognize that the image in the mirror is of the self, and that the rouge violates the internalized representation one has of one's face. Facial recognition, therefore, represents a major developmental turning point in self-knowledge.

With increasing cognitive development and the advent of language, other forms of self-knowledge emerge. By the age of 18 months, the toddler can state his or her name and can identify the self in pictures, distinguishing between the self and other toddlers. These developmental acquisitions are quickly followed by the first category labels that come to define the self, in that the 2-year old can state "I am a girl, not a boy" (gender category) as well as "I am a baby or child, not a grownup" (age categories). However, this is a far cry from the elaborate system of categories and self-descriptions used by adolescents and adults. Thus, we turn next to an examination of the developmental stages of self-knowledge that emerge during early childhood, middle childhood, and adolescence.

The Construction of the Self During Early Childhood

If we were to give preschoolers an age-appropriate version of the "Who am I" question, asking them to describe themselves, we would obtain the following type of self-descriptions:

> I am a boy, my name is Jason. I live with my mother and father in a big house. I have a kitty that's orange and a sister named Lisa and a television that's in my *own* room. I'm four years old and I know all my A,B,C's. Listen to me say them, A, B, C, D, E, F, G, H, J, L, K, O, M, P, R, Q, X, Z. I can run faster than anyone. I like pizza and I have a nice teacher. I can count up to 100, want to hear me? I love my dog, Skipper. I can climb to the top of the jungle gym. I have brown hair and I go to preschool. I'm really strong, I can lift this chair, watch me!

Major Features.   How can we best extract the characteristics of the young child's self-portrait? First and foremost, the preschooler describes concrete, *observable* behaviors or characteristics (Montemayor & Eisen, 1977; Rosenberg, 1979); that is, anyone could verify these attributes by observing Jason directly. Moreover, they give *specific* examples rather than generalizations. Thus, we learn about Jason's cat and dog, rather than that he likes animals. Similarly, particular skills are touted (numbers, letters, running, and climbing) rather than more general references to being smart or good at sports. Moreover, often these descriptions spill over into actual demonstrations of one's abilities, suggesting that these emerging self-attributes are very directly tied to behavior. They do not represent higher order conceptual categories through which the self is defined. Nor are they likely to be very realistic appraisals of the self (witness Jason's knowledge of the alphabet!).

In addition to the description of behaviors, the young child also expresses *preferences* (e.g., Jason likes pizza) and identifies *possessions* (he has a cat and a television in his own room). Specific *physical* characteristics are also often mentioned, as are other *family members*. Note two more general features: There is *little organization* to the description, nor is there any *negativity*. Rather, we have a rather disjointed account of "all things bright and beautiful" about the self.

Cognitive Limitations.   The preschooler's protrait of the self reflects, to a large degree, certain cognitive limitations of what Piaget (1960, 1963) termed the *preoperational* or prelogical period of development. At this stage, the child is not yet capable of understanding logical relations; for example, Jason cannot relate his counting ability to his facility with the alphabet in order to come up with the generalized concept of smartness nor can his adeptness on the jungle gym be combined with observations of his strength in order to arrive at a generalization concerning his physical abilities. The child can only make reference to a variety of very specific behaviors or characteristics rather than higher order concepts about the self.

Furthermore, the positivity observed in all likihood reflects an inflated sense of one's abilities because the young child does not have the cognitive ability to test or logically deduce whether these judgments are realistic. In fact, findings clearly demonstrate that the young child is very inaccurate in judging his or her abilities, if one compares the child's self-perceptions to more objective standards such as teachers' ratings (Harter & Pike, 1984). There we find that with skills such as running, counting, and knowing one's letters and colors, the child typically evaluates the self as more skillful than does the teacher. This results from the fact that most young children *confuse* the *wish* to be competent with reality, and as a result their self-judgments represent overestimations of their true abilities. It is important to note, however, that these distortions are due to the cognitive limitations of this period. The child is not willfully misrepresenting his or her competencies but is simply unable to realistically or logically test the postulates in his or her self-theory. Thus, the child cannot differentiate one's *real* from one's *ideal* self-image.

The rather disjointed nature of Jason's narrative results from the fact that the young child does not yet have the ability to organize logically these self-descriptions into any coherent picture of the self. Moreover, if one were to obtain a different description from the same child, at another point in time, it might well be somewhat inconsistent with the first self-description. The child, however, is unable to recognize such contradictions and is thus unconcerned about the lack of logical consistency.

We can relate this latter point to Piaget's observations with regard to the concept of *conservation*. In the classic water beaker experiment, where water is poured from a short, wide beaker into a tall, thin beaker, the preoperational child will assert that the quantity of liquid has changed. There is now more water in the tall beaker because it is higher; that is, the amount of water is not conserved in the mind of the young child. Similarly, when transformations occur in the life of the child at this age, one's attributes may well change, and we observe lack of "conservation of self." This phenomenon has been most dramatically demonstrated by Kohlberg (1966), who found that *gender constancy,* the appreciation that one's gender does not change, is not achieved until the ages of 5 to 7. Thus, whereas preschoolers may readily provide an account of their attributes, these descriptions do not necessarily represent a stable conceptualization of the self. (See Table 3.1 where the various features of the young child's self-description are summarized.)

Self-Descriptions in Middle Childhood

Contrast the preschooler's self-description with that of a child in the middle to late elementary school grades, Jason's sister, Lisa:

> I'm in the fifth grade this year at Rockland Elementary School. I'm pretty popular. That's because I'm nice and helpful, the other girls in my class say that I am. I have two girlfriends who are really close friends, and I'm good at keeping their secrets. Most of the boys are pretty yukky. My brother Jason is younger and I don't feel that way about him, tho' sometimes he gets on my nerves too. But I control my temper most of the time and don't get toó angry and I'd be ashamed of myself if I got really mad at him. I've always been smart at school, ever since the first grade and I'm proud of myself for that. This year I'm doing really well in reading, social studies, and science, better than the other kids. But some of them do better than me in math, like on tests where sometimes I goof up. When that happens, I feel really dumb, but usually not for long. I don't worry about it that much, and most of the time I feel like I'm smart. I'm not very good at sports, like I don't do well at baseball, soccer, or gymnastics. I don't really see why they even have sports in school since they just aren't that important. I'd like to be an actress when I grow up but nobody thinks I am pretty enough. Jennifer, my older sister is really really pretty, but I'm smarter than she is. I know I would make a good teacher, that's what my friends say and that's what I'll probably be. Mostly I am just me. Some things about me might change when I get older but alot of them will probably stay the same. I'm a pretty OK person.

Major Features.   Self-descriptions at this age are different from those of younger children on a number of dimensions (see Table 3.1). One major difference is the emergence of *trait* labels such as popular, helpful, smart, and references to athletic ability and physical attractiveness. The child at this age combines a number of specific behaviors into a more generalized concept about the self. Moreover, children often indicate the process through which they arrive at such a generalization. For example, Lisa infers smartness from her perfor-

TABLE 3.1
Features of Self–Description to Emerge
at Three Developmental Periods

	Early Childhood	Middle Childhood	Adolescence
Structure Content	Specific examples of observable physical characteristics, behaviors, abilities, preferences, possessions.	Trait labels reflecting the ability to integrate behaviors into generalized concepts about the self. Focus on abilities, interpersonal characteristics, and emotional atributes, including self-affects.	Abstractions about the self involving psychological constructs, due to ability to integrate traits into higher order generalizations. Abstractions focus on different roles and relationships.
Organization	Little coherence to description of self, due to inability to logically organize single self-descriptions.	Self-attributes logically organized, integrated within domains which are differentiated from one another.	Ability to construct a formal theory of the self in which all attributes across and within role domain are integrated and should be internally consistent.
Stability, Interest	Self-descriptions not stable over time, little constancy, although no recognition, interest, or concern.	Recognition of, interest in, continuity and stability of self-attributes over time.	Intrapsychic conflict and confusion over contradictions and instability within the self, concern with creation of an integrated identity. Intense preoccupation with the self.
Bases, Criteria	Fantacies, wishes dominate description of behaviors and abilities rather than direct self-observation.	Use of social comparison due to ability to simultaneously observe and evaluate the self in relation to others in one's reference group.	Intense focus on the opinions which significant others hold of the self, particularly opinions of peers and close friends.
Ability to Evaluate	Criticism of others, but inability to critically observe and evaluate the self.	Aware that others are critically evaluating the self; adopts these attitudes and standards in forming the looking-glass self.	Creation of imaginary audience which is critically evaluating the self. Blurs the distinction between this evaluation and self-criticism.

(*Continued*)

TABLE 3.1   (*Continued*)

	Early Childhood	Middle Childhood	Adolescence
Valence, Accuracy	Self-statements extremely positive, inflated sense of self. Inaccuracies due to confusion between the ideal and the real self.	More accurate appraisal of self due to ability to use social comparison and to realistically observe the self. Both positive and negative self-evaluation.	Adolescent egocentrism may preclude accurate appraisals of abstractions which define the self and are less testable. Vacillation from positive to negative self-evaluations within the same domain or role.

mance in specific school subjects. Her poor athletic ability is based on her performance across several different sports. Her popularity and social acceptance are based on the fact that she is nice, helpful, and keeps secrets. Lisa's self-description is typical of children moving into late childhood, in that the trait labels applied to the self become increasingly interpersonal (Rosenberg, 1979); that is, one's relationship to others, particularly peers and close friends, becomes more salient dimensions of the self.

In providing the behavioral evidence for these trait labels, we find a much more coherent self-portrait than we observed in young children. Lisa's account is logically organized around particular themes that represent the different domains relevant to her self-definition, and the narrative flows smoothly from one topic to the next.

We also see the effect of *other's opinion* on Lisa's self-evaluation. She is concerned about what others think about her sociability, her attractiveness, and her potential as a good teacher. The incorporation of these opinions into her own self-description represents an example of what Cooley (1902) termed the *looking-glass-self;* that is, the significant others in one's life become social mirrors, as it were, and one gazes into these mirrors in order to determine others' opinions of oneself. One then adopts this opinion in forming one's self-definition. Lisa is particularly sensitive to the opinion of her peers, whereas a few years earlier, parental opinion was more salient (Rosenberg, 1979).

Another feature of self-description at this stage is the use of *social comparison* as a means of determining the competence or adequacy of the self. Lisa's judgment of her academic competence is based on a comparison of her performance with that of her classmates, whereas her opinion of her attractiveness involves a comparison with her older sister. In making these comparisons, Lisa arrives at a more balanced self-portrait than her younger brother Jason. Thus, in the domain of academics she concludes that she is reasonably competent, whereas her judgment is more negative with regard to her appearance. Sports is another arena where she feels relatively incompetent, indicating that she can make distinctions between the different domains of relevance to the self. It is also likely that her judgments are reasonably *accurate,* in contrast to the self-descriptions of her younger brother.

Although one finds mention of negative self-attributes at this age level, one also observes the emergence of mechanisms through which the potentially damaging impact to the self can be reduced. For example, although Lisa admits her lack of ability in sports, she also considers this domain to be relatively *unimportant.* Her anticipated career as a teacher rather than an actress also represents an attempt to highlight her strengths. In a subsequent section on self-worth, we return to this issue of the mechanisms that children come to develop in order to protect and enhance the self.

On another point, we find the introduction of *emotion concepts* as self-descriptors during middle and later childhood. In Lisa's account, we find references to feeling proud, not that worried, and not too angry. The ability to control one's emotions and related behavior, particularly anger, becomes an important dimension of self-evaluation during this period. The emergence of self-control as a salient criterion for evaluating one's worth as a person has been noted elsewhere in the literature (Minton, 1981; Rosenberg, 1979). It is of interest that whereas very young children obviously experience a range of emotions, often very intensely, neither the expression nor the control of these emotions finds its way into the self-descriptions at younger age levels; that is, they are not yet defining characteristics of the self.

Furthermore, we not only find emotion concepts in Lisa's self-description, but we observe the emergence of *self-affects,* namely emotions directed toward the self. For example, Lisa would be *ashamed* of *herself* if she lost her temper. She is *proud* of *herself* because she does well at school. The ability to experience these emotions directed toward the self does not emerge until middle childhood (Harter, 1983). The very young child may experience pride and shame, if one's parents express the fact that they are proud of the child's accomplishments or ashamed of the child's transgressions. It is not until approximately third grade, however, that children can, in the absence of parental observations of their behavior, feel proud or ashamed of *themselves.* Moreover, not only does the child develop the ability to experience these self-affects, but they find their way into one's self-descriptions.

Self-descriptions in middle childhood also reflect an interest in the *continuity* of the self over time. Lisa's references to her scholastic competence imply stability with the past (she notes that she has done well in school since first grade) as well as some projection into the future. She gives some thought to the general issue of whether she will change or stay the same, concluding that she will probably be a teacher. During this period, children begin to think about the issue of trait stability or the constancy of attributes that define the self (Dweck &

Elliot, 1983; Guardo & Bohan, 1971; Ruble, in press), an issue that was not of interest or concern when they were younger.

Underlying Cognitive Abilities During Middle Childhood.   With these various features in mind, how can such developmental shifts in self-description be explained in terms of the emerging cognitive abilities during middle childhood? Cognitive-developmental theory (Fischer, 1980; Piaget, 1960, 1963) alerts us to many relevant skills that emerge during the period of *concrete operations.* At this particular stage, beginning at approximately the age of 6, the child is now able to begin to think logically at least with regard to the concrete, observable elements of one's world, including the behaviors or the self. The child can classify events into *categories* and can begin to develop conceptual hierarchies within these categories. For example, the category of animals can be divided into wild and domestic, and within each of these subcategories the child can identify any number of exemplars, e.g., lions, tigers, elephants, and bears (wild animals) versus dogs, cats, cows, and horses (domestic animals).

Thus, a major cognitive advance in middle childhood results from newfound abilities at *conceptual integration.* Moreover, the child's ability to classify and hierarchize concepts logically extends to attempts at self-definition. In particular, it provides the skills whereby particular behaviors can be organized and categorized into *trait labels.* We observed earlier that the young child is conceptually ill equipped to relate one self-descriptor to another. Thus, Jason could not observe the links between potentially related characteristics such as his strength and his ability to climb the jungle gym. In contrast, Lisa is able to integrate the observations of her successes across various school subjects in order to arrive at a trait label or conceptual generalization about her school performance, namely that she is *smart.*

Lisa employs a similar process within the domain of athletics, integrating the observations of her performance at several sports, which lead to the generalized conclusion that she is not good at sports. What has been emphasized by cognitive-developmental theorists in the tradition of Piaget is that not only do these new conceptual abilities emerge, but that the child has a penchant for utilizing these new cognitive structures. Thus, the child is eager to organize, classify, and hierarchize the elements of his or her world, as well as attributes of the self. This organizational penchant also accounts for the greater coherence observed in the self-descriptions of children in middle childhood.

The ability to relate one concept to another, to compare two elements simultaneously, is also a prerequisite to both an interest in the *continuity* of the self and the use of *social comparison* information. With regard to the continuity of the self, the child is now able to compare the self in the present with the self in the past, holding these aspects in mind simultaneously. To the extent that one attempts to focus on similarities, to integrate these self-observations, one comes to the conclusion that one's attributes are conserved over time.

The basic ability to compare different elements or features simultaneously is also necessary in order to appreciate the implications that social comparison has for the evaluation of the self. The child must be able to compare simultaneously the characteristics of another child to the attributes of the self, in order to detect differences or similarites. These comparisons are likely to take on greater meaning, against a backdrop of trait labels that the child may well view as relatively stable (Ruble, in press). Through this type of analysis we come to see how changes in one's concept of self are very intimately related to changes in the child's cognitive abilities.

Self-Descriptions During Adolescence

Having provided an analysis of the self-descriptions of early and middle childhood, we now turn to a cameo of the self provided by the adolescent, in the words of Jennifer, the 15-year-old sister of Jason and Lisa.

> I'm pretty complicated, actually. Most people don't understand me, *especially* my parents! I'm sensitive, moody, affectionate, and sometimes self-conscious. It depends on who I am with. When I'm with my *friends,* mostly my *best* friends that is, I'm sensitive and understanding. But sometimes I can also be extremely uncaring and selfish. At home, with my parents I'm affectionate, but I can also get very moody; sometimes I get really depressed and go the the opposite extreme. I'm usually pretty tolerant of my little brother and sister. But I'm a different person on a date. I'm outgoing and I can be alot of fun. There's this one guy I went out with, tho', and I know he was trying to analyze me! When that happens I just change on the spot! I get self-conscious and nervous and then I become a *total* introvert. I don't know what to say or how to act. It really bugs me too. I mean the *real* me is fun-loving so why do I have to act so *weird?* I also don't really understand why I treat my friends the way I do. I'm a naturally sensitive person and I care alot about their feelings, but sometimes I say really nasty things to them. I'm not a horrible person, I know that, but then how can I *say* horrible things that I don't really mean? Sometimes I feel pretty confused and mixed up about it. Talking to my best girl friends, Tammy and Sharon, helps. We talk on the phone for hours. They understand me better than anyone else, and they care about me. You probably don't understand what I'm trying to say. What I mean is that I can be pretty obnoxious with my friends sometimes, but that's not who I *really* am as a *person.* That's not part of my personality, its just the way I act sometimes, and its not that important, actually, so I probably shouldn't even have mentioned it. There are things that are much more important, for example, I think I am good-looking. Not exactly Brook Shields, understand, but I'm really attractive compared to the other girls in my school, or at least in the group I go around with, *they* think I'm good-looking. My little sister Lisa tells me I'm pretty too, but she really bugs me because there are days when I look at myself in the mirror and think I look absolutely, totally, atrocious, I'm the ugliest person in the *entire world!* She tries to talk me out of it, but what does she know about looks, she's only 10! My mother is the same way. She'll say "you look lovely, dear" when I really look like a total zero! But then

there are days when I look great, and my mom says "Are you going out with your hair like *that*?" I hate to go to school on days like that, I get really depressed. Besides, I'm pretty bored at school anyway. Nothing they teach is *relevant* to anything in *life!* I think of myself as an inquisitive person but there's nothing about school subjects to be curious about. So I'm a pretty mediocre student, I just do what I have to in order to get by, but it doesn't bother me that much, its just not that important. I know *everyone* in class is looking at me thinking I'm really dumb, but I only care about what my friends think. Besides I'm going to be an airline stewardness, anyway. Well *probably*. So are my best friends, Tammy and Sharon, we're all going to airline school together after we graduate, *if* we graduate. I'm confused about what to do. Subconsciously I want to quit, but then the real me knows I should stay in school for my own good. I really don't know. There are days when I wish I could just become immune to myself!

Major Features and Cognitive Underpinnings.   How can we summarize the primary features of self-description in adolescence, and how are these features dependent, in part, on cognitive-developmental change during this period? A major characteristic of adolescent self-description is the use of *abstract concepts* in making reference to the self. For example, Jennifer refers to herself as sensitive, moody, self-conscious, affectionate, obnoxious, attractive, tolerant, a total introvert, etc. As Rosenberg (1979) has pointed out, the adolescent describes his or her *psychological interior,* characteristics that describe the inner world of one's feelings, thoughts, and personality.

These abstractions represent a cognitive advance over the preadolescent who could only combine particular behaviors into trait labels. The adolescent, at a new stage of cognitive development, can now integrate one's tendencies to be both depressed and fun loving into the abstraction "moody." To consider oneself "sensitive" one must combine such traits as friendly, helpful, caring, and good listener. This new level of intergrative abilities comes about with the entrance into Piaget's period of *formal operations.* The adolescent is now able to apply one's logical operations to constructs about the self that are unobservable and hypothetical, which are abstract generalizations about the self; that is, these self attributes require much more inference about one's latent characteristics than do the self-descriptions of the younger child.

At the same time that the adolescent is integrating concepts about the self in the form of such abstractions, there is also *differentiation* within the self based on the various roles that one must adopt. Thus, Jennifer presents one set of self-abstractions in relationship to her family, whereas the self is quite different with friends. Yet another set of characteristics surfaces in her self-description within romantic relationships. Thus, one possesses different selves depending on the particular role or context.

Contradictions Within the Self.   These different selves represent an underlying cognitive advance in the form of ability to differentiate; yet they also pose what William James (1892) initially entitled the "conflict of the different Me's"; that is, one may well recognize contradictions within the self. For example, Jennifer is understanding with her friends, but moody with her family. In addition, she experiences conflict *within* the various roles she plays. She is outgoing on a date and then becomes a total introvert. She is caring with her friends but then says horrible things to them. She is affectionate with her parents but then gets depressed and goes to the opposite extreme.

The self-descriptions of the adolescent are not stable, therefore, but vacillate from the display of a given attribute to its opposite. In these observations, we see a more advanced form of lack of conservation of self that typically accompanies movement to a new stage of cognitive development. Furthermore, these contradictions within the self become quite bothersome to the adolescent. In fact, it has been demonstrated that adolescents perceive these inconsistencies as clashes within one's personality, clashes that are a major source of distress and confusion (Harter, 1986; Monsour, 1985); that is, they cause considerable intrapsychic conflict. Such conflict becomes particularly apparent at about the age of 15.

The structure of Jennifer's self-portrait, including the inconsistencies within her personality that cause such conflict, is depicted in Fig. 3.1. This particular self-portrait is adapted from our findings with ninth graders. We ask subjects to first make lists of self-attributes in four different roles or contexts: how they are with their friends, with their family, at school, and in romantic relationships. They then organize these attributes into clusters and also indicate which are the most important, less important, and the least important aspects of their personality. Finally, they are asked to indicate whether any of these attributes are clashing, fighting, or at war with each other within their personality. The conflicts are represented by the double-headed arrows in the portrait depicted in Fig. 3.1.

As Jennifer's self-picture reveals, her attributes are organized around the four roles we inquired about, such that there are four clusters of self-descriptions according to how she sees herself with friends, with family, in school, and in romantic relationships. This figure also depicts the various conflicts she is experiencing, most of which are *within* each of the roles depicted. It is interesting that we do not find evidence for much conflict prior to the ninth grade. This raises the question of why it does not emerge until middle adolescence.

The tendency for contradictions within the self to be observed and to cause conflict is in large part based on new cognitive abilities now possessed in middle adolescence. One is now capable of constructing a *theory* of the self, which involves the *integration* of the multiple concepts of the self; that is, one can relate one abstraction about the self to another (Fischer, 1980). Note that a major criterion for any good theory, be it a theory in science or a theory about the self, is that all the postulates of the theory be *internally consistant* (Epstein, 1973). However, given the role experimentation, the physiological changes, new social demands, and mood swings of adolescence, one's self-expression is often not

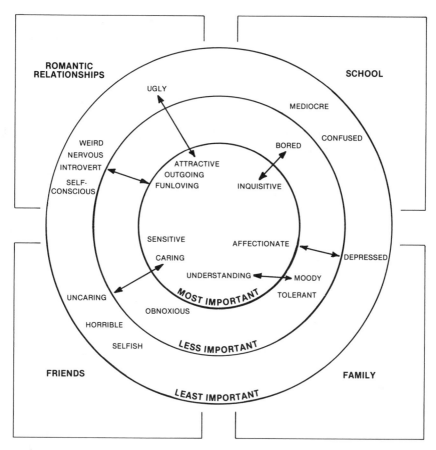

FIG. 3.1. Prototypical self-protrait of a ninth grader, as exemplified by Jennifer's self-description.

consistent, either across roles or within roles. Yet the adolescent has the cognitive ability to detect these inconsistencies as one attempts to construct a general theory of one's personality, an integrated identity. The realization of these contradictions, therefore, creates considerable conflict within the self-system, conflict that leads to a sense of confusion and psychological distress. In Jennifer's account, for example, we see her agonizing over these inconsistencies, particularly those that occur within a particular role or interpersonal context.

Adolescent Preoccupation with the Self. The penchant for constructing an entire portrait of the self in which the different characteristics of the self are integrated helps to explain why the adolescent appears so *preoccupied* with his or her own personality. The canvas for such a portrait is overwhelmingly large, the

57

elements to integrate are numerous, and therefore the task becomes all consuming. Unlike the younger children, whose descriptions were relatively brief and direct, the lengthy and often tortured self-descriptions provided by Jennifer convey the intensity of these processes during adolescence.

This introspectiveness, this intense preoccupation with the self, is not conducted in isolation. Rather, the adolescent turns to one's friends for support and self-clarification. Lisa turns to her girlfriends, to help her sort things out. It is their opinion of her that is most critical to her emerging self-definition. In so doing, we see an intensification of the *looking-glass self* phenomenon that began in middle childhood. As Rosenberg (1979) has pointed out, one's *best friends* become the major source of reflected appraisals; they become the social mirror into which the adolescent anxiously stares.

The self-consciousness and preoccupation with a theory of self represents one form of what Elkind (1967) has termed *adolescent egocentrism*. As Elkind observed, the adolescent often concludes that others are as preoccupied with his or her appearance as he or she. Thus, *others* are analyzing or thinking about the self, as in Jennifer's account of her date, or her classmates thinking she was dumb. The construction of this *imaginary audience,* to use Elkind's label, reflects the convergence of intense self-consciousness, the heightened importance of the looking-glass self, and some difficulty in differentiating one's own thoughts and preoccupations from those of others.

There is another element of adolescent egocentrism that Elkind identifies as the *personal fable.* The adolescent tends to feel that one's own experiences are so unique and novel that no one else could possibly appreciate them, particularly one's parents and those outside one's circle of close friends. In Jennifer's self-description we learn that neither her parents nor her younger sister really understand her. Neither does the interviewer, a neutral adult who was merely recording her self-descriptions!

Mechanisms to Protect the Self.   Despite the confusion and sense of conflict provoked by these introspective attempts to fathom the self, we see evidence of mechanisms designed to protect and enhance the self. It is most evident in Jennifer's descriptions of those contradictions in herself that occurred within a particular interpersonal role. She laments the fact that she sometimes says nasty things to her friends even though she is not a horrible person. Yet in so doing, she sees her *real* self as naturally sensitive and caring, *not* a horrible *person.* Rather, from time to time negative behaviors may inexplicably be displayed, but these are *not* at the core of her personality. In fact, she denies their importance. In another sphere, she sees herself as basically inquisitive. She admits she is bored and a mediocre student in school but denies the importance of her behavior in this context.

This tendency to deny the importance of one's negative characteristics has been systematically documented in our own research (Harter, 1986; Monsour,

1985). As Fig. 3.1 indicates, when we have adolescents sort their various self-descriptive labels into those that are at the center of their personality, those that are less important, and those that are the least important, there is a definite pattern. Adolescents very consistently identify positive attributes as the core constructs in their self-portrait, whereas negative attributes are relegated to the periphery of one's personality. For example, in Jennifer's depiction, attributes such as attractive, fun loving, sensitive, affectionate, and inquisitive are located at the center of the self. In contrast, the most negative self-descriptions, e.g., ugly, mediocre, depressed, selfish, nervous, are placed in the outer ring, as the least important attributes of the self. By depicting one's personality in this manner, the adolescent is able to maintain a reasonably positive self-image, touting one's admirable qualities as central to the self. The importance of behaviors that are less than admirable is minimized and they are perceived as foreign to one's true self.

This analysis highlights the fact that not only does the nature of self-description change dramatically over the course of development, but that these changes are very dependent on the emergence of new cognitive abilities. Generally, in treatments of cognitive development, advances to new levels of thinking are discussed in terms of their positive implications. We can also see from our analysis, however, that the emergence of a higher level of cognitive development also brings with it certain vulnerabilities for the self. The child moving into the period of concrete operations, with the newfound capacity for social comparison, must now run the risk of realizing that one may not be as smart or as athletic or as attractive as others within one's reference group (Maccoby & Martin, 1983). The adolescent, moving solidly into the period of formal operations, must now run the risk of realizing that there are serious contradictions within the self-theory that one is trying so valiantly to construct. We need to appreciate the fact that developmental strides bring with them new organizational capacities that directly impact the self. However, they also present new challenges and stresses with which the individual must cope.

Developmental Stages in Self-Awareness

The previous sections have documented age differences in the nature of children's self-description, focusing primarily on the cognitive-developmental factors responsible for these changes. However, the child obviously does not develop in a vacuum. The significant others in one's life have a major impact on one's evolving self-image. These socializing influences operate in conjunction with cognitive-developmental change.

Consider the concept of the looking-glass self. We noted earlier that our sense of self is in part determined by the opinions that we feel others hold about us. We incorporate those perceptions into our self-image. However, the very ability to recognize that others are evaluating the self must develop; it is not present in the young child. This recognition is a prerequisite to self-awareness. From two sources, the descriptive accounts of development provided by Gesell and Ilg (1946) and the theorizing of Selman (1980), we can piece together a picture of the stages of self-awareness. As depicted in Fig. 3.2, we first need to distinguish between two separate aspects of the self and other. One can be an observer but one can also be observed.

At the *first* stage, which occurs at approximately age 5, the child can observe others, but does not realize that others can observe the self. Thus, the 5-year old seems preoccupied with evaluating the conduct and correctness of one's friends' or classmates' behavior, frequently criticizing them on this account. However, the very young child is unable to recognize that friends are also observing him or her in this same light, nor can the young child observe or critically evaluate the self directly.

At the *second stage*, the child comes to appreciate the fact that others are observing and evaluating the self. Moreover, as Gesell and Ilg note, children become concerned about what others might think of them and are careful not to

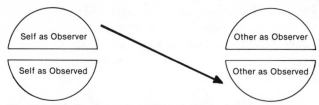
Stage 1. Self as Observer evaluates Other as Observed. I am evaluating you.

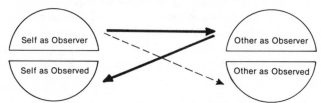
Stage 2. Self as Observer is aware that Other as Observer is evaluating the Self as Observed. I'm aware that you are evaluating me.

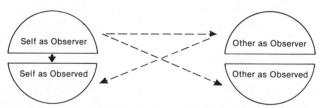
Stage 3. Self as Observer evaluates Self as Observed. I can evaluate myself.

FIG. 3.2.   Stages leading to self-awareness.

expose themselves to criticism. They worry about making mistakes and cringe when they are laughed at or made fun of. This second stage, therefore, sets the stage for the looking-glass self in that the child becomes aware that others are appraising the self. The limitation of this stage, however, can be seen in the fact that the child cannot critically observe the self directly.

At the third stage, which emerges around the age of 8, the child can begin to incorporate the observations of others into one's own self-perceptions and can directly evaluate the self. Children become interested in evaluating their own performance, based on the standards that other people have for the self. During this period, they internalize these expectations into self-standards. In so doing, they also develop the capacity for self-criticism, if they feel that they fail to meet these standards.

This third stage also marks the emergence of the ability to *compare oneself* to *others*. The child can now simultaneously observe both self and other, and this ability to engage in social comparison provides a major index of the self's adequacy. As we noted earlier, the very young child's self-descriptions often represent quite an unrealistic inflation of their competencies, in part because they do not yet have the ability to compare their performance to that of others. Thus, the ability to observe, evaluate, and criticize the self must develop through a series of stages that begin with an awareness that others are evaluating the self and with the ability to compare oneself to one's social reference group.

A Domain-Specific Approach to Self-Evaluation

As we have seen in the preceding sections, one's self-portrait is not merely a description of one's attributes, but it contains critical *evaluations* of judgments about the adequacy of the self. This evaluative component forms the basis for what many have labelled one's *self-esteem* or self-image. Do we hold the self in high regard, or do we have a negative opinion of the self? From the types of spontaneous self-descriptions presented, we might be able to infer each child's self-esteem. Psychologists, however, have been interested in obtaining a more precise index of the *level* of a child's regard for the self. Thus, there have been attempts to *quantify* self-esteem.

Until recently, theorists and investigators treated self-esteem as a general judgment about the self that could be represented by a single score (Coopersmith, 1967; Piers & Harris, 1969). Questionnaires designed to assess self-esteem typically included items that tapped the children's evaluation of their performance across numerous areas of their life. Self-evaluative judgments about school performance, interactions with family members, peer relationships, emotional reactivity, conduct, appearance, and so forth were elicited by giving the following types of true-false questions: I do well at school, My family understands me, I am easy to like, I hardly ever get upset, I usually behave myself, I have a nice appearance. The evaluative responses to such an aggregate of items (which typically number from 40 to 60) are then summed into a total score which represents the level of one's self-esteem from extremely positive (if the subject responds affirmatively to most or all items) to extremely negative (if the subject indicates that these statements are false, that is, they do not characterize the self).

More recently, theorists and investigators of the self have questioned whether this framework and method of assessment provides a sensitive enough appraisal of the child's self-esteem (see Harter, 1982, 1983, 1986). The single score approach implies that one's sense of esteem is at the same level across all areas of one's life. However, the child may well evaluate the self differently depending upon the particular domain in question. For example, a child may feel very competent at schoolwork, somewhat less adequate in the realm of peer relationships, and relatively incompetent in the domain of athletics. The single-score approach, however, would mask these differences in self-evaluation. If one merely summed scores across these different domains, one would falsely conclude that the child's self-esteem was neither high nor low, but average in all areas.

As an alternative to the single-score approach, a number of theorists have put forth domain-specific models in which one assesses each domain separately (see Harter, 1983, 1986). This domain-specific approach provides a *profile* of scores that depict differences in the child's sense of adequacy across the various domains identified by the investigator. That is, the child's responses to a questionnaire lead to separate scores for each domain.

We have adopted such a domain-specific approach in our own work (see Harter, 1982; 1983; 1985a; 1985b; 1986). Our Self-Perception Profile for Children (1985b) taps five specific domains in the lives of children age 8 and older. These are:

1. *Scholastic Competence:* How competent, smart, the child feels with regard to schoolwork.
2. *Athletic Competence:* How competent the child feels at sports and games requiring physical skill, athletic ability.
3. *Social Acceptance:* How popular or socially accepted the child feels in social interactions with peers.
4. *Behavioral Conduct:* How adequate the child feels with regard to behaving the way one is supposed to.
5. *Physical Appearance.* How good looking the child feels, how much one likes such physical characteristics as height, weight, face, hair.

The Issue of Question Format.   Typically, on earlier self-esteem measures, a two-choice response format has been employed where the child indicates whether a statement (e.g., I have alot of friends) is true or false for the self. Investigators have found, however, that this type of format does not provide a broad enough range of options. As a result, when forced with only two choices, children often give the socially desirable response, that is, they typically endorse the positive choice (see Harter, 1982). Thus, their responses may not provide an accurate self-evaluation.

On our Self-Perception Profile for Children, we have sought to avoid this problem by devising an alternative question format. The child is presented with items in the form depicted in Table 3.2 where there is a sample item for each domain. The child's task is to first decide whether he or she is more like the kids described in the first half of the statement on the left, or more like the kids described in the second half of the statement on the right. Once having made this decision, the child next indicates whether the half of the statement that best characterizes the self is only Sort of True or Really True. Thus, the child checks one of the four boxes for each item.

Items are scored according to a 4-point scale. If children pick the statement describing the mark competent or adequate kids and indicate that this is Very True for the self, they receive a score of 4. If the check that this statement is only Sort of True for them, they receive a score of 3. If they endorse the side of the statement depicting less competent kids and indicate that this description is just

TABLE 3.2
Sample Items from the Self-Perception Profile for Children

Really True for me	Sort of True for me			Sort of True for me	Really True for me
1	2	Some kids have *trouble* figuring out the answers in school	BUT	Other kids almost *always* can figure out the answers.	3	4
4	3	Some kids do very *well* at all kinds of sports	BUT	Others *don't* feel that they are very good when it comes to sports.	2	1
4	3	Some kids are *popular* with others their age	BUT	Other kids are *not* very popular.	2	1
1	2	Some kids usually get in *trouble* because of things they do	BUT	Other kids usually *don't* do things that get them in trouble.	3	4
1	2	Some kids wish their physical appearance was *different*	BUT	Other kids *like* their physical appearance the way it is.	3	4
4	3	Some kids *like* the kind of *person* they are	BUT	Other kids often wish they were someone else.	2	1

Sort of True for Me, they receive a score of 2. If they indicate that the less competent description is Really True for the self, they receive a score of 1.

These scores are not printed on the actual form that the child fills out. They are presented in the table merely to illustrate the scoring procedure. Also note that half the items begin with a statement describing the more competent or adequate kids, whereas the other half begin with a statement describing less competent kids. This is done so that we know that child respondents are actually reading the items and tracking their content. The actual form of the scale that the child fills out has six items for each domain. The average of the six scores for each separate domain is calculated, leading to a profile of scores across these domains.

We have found this question format to be very effective in reducing children's tendency to give the socially desirable response, for several reasons. Children do not have to endorse or deny bold "I" statements about the self. Rather, our items present descriptions of how existing types of kids feel about themselves, and we invite the child respondent to *identify* with one group; that is, they legitimize the child's choice. For the child who is not very competent, such an item conveys the fact that lots of kids in the real world feel the same way, and thus the items allow the child to admit that he or she is a member of this existing group.

In addition, we have found that the option of checking either Sort of True for Me or Really True for Me allows the child a greater range of responses than the typical two-choice format. For example, a child who questions his competency at schoolwork is more likely to check that side of the statement if it is possible to indicate that this is only sort of true. In general, therefore, we feel that we are obtaining a reasonably accurate portrayal of most children's sense of adequacy in these domains.

With younger children the task of obtaining an accurate portrayal of one's competencies is somewhat more difficult. As we pointed out in our discussion of Jason's self-description, the young child is likely to inflate his sense of competence. We can directly assess this feature of young children's judgments, however, by employing a pictorial version that shares certain features with the questionnaire (Harter & Pike, 1984). Each plate contains two pictures, one depicting a child who is competent (e.g., gets stars on his school papers) and one depicting a child who is not very competent (e.g., does not get stars on his papers). The subject picks which child is most like him and then indicates whether this is just a little like the self (points to a small circle underneath) or alot like the self (points to a large circle).

Sample Self-Perception Profiles.   Before presenting some sample profiles of actual children from our studies, it is important to point out that there are any number of profiles that children can display. In this chapter we are only able to present a few. Think about yourself, for example, as a fifth grader. How would you reconstruct your remembrance of how you felt about yourself? What would have been your sense of adequacy across these domains? What would your unique profile have looked like?

In Fig. 3.3, we present the profiles of six different children who are in the late elementary grades. What should be noted first is that children can and do make distinctions among the different areas of their lives. They do not feel equally adequate in all domains. (If they did, they would have approximately the same subscale score in every area.) For the moment we are concentrating on the specific domain scores. We deal with the self-worth score in a subsequent section.

Consider Child A. This particular child feels very good about her scholastic performance, although this is in sharp contrast to her opinion of her athletic ability. Socially, this child feels reasonably well accepted by her peers. In addition, she considers herself to be well behaved. Her feelings about her appearance, however, are only average. This particular profile is very much like what we would expect from a child like Lisa.

Child B has a very different configuration of subscale scores across these domains. This is a boy who feels very incompetent when it comes to schoolwork. However, he feels very competent athletically and is well received by his peers. He feels that his behavioral conduct is less commendable. In contrast, he thinks he is relatively good looking.

Child A and Child B both represent children whose scores vary markedly across domains. There are other children whose profiles do not display such dramatic differences, although they make some distinction among domains. Child C represents a child who feels relatively competent in almost all domains. Whereas there are some dips in this profile with regard to athletic competence and appearance, they are not nearly as dramatic as those shown by Child A. Child D is an example of an individual who feels relatively inadequate across all domains. Nevertheless, this boy's profile is not entirely flat. He feels slightly better about himself in some domains, for example, in scholastic competence and conduct, than in others.

Child E and Child F represent two children, neither of whom feel very good about themselves scholastically or athletically. They feel much better about their social acceptance, conduct, and physical appearance. In fact, their profiles are quite similar to each other across these specific domains. Yet why, then, are they so *different* with regard to the self-worth score that is also presented? How is this to be explained? In order to understand this difference, we must next turn to a discussion of what is meant by self-worth.

Children's Perceptions of Their Global Self-Worth

There is ample evidence that most children, age 8 and older, evaluate their performance differently in the various areas of their lives. Thus, if we were to combine these subscale scores into a single score, we would mask or obscure important self-evaluative distinctions that children clearly make. If we wish to

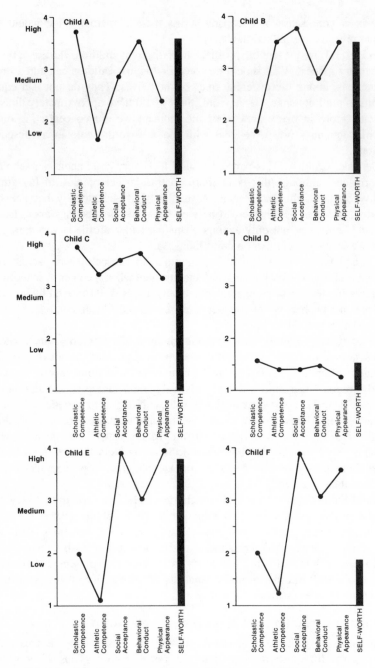

FIG. 3.3.   Sample self-perception profiles from six children.

truly understand a given child, we must take these context-specific judgments into account.

We also now know that beginning at about the third grade, children are able to make a *global* judgment about their overall *worth as a person* (Harter, 1982, 1985a,b, 1986; Rosenberg, 1979). (Prior to age 8, children are not capable of constructing a global concept of themselves as a person that can be evaluated in terms of overall worth.) Among *older* children this judgment is tapped by items that ask how much one likes oneself as a person, likes the way one is in general, is pleased with oneself, likes the way one is leading one's life, etc. A sample from the Self-Perception Profile for Children would be:

Really true for me	Sort of True for me				Sort of True for me	Really True for me
☐	☐	Some kids like the way they are leading their life	**BUT**	Other kids *don't* like the way they are leading their life.	☐	☐

There are six of these items that form the global self-worth subscale. It is important to appreciate the fact that gobal self-worth is measured directly and *independently* of the specific domains we have discussed; that is, it has its own unique set of items that inquire into one's overall judgment about how much one likes oneself as a person. (It is *not* a combination of domain-specific items.)

The concept of global self-worth has its historical roots in the writings of William James (1892) and Charles H. Cooley (1902). These scholars of the self both observed that we carry around an overall feeling about ourselves, about our worth as a human being. We make a global judgment that somehow transcends the sum of our specific self-evaluations. Many decades later, certain psychologists have documented the fact that global feelings of self-worth can be reliably measured in adults and adolescents (Rosenberg, 1979) as well as in older elementary, and middle schoolchildren (Harter, 1985a, 1985b, 1986). However, an intriguing question remains. What determines the level of one's global self-worth; why do some children have a very positive overall evaluation of the self, whereas other children have a very negative opinion of their overall worth?

The Determinants of Global Self-Worth

Both Cooley and James speculated on the antecedents of self-worth, although their formulations were quite different from each other. We have already encountered Cooley's basic formulation as represented by this concept of the looking-glass self. For Cooley, the self represented the internalized opinions that we perceive others to hold about us. *Acceptance* and *positive regard* from *others,* therefore, was an important source of one's own sense of worth as a person. For James, the evaluation of one's *competence,* one's *achievements,* was a primary determinant of self-worth. More specifically, he postulated that displays of competence in those areas where it was *important* to be *successful* were the most critical to one's overall self-esteem. We turn to each of these formulations in more detail and examine their applicability to children, ages 8 and older, who possess a sense of global self-worth.

Acceptance and Regard from Others.   We first introduced Cooley's notion of the looking-glass self in relation to the specific judgments encountered within the self-descriptions of our prototypical children. Recall that 10-year-old Lisa was concerned about what her friends thought about her appearance and her school competence. However, this formulation not only applies to domain-specific judgments but to one's sense of global self-worth as well. According to this analysis, we will have a very positive judgment about our overall worth if we perceive that significant others hold us in high regard. If we perceive that others feel negatively about us, we will internalize this attitude and have a very low opinion of ourselves, in general.

A more circumscribed version of this formulation can be seen in the writings of other theorists who have underscored the importance of feeling accepted by the important others in one's life, beginning with one's parents. Epstein (1973) emphasized what he terms *love worthiness.* Coopersmith (1967) described it as *significance,* namely acceptance, attention, and affection from others. White (1963) also highlighted this source of general self-esteem, noting that the esteem in which we are held by others begins to assume importance as soon as the child can sense that others are a source of attitudes. With this comes the realization that one's parents, in particular, possess and convey an attitude about one's worth as a child.

Competence as a Source of Self-Worth.   As a general dimension, competence has appeared in several models of self-esteem or self-worth. Both Epstein (1973) and Coopersmith (1967) included competence or success at meeting achievement demands as a determinant of global self-esteem. White (1963) placed more emphasis on the early experience of efficacy, the sense that one can make things happen in one's world.

James took his analysis a step further, asserting that it was primarily one's achievements in those areas that were deemed *important* that were the critical determinates of one's overall sense of esteem. He formalized this position, in an equation in which self-esteem equalled the *ratio* of one's *successes* to one's *pretensions.* Pretensions for James represented those domains in which it was important to achieve success. Thus, if one's level of success was comparable to one's desire for success, then positive self-esteem would result. If one's level of success fell short of one's pretensions or desires for success, negative self-esteem would result. It is important to note that according to this position, one would *not* simply sum or average one's competencies across domains in order to predict self-worth. Rather, one would only take into account those domains that were related as *important* to the subject. We explore the applicability of this model to predicting children's self-worth in the next section.

Applicability of Cooley's and James' Formulations to the Self-Worth of Children

In our own work (see Harter, 1986) we have sought to determine whether either of these two models accounts for the tremendous individual differences we find in children's self-worth. In order to examine these formulations, it is necessary to first *quantify* each of the relevant variables. Our self-worth subscale provides a score of the child's overall sense of worth. However, we also need to assess the child's sense of acceptance, support, and regard from significant others. In addition, we need a measure of the importance of success for each domain that we can then compare to the child's perceived competence or adequacy in each domain.

Acceptance, Support, Regard.   In order to assess this constellation of perceptions, we designed a new questionnaire that focussed on the degree to which children felt that their parents and peers accepted them, supported them, and treated them with regard. Parent items tapped the degree to which children felt that their parents treated them like a person, cared about their childrens feelings, listened to their problems, understood them, and treated them like someone who really mattered. We employed the same question format we had constructed for the Self-Perception Profile described earlier. A sample item from the parent scale would be:

Really true for me	Sort of True for me					Sort of True for me	Really True for me
☐	☐	Some kids have parents who treat their children like a *person* who really matters	**BUT**	Other kids have parents who *don't* usually treat their children like a person who matters.		☐	☐

The peer items assessed the degree to which others their age treated them like a person, helped them with problems, cared how they felt, kept their secrets, etc. (These items were cast into the same question format.)

We have examined the relationship between these scores and children's self-worth scores for numerous children between the ages of 10 and 13. For example, if we divide children into those that have high self-worth and those that have low self-worth, the pattern is very clear. Children with high self-worth feel that the significant others in their lives, both parents and peers, accept them, support them, and hold them in high regard. That is, they have high scores on the parent and peer measures just described. Conversely, children with low self-worth feel that they are not accepted or supported by parents and peers, that they are not

TABLE 3.3
Features of High and Low Self-Worth Children

	Child E. High Self-Worth		Child F. Low Self-Worth	
	(Self-Worth Score = 3.7) Child feels that parents and peers accept, support, have regard for the self.		(Self-Worth Score = 1.5) Child feels that parents and peers do *not* accept, support, have regard for the self.	
	Competence Adequacy	Importance of Success	Competence Adequacy	Importance of Success
Popularity	Very Popular (4) =	Very Important (4)	Very Popular (4) =	Very Important (4)
Appearance	Very Attractive (4) =	Very Important (4)	Very Attractive (4) =	Very Important (4)
Conduct	Pretty Good (3) =	Pretty Important (3)	Pretty Good (3) =	Very Important (4)
Schoolwork	Not Very Good (2) =	Not Very Important (2)	Not Very Good (2) =	Very Important (4)
Sports	Pretty Bad (1) =	Not at all Important (1)	Pretty Bad (1) =	Pretty Important (3)

treated as a person who matters (see top of Table 3.3). Thus, there is strong support for Cooley's view that the regard that significant others have for the self influences one's own sense of self-worth. The acceptance, support, and positive regard from others is a critical determinant of one's overall sense of worth as a person.

The Relationship Between Competence and the Importance of Success.   The essence of James' formulation is that high self-worth individuals are competent in domains where success is important. Low self-worth individuals are *not* competent in areas where they wish to be successful. In order to examine this theoretical proposition, it was first necessary to ascertain how important each child considered the five specific domains to be. Using the same kids—other kids question format—we devised questions in which we asked how important scholastic success, athletic success, popularity, behavioral conduct, and attractiveness were to the child's worth as a person.

For illustrative purposes, consider Child E and Child F whose profiles are presented at the bottom of Fig. 3.3. Each of these children has a very similar profile across the five domains. They feel *very good* about themselves with regard to their popularity and physical appearance. They feel *pretty* good about their behavioral conduct, *not very good* about their schoolwork, and *pretty bad* about their athletic ability. Thus, their profiles across the specific domains are virtually identical. However, Child E has very *high* self-worth (3.7) and Child F has very *low* self-worth (1.5). How can their self-worth scores be so different?

The answer lies in the differences in importance that each of these children attaches to the various domains. These differences are presented in the bottom of Table 3.3. First note that the *competence* or *adequacy* judgments of these two children are *identical,* as we also saw from Fig. 3.3. The domains are arranged here from the highest domain (popularity) to the lowest (sports), with the competence/adequacy scores in parenthesis. However, their importance scores differ in critical ways. For Child E, competence/adequacy judgments and importance scores are comparable to one another. Domains in which Child E is performing well (popularity and appearance) are rated as *very* important. An area in which she is only pretty good (behavioral conduct) is rated as just *pretty* important. The domain of schoolwork, where she is not very good, is rated *not very important.* And her worst domain, sports, is rated *not at all* important.

To summarize Child E, her competence/adequacy scores are *comparable* to her importance judgments. She has a hierarchy of competence scores that is very *congruent* with her hierarchy of importance scores. She is doing well in areas that are important to her. Popularity and attractiveness are very important to her and she considers herself very popular and very attractive. She is not uniformly competent in all areas. She admits that she does not do well at schoolwork and sports. However, she does not feel that these areas are that important to her. It does not bother her that she gets C's on her report card and that she is not chosen to be on athletic teams; that is, she is able to *discount* the *importance* of things she is *not good at* and *emphasize* those areas where she *is* doing well. In this way, she can maintain her sense of high self-worth.

Child F has a different pattern of *importance* scores for his less competent domains. For example, he considers his behavioral conduct to be only *pretty* good, yet he still considers it to be *very* important. His schoolwork is even worse, yet he continues to regard it as *very* important. In his worst area, sports, success is still *pretty* important. Thus, we have a child whose competence hierarchy and whose importance hierarchy are *not* congruent with each other. This is most evident for those domains in which competence is lacking, where importance scores are higher than his competence/adequacy judgments; that is, he is *unable* to discount the importance of things he is not good at. This is a boy for whom scholastic success is very important, despite his poor showing. This is a boy who very badly wants to be on the school soccer team; this is very important to him, yet he does not have the athletic skills to make the team. Because he is not competent in a number of areas where success is important to him, his self-worth suffers. He cannot live up to his expectations and desired competence.

This is but one illustrative example involving only two children. When we examine the pattern of scores across large numbers of children, however, we find clear support for James' notion that one's level of competence or perceived adequacy in areas where success is important strongly impacts one's overall sense of worth as a person. Children with high self-worth are children who are doing well in areas where success is important, and who can discount the importance of their less competent areas. Children who are not doing well in certain areas but continue to assert that these domains are important will suffer in terms of low self-worth.

Summary of the Determinantsof Self-Worth.   The evidence provides clear support for the formulations of both Cooley and James. Perceived positive regard from significant others is strongly related to self-worth, suggesting that children (ages 10 to 13) adopt the attitudes and opinions that they feel others hold toward the self. In addition, the degree to which one feels one is competent in areas where success is important, and has the ability to discount the importance of domains where one feels less adequate, is also an important determinant of self-worth. Moreover, these effects appear to be *additive*. Thus, the child with the *highest* sense of overall worth as a person will acknowledge the regard or esteem of others *as well as* feel competent in areas of importance. The child with the *lowest* sense of self-worth feels that significant others are not accepting *as well as* that he or she is not performing competently in areas of importance. Both of these factors, therefore, need to be taken into account in order for us to understand the reasons why a child does, or does not, feel good about the self, in general.

The Stability of Self-Judgments

A question that is often asked concerns the stability of self-judgments, both domain-specific evaluations and global self-worth. Should one's sense of self be regarded as trait like, a relatively enduring characteristic of the individual? Or is it susceptible to change? If it can and does change, what factors are responsible?

The answers to these questions hinge on both developmental and environmental factors. Over relatively short periods of time, for example, within a single school year, one's domain-specific judgments and one's self-worth are *moderately* stable for *most* children (Coopersmith, 1967; Harter, 1982; Wylie, 1979). In addition, self-judgments are more likely to be stable *within* particular periods of development, e.g., middle to late elementary school grades, then *across* periods of developmental and/or environmental change.

The transition to junior high school, for example, is likely to have an influence on self-judgments. There is some evidence that self-esteem is lowered as pupils move into the new school environment of junior high (Harter & Kowalski, 1985; Simmons, Rosenberg, & Rosenberg, 1971). However, these effects depend on the individual pupil. Our own data suggest that for certain children the transition to seventh grade takes a major toll in terms of a lowered sense of competency and self-worth. For other children, however, there is little effect, and some children actually show increases in their sense of competence, popularity, and self-worth.

In one interesting comparison, we looked at two groups of children making the transition from a sixth-grade elementary school to a seventh-grade junior high school, those whose self-worth increased and those whose self-worth decreased (Harter, 1986). In keeping with James' formulation, we found that pupils whose self-worth increased had a greater *congruence* between their competence scores and their importance ratings in seventh grade than they did in sixth grade. Certain students in this group became more competent in areas that were important to them; for example, appearance remained important and they felt that they became more attractive. Other students adjusted their importance rating, that is, they became able to discount the importance of domains in which they were not competent; for example, they may have decided that scholastic success was not as important now, whereas their popularity became more important.

In contrast, pupils whose self-worth *decreased* as they moved into seventh grade had *greater discrepancies* between competence and importance compared to sixth grade. Some felt that they were becoming *less* competent in areas that were still important; for example, they were doing less well scholastically, though still asserting the importance of academic competence. Others were increasing the importance of domains that were not their most competent; for example, popularity or attractiveness became more important, though their adequacy in these domains did not. These different patterns alert us to the fact that we should not expect entrance into new school environments or life situations to have the same effect on all individuals. It depends on the relationship between their particular competencies, the importance of these domains, and the priorities of the peer culture.

The *accuracy* of self-judgments also changes with development and with transitions to new environments. In the scholastic domain, children become increasingly more accurate over the grade-school years, as evidenced by a systematic increase in the correlation between their perceived scholastic competence and either teacher's ratings or achievement scores (Harter, 1982). However, the accuracy of judgments about one's scholastic competence takes a nose dive in seventh grade for students making the transition to a junior high school. The new school structure, bringing with it new academic challenges and a new group of students with whom to compare the self, disrupts the self-evaluative process. Accuracy shows a marked recovery in eighth grade, as students begin to make more realistic judgments of their abilities in relation to the academic demands and the performance of others in their reference group. The overall pattern, therefore, suggests that self-judgments are not as stable as theorists might have previously believed. When one considers the interaction between the developmental level of the child and his or her particular environment, one comes to appreciate how factors act to cause changes in one's sense of self.

The Effects of Self-Judgments
on Emotions, Motivation, and Behavior

In the preceding sections we have dealt with the nature of self-description, the self-evaluation process, the antecedents of one's sense of worth, and the stability of self-judgments. Yet one critical question still remains. Does one's sense of self influence one's emotional life, one's motivation, one's performance at life's tasks? We can ask this question both at the level of domain-specific judgments and at the level of one's sense of global self-worth.

At the domain-specific level, the primary evidence comes from the scholastic domain. In the 1960s and 1970s numerous studies (see Harter, 1983; Purkey, 1970) were conducted on the relationship between academic self-concept and achievement. These findings revealed a positive relationship between perceived academic competence and one's actual school achievement level. Children who perceive their academic competence to be high are more likely to be academic achievers, whereas those whose perceived academic competence is low are more likely to be the poorer students.

In recent years, there has been an attempt to examine a broader network of relationships. Within the scholastic domain, for example, investigators have been interested in the *emotional* or affective reactions that children have in response to their academic performance, as well as in children's *motivation* for classroom learning. The findings suggest the network or chain of relationships depicted in Fig. 3.4 (adapted from Harter & Connell, 1984).

The children who are achieving scholastically typically perceive their scholastic competence to be relatively high. Such children, in turn, have a positive affective reaction to their schoolwork; they feel good about their performance. This emotional reaction, in turn, seems to provide the impetus for classroom

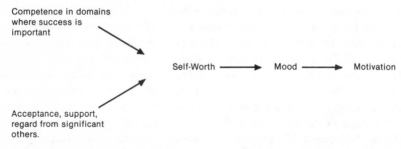

FIG. 3.4.   Determinants of self-worth and the impact of self-worth on mood and motivation.

learning. Specifically, children who feel good about their schoolwork are more likely to be *intrinsically* motivated, namely to be curious, to find schoolwork interesting, and to prefer challenge. This motivational orientation, in turn, leads to a relatively high level of achievement.

In contrast, there are children who get into a more negative cycle. Their achievement level is low, they perceive themselves to be relatively incompetent, they feel badly about their performance, which in turn leads to a more extrinsic classroom orientation in which they avoid challenge in favor of easy assignments and show little interest or pleasure in classroom learning; they tend to do the minimum that the school system requires. This orientation, in turn, leads to lower levels of actual achievement. This pattern of findings indicates that within the specific domain of academic performance one's sense of self, as defined by perceived scholastic competence, is intimately related to other systems within the individual, namely emotional reactions, motivational patterns, and actual academic behavior.

The Effects of Global Self-Worth

One can find similar relationships at a more global level if one examines the effects of self-worth on one's emotional and motivational responses. This larger question has been addressed within the study on the determinants of self-worth. Having established that positive regard from significant others and competence in domains deemed important to the individual were critical antecedents, we were interested in the impact that self-worth had on children's general mood and motivation (Harter & Hogan, 1985).

By *mood,* we mean one's general affective reaction or state along a dimension of happy or cheerful to sad or depressed. We assessed mood through a series of questions in which we asked about the degree to which children generally felt happy versus sad, cheerful versus depressed, up versus down, employing the same kids—other kids question format.

Motivation was defined as the degree to which one was interested, and had the energy to engage, in age-appropriate activities. Thus, question (in the same format) asked children whether they had enough energy to get them through the day, whether they enjoyed doing the kinds of things most kids their age liked to do, whether they were interested in the things they were supposed to do each day, etc. Both mood and motivation questions were designed to be general, because we wanted global judgments that we could then relate to children's judgment of their overall sense of worth. (See Fig. 3.5 that depicts these components within the larger model.)

The findings revealed a chain of casual effects. As reported earlier, competence in domains where success was important, and positive regard from others, strongly influenced self-worth. Self-worth, in turn, had a very dramatic impact on children's mood. Mood, in turn, had a large effect on motivation. These

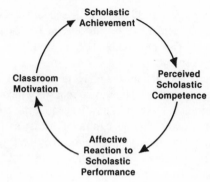

FIG. 3.5.   Relationships among actual achievement, perceived competence, affective reaction, and motivation within the scholastic domain.

relationships reveal that the high self-worth child is typically in a cheerful mood; positive judgments about the self in general lead one to feel relatively happy. These feelings of happines, in turn, seem to fuel the child, leading one to have the energy and interest to do things that children one's age should be doing or like to do. At the other extreme are children whose low self-worth causes them to be unhappy or depressed, which in turn seems to sap them of the energy and interest to engage in age-appropriate activities. These findings are important because they reveal that self-worth does not manifest itself in isolation of other very critical systems within the child. Rather, self-worth is intimately linked to emotional and motivational systems that propel the child toward the development of an ever-expanding repertoire of new skills. One's sense of self, therefore, is very central to those processes that promote adjustment and continued psychological growth.

Summary and Conclusions

This chapter began with a developmental analysis of self-description. There we saw how the self changes dramatically with development. The attributes that define the self-concept, their organization, their stability, their accuracy, the critera on which they are based, the very ability to observe the self, all change with age. These differences are in large part due to cognitive-developmental changes in interaction with the child's socialization experiences.

The nature of the self-evaluation process was also examined. The evidence indicates that children evaluate their performance differently, depending on the particular domain. Five domains were emphasized, scholastic competence, athletic competence, popularity, behavioral conduct, and physical appearance. It was urged that one approach the issue of self-evaluation by considering a child's profile of scores across these domains.

In addition to these domain-specific judgments, children age 8 and older are capable of making a global judgment of their overall worth as a person. Evidence indicates that there are two primary determinants of a child's self-worth. The first involves the internalization of attitudes that significant others hold toward the self. The more one feels that others accept, support, and have regard for the self, the higher one's self-worth. The second determinant involves the degree to which one feels competent or adequate in areas where success is important. If one meets one's performance standards in these areas, and can discount the importance of domains in which one is not competent, high self-worth will result.

The stability of children's self-judgments was also examined. The findings indicate that self-judgments are moderately stable over short periods of time during which the child is not faced with major change. During periods of developmental and/or environmental change, for example, the transition to junior high school, self-judgments may well undergo change.

Finally, we explored the question of whether self-judgments have any impact on the child's emotions, motivation, and behavior. For domain-specific judgments as well as global self-worth, the findings indicate that one's sense of self has a major impact on one's emotional life, which in turn influences children's motivation and behavior. Thus, self-judgments are intimately related to other systems within the child that are critical for development.

REFERENCES

Amsterdam, B. K. (1972). Mirror self-image reactions before age two. *Developmental Psychology, 5*, 297–305.

Bertenthal, B. I., & Fischer, K. W. (1978). Development of self-recognition in the infant. *Developmental Psychology, 14*, 44–50.

Cooley, C. H. (1902). *Human nature and the social order*. New York: Schribners's.

Coopersmith, S. (1967). *The antecedents of self-esteem*. San Francisco: W. H. Freeman.

Dweck, C., & Elliot, E. S. (1983). Achievement motivation. In E. M. Hetherington (Ed.), *Handbook of child psychology: Socialization. Personality and social development* (Vol. 4). New York: Wiley.

Elkind, D. (1967). Egocentrism in adolescence. *Child Development, 38*, 1025–1034.

Epstein, S. (1973). The self-concept revisited or a theory of a theory. *American Psychologist, 28*, 405–416.

Fischer, K. W. (1980). A theory of cognitive development: The control and construction of hierarchies of skills. *Psychological Review, 87*, 477–531.

Gesell, A., & Ilg, F. (1946). *The child from five to ten*. New York: Harper & Row.

Guardo, C. J., & Bohan, J. B. (1971). Development of a sense of self-identity in children. *Child Development, 42*, 1909–1921.

Harter, S. (1982). The perceived competence scale for children. *Child Development, 53*, 87–97.

Harter, S. (1983). Developmental perspectives on the self-system. In M. Hetherington (Ed.), *Handbook of child psychology, Vol. 4, Socialization, personality, and social development*. New York: Wiley.

Harter, S. (1985a). Competence as a dimension of self-evaluation: Toward a comprehensive model of self-worth. In R. Leahy (Ed.), *The development of the self*. New York: Academic Press.

Harter, S. (1985b). *The self-perception profile for children.* Unpublished manuscript, University of Denver.

Harter, S. (1986). Processes underlying the construction, maintenance and enhancement of the self-concept in children. In J. Suls & A. Greenwald (Eds.), *Psychological perspectives on the self* (Vol. 3, pp. 136–182). Hillsdale, NJ: Lawrence Erlbaum Associates.

Harter, S., & Connell, J. P. (1984). A structural model of the relationships among academic achievement and children's self-perceptions of competence, control, and motivational orientation in the cognitive domain. In J. Nicholls (Ed.), *The development of achievement motivation.* Greenwich, CT: JAI Press.

Harter, S., & Hogan, A. (1985). *A causal model of the determinants and mediational role of global self-worth in middle-school children.* S.R.C.D. presentation, Toronto,.

Harter, S., & Kowalski, P. (1985). *The relationship between perceived competence and self-reported affects.* Unpublished manuscript, University of Denver.

Harter, S., & Pike, R. (1984). The pictorial scale of perceived competence and social acceptance for young children. *Child Development, 55,* 1969–1982.

James, W. (1963). *Psychology.* New York: Fawcett Publications. (originally published in 1892)

Kohlberg, L. (1966). A cognitive-developmental analysis of children's sex-role concepts and attitudes. In E. Maccoby (Ed.), *The development of sex differences* (pp. 82–172). Stanford, CA: Stanford University Press.

Lewis, M., & Brooks-Gunn, J. (1979). Toward a theory of social cognition: The development of the self. In I. Uzgiris (Ed.), *New directions in child development: Social interaction and communication during infancy.* San Francisco: Jossey-Bass.

Maccoby, E. E. & Martin, J. A. (1983). Socio-emotional development and response to stressors. In N. Garmazy & M. Rutter (Eds.), *Stress, coping, and development in children* (pp. 1–102). New York: McGraw Hill.

Minton, B. (1979). Dimensions of information underlying children's judgments of their competence. Unpublished master's thesis, University of Denver.

Monsour, A. (1985). *The structure and dynamics of the adolescent self-concept.* Doctoral dissertation, University of Denver.

Montemayor, R., & Eisen, M. (1977). The development of self-conceptions from childhood to adolescence. *Developmental Psychology, 13,* 314–319.

Piaget, J. (1960). *The psychology of intelligence.* Paterson, NJ: Littlefield, Adams.

Piaget, J. (1963). *The origins of intelligence in children.* New York: Norton.

Piers, E., & Harris, D. (1969). *The Piers–Harris Children's Self-Concept Scale.* Nashville, TN: Counselor Recordings and Tests.

Purkey, W. W. (1970). *Self-concept and school achievement.* Englewood Cliffs, NJ: Prentice-Hall.

Rosenberg, M. (1979). *Conceiving the self.* New York: Basic Books.

Ruble, D. N. (In press). The development of social comparison processes and their role in achievement-related self-socialization. In E. T. Higgins, D. N. Ruble, & W. W. Hartup (Eds.), *Developmental Social Cognition: A socio-cultural perspective.* Hillsdale, NJ: Lawrence Erlbaum Associates.

Selman, R. (1980). *The growth of interpersonal understanding.* New York: Academic Press.

Simmons, R. G., Rosenberg, F., & Rosenberg, M. (1971). Disturbance in the self-image at adolescence. *American Sociological Review, 38,* 553–568.

White, R. W. (1963). Ego and reality in psychoanalytic theory. *Psychological Issues,* Monograph 3.

Wylie, R. (1979). *The self concept, Vol 2. Theory and research on selected topics.* Lincoln: University of Nebraska Press.

Social Cognition

4

Linda Rose-Krasnor
Brock University

Over 100 years ago, G. Stanley Hall attempted to determine the contents of young children's minds (Hall, 1883). In this ambitious project, more than 400 children were asked approximately 140 questions. Items were drawn from many different content domains, including animals, body parts, shapes, color, origins of foodstuffs, and vocabulary. On the basis of this survey, Hall concluded, "there is next to nothing of pedogic value the knowledge of which it is safe to assume at the onset of school life" (p. 137). Only one of Hall's published questions, however, even remotely sampled social understanding ("Name three right and three wrong things"). This neglect of the child's social world reflected the predominantly cognitive and physical priorities of the early child study movement.

By the 1930s, children's social behavior had emerged as a major research topic. Sociometrics and the study of children's relationship patterns rose to popularity in the 1950s. It was not until the 1970s, however, that children's social knowledge entered the mainstream of developmental research. Social cognitions have since become one of the most active areas of study for researchers from a variety of theoretical orientations (Fiske & Taylor, 1984).

From modern perspectives, then, Hall missed perhaps the most important knowledge base that a young child brings to school—knowledge of social phenomena. A child who cannot draw social inferences (e.g., judging motives and emotions, anticipating others' actions) is ill equipped for social interaction. Similarly, a child who lacks social knowledge (e.g., is not aware of social norms, insensitive to role relationships) is at a considerably social disadvantage.

This is a difficult domain to master. In fact, acquiring accurate and useful social knowledge may be more difficult than learning about the nonsocial world

(Humphrey, 1976). Social objects, unlike physical ones, have motives of their own and may even deliberately misrepresent their true state. Social information is often ambiguous, and people's actions are far less predictable than those of objects. An individual's knowledge of the social world, and the processes by which this knowledge is acquired, is the domain of social cognition.

Social-cognitive content includes knowledge and inferences about the characteristics of people (e.g., traits), their behaviors (e.g., aggression), and their motivations (e.g., frustration). Social cognition also encompasses the relationships between people (e.g., authority, friendship) and the structure of these interpersonal relationships within groups (Shantz, 1983). Knowledge about the social characteristics of the self and relationships between the self and others is also included. Social cognitions may be about people in general (e.g., "Absence makes the heart grow fonder") or be person specific (e.g., "Janet hates to be teased"). They may also include thoughts about the nature and use of social-cognitive knowledge itself (Flavell, 1981).

Several general research issues have recently emerged from this rich domain. First, there has been a steadily growing interest in describing developmental changes in social cognition (see reviews by Chandler, 1977; Shantz, 1983) and in identifying the correlates of social-cognitive abilities (e.g., Pellegrini, 1985). Two other major research goals have been to specify the relationship between social cognition and behavior (e.g., Lefebvre-Pinard, Bufford-Bouchard, & Feidler, 1982) and to identify effective social-cognitive training methods (e.g., Spivack & Shure, 1974). A fifth general research direction has been to show how different social-cognitive components are coordinated within individuals. In the following pages, I address some of the issues and data relevant to this intraindividual integration. First, however, it is important to make a theoretical distinction between process and product orientations to social cognition, such as that proposed by Fiske and Taylor (1984).

The dominant approach in social-cognitive research has been product oriented. Products can be conceptualized as the "outputs" of a social-cognitive process. Examples of these products are conventional thinking level (Turiel, 1983), perspective-taking level (e.g., Selman, 1980), and causal attributions (e.g., Goetz & Dweck, 1980). Products can be counted and classified as discreet, isolated units. In product-oriented research, there is characteristically little specification of the process that generated the products. In addition, few references are made concerning how products function as inputs to subsequent steps.

In contrast, process-oriented research has focused primarily on the mechanisms by which social-cognitive products are produced and how they are used. This research approach is most clearly represented by investigators who have articulated step-by-step sequential models of social cognition. Flavell (1974), for example, presented one of the earliest descriptions of a social-cognitive process. In this seminal model of role taking, four sequential steps were identified: (1) recognizing that others have a perspective different than one's own; (2) realizing the need to take the other's perspective; (3) inferring the other's perspective; and (4) applying the inference to subsequent behavior or social-cognitive activity.

In recent years processing orientations to social cognition have become popular. Current models have been heavily influenced by information processing and cybernetic frameworks. Models by Ford (1982) for social behavior, by Hastie (1984) for social attributions, by Smith (1984) for social inferences, and by Dodge (1986) for social information processing are representative of these recent developments. Krasnor and Rubin's description of social problem solving (Krasnor & Rubin, 1981; Rubin & Krasnor, 1986) is another example. This latter model is examined in some detail in order to illustrate process and product orientations to social cognition.

In its broadest sense, social problem solving is the process of achieving personal goals in social interaction (Krasnor & Rubin, 1983). Social problem-solving cognitions have been recognized as important components of social competence (see review by Rubin & Krasnor, 1986) and have been investigated at both product and process levels.

A potential path for social problem-solving cognitions can be described in several major steps. In the first step, a social goal (e.g., making a friend, getting a toy away from a peer) is selected. Next, information relevant to the goal is extracted from the environment (e.g., identification of potential allies, proximity of the teacher). The third step is to produce potential social strategies (e.g., asking, bribing, grabbing). An individual may access strategies already stored in memory or may generate new ones. Selecting a strategy on the basis of some criteria (e.g., social acceptability or prior utility) is the fourth step in the sequence; implementing the strategy is the fifth. Once implemented, the individual must assess its success or failure in achieving the goal. A successful outcome results in termination of the process. A failure, however, is followed by a decision process that results in trying the goal again or "giving up." If the goal is reattempted, the process will return to an earlier step in the sequence (e.g., get more information, reimplement the same strategy, generate new potential strategies).

Several process-oriented dimensions can be derived from this model. The time taken to complete the process, for example, can be used to measure efficiency. The tendency to repeat a failed strategy (perseveration) is another process measure (Krasnor & Rubin, 1983). The model also helps to identify relevant products. Product measures include, for example, the type of information extracted (Dodge, 1986) and goal chosen (Renshaw & Asher, 1982). The most common product measure has been the quantity and quality of alternate strategies produced in the third step (e.g., Spivack & Shure, 1974).

At this point, it is important to note that the distinction between process and product may be more theoretical than real. This differentiation, however, does provide a useful framework for examining social-cognitive integration. The integration of process is conceptually distinct from the integration of product. A "vertical," sequential form of integration corresponds to a process orientation: a "horizontal," stage-like form of integration more closely parallels a product orientation. This distinction is expanded in the following sections.

PRODUCT INTEGRATION

Social-cognitive products are integrated when similar levels of skill are apparent across structurally similar tasks. From this perspective, performance will depend heavily on a general ability factor. The influence of this general ability level will appear as a stable individual difference across tasks and occasions. If product integration is strong, variations in specific task content would explain little of performance variance, compared to that explained by reliable differences among people. Product integration would also be reflected in strong transfer across social-cognitive activities. In contrast (Flavell, 1982), extreme nonintegration would appear as "a chaotic hodgepodge of isolated and unconnected learnings and maturings" (p. 2). Variance in performance would be largely explained by task and situational factors, rather than by stable individual differences.

The study of product integration has been popular with researchers who support a stage model of social-cognitive development (e.g., Damon, 1977; Selman, 1980; Turiel, 1983). Within stages, individuals should show relative homogeneity in social-cognitive levels. Common analytic models for assessing homogeneity have been to measure the correlations among structurally similar tasks or to compare an individual's stage classification on related tasks.

In one of the first major investigations of social-cognitive integration, Damon (1977) examined performance in two relational (friendship and authority) and two regulatory (positive justice and social convention) domains. Because social-cognitive skill was assumed to depend on general logical structures, some intra-individual integration across task domains was expected. Furthermore, task per-formances within a domain were expected to be more closely related to each other than to tasks from another domain. Damon's data provided support for the existence of both partial and general social-cognitive structures.

Selman (1980) also examined consistency in individual performance across and within social-cognitive domains. Both correlational and factor analytic anal-yses of social perspective taking generally supported the existence of significant intrapersonal coherence in perspective taking. In addition, the scatter of indi-vidual's scores across domains indicated a relatively tight clustering around a modal stage. Both Selman and Damon, therefore, provided consistent evidence for a moderate level of intraindividual integration in social-cognitive skills.

After extensive literature reviews, both Chandler (1977) and Shantz (1983) reported the existence of significant low to moderate correlations between similar social-cognitive tasks. Both reviewers, however, qualified their conclusions. Chandler (1977) noted that the correlations typically disappeared when mental and chronological age were partialled out, and Shantz (1983) observed that correlations among tasks within a social-cognitive domain were not necessarily stronger than those found between domains of different content.

Few, if any, current stage theorists would predict complete homogeneity of an individual's performance across related tasks. Although the level of social-cognitive skill shown by a child on a task depends on general logical structures, it is not totally determined by it (Damon, 1977; Turiel, 1983). Other important influences on performance are the specific task demands (Messick, 1983). Wide variations in task format may explain more of the variance in performance than individual differences in the general social-cognitive skill being assessed (Chandler, 1977; Shantz, 1983). Uneven performance across related tasks, therefore, may be due to factors such as presentation form (written, verbal, pictoral), complexity (number, novelty), or response format (recall, recognition, explanation).

In addition, tasks that differ in content are also likely to elicit individual differences in interest and motivation. For example, asking for alternate strategies for joining an ongoing baseball game may be a more interesting problem for some children than generating strategies for joining an ongoing art activity. Similarly, differences in familarity with task content or materials task will affect performance. Thus, wide variation in responses to task content may result in an apparent low level of integration in social-cognitive product.

Although many researchers have attempted to study product integration across related tasks, there has been little systematic control of task variance or analysis of task characteristics. This methodological variance is largely unexplored and unmeasured and thus attempts to assess homogeneity of performance across tasks have been difficult to interprete.

Developmental patterns in product integration have also been seriously understudied. In fact, three divergent developmental predictions can be made, each with its own theoretical and empirical basis. Product integration may increase, decrease, or show nonmonotonic change with age.

A rational for the hypothesis that product integration increases with development can be drawn from Piaget's description of developmental changes in cognition (Piaget & Inhelder, 1969). Building on Piaget's stage theory, Damon (1977) suggested that there would be only limited overlap among social-cognitive domains in the young child, because early knowledge is characteristically fragmented. Knowledge should become more systematic, coordinated, and integrated, however, with the emergence of formal operations in adolescence (Damon, 1977; Selman, 1980). Selman (1980) further proposed that "cross fertilization among issues" within an individual should be characteristic of the more advanced cognitive stages.

Further bases for predicting a developmental increase in product integration comes from the skill-acquisition literature. As a person becomes more expert in a domain, transfer across tasks is facilitated. With development, cognitive operations become more mobile and less tied to the specific context in which they were learned (Brown, Bransford, Ferrara, & Campione, 1983). Young children's strategy applications, therefore, tend to be unstable, fragmentary, and constrained to limited domains. Older children's use of cognitive strategies show more coherence and robustness across problem types (Case, 1978); thus, they would should show greater product integration. For social-cognitive skills that increase with age (e.g., role taking), we would expect corresponding increases in the range of applications and consistency across related tasks.

In spite of this evidence, there is reason to suspect that product integration may show a nonmonotonic developmental pattern. The degree of product integration across related tasks may both increase *and* decrease within a single stage (Flavell, 1982). In the beginning of a stage, a new social-cognitive skill is just emerging. It exists in a fragile state with limited applicability. Performance will look relatively homogeneous because the child will be consistently unsuccessful across tasks requiring that skill. At the end of a stage, the child will show a similar product integration because she or he succeeds on all tasks. Performance would be most uneven in the middle of a stage when the child would successfully use the skill in the easier tasks but fail in the harder ones. This cycle should repeat for each stage, resulting in nonmonotonic age-related changes in product integration.

A third potential developmental pattern is that product integration across tasks may decrease with age. Systems become differentiated with experience and maturation, and subsystems become "fine tuned" to specific tasks (Berrien, 1965; Werner, 1948). Children may learn to respond to routine and familar tasks with situation-specific social cognitions. This specialization is likely to enhance cognitive efficency (Flavell, 1981) and also represents sensitivity to potentially important environmental factors. In fact, differentiation of activity by situation is considered to be a sign of competence (Nakamuri & Finck, 1980). In addition, differentiation of strategy by target (e.g., boy, teacher) and goal has been correlated with social success (Krasnor, 1982). This fine tuning should increase with age due to greater opportunities for experience, practice, and direct instruction. Tasks or situations that evoke differentiated and situation-specific social cognitions are not likely to show the same performance patterns as those that do not.

We have hypothesized age-related increases in product integration, decreases in integration, and nonmonotonic change. The small amount of currently available data provides little basis for discriminating among these three predictions. In the next section, I present some data describing developmental changes in the product integration of one social problem-solving skill over the elementary school years.

PRODUCT INTEGRATION IN SOCIAL PROBLEM SOLVING:
AN EXAMPLE

Social problem-solving skill has been studied through many different social-cognitive products. These include sensitivity to social problems and social consequences (Spivack & Shure, 1974), goal setting (Renshaw & Asher, 1982), and causal thinking (Elias, Larcen, Zlotlow, & Chinsky, 1978). The product that has been studied most frequently is social-strategy repertoire (Rubin & Krasnor, 1983; Spivack & Shure, 1974). The quantity and quality of an individual's social strategies have been significant predictors of social competence. In addition, alternate strategies are the outputs of a theoretically critical processing step.

For several years, measures of children's strategy repertoires have been available (e.g., Elias et al., 1978; Ladd & Oden, 1979; Polifka, Weissberg, Gesten, de Apodaca & Piccoli, 1981; Rubin, 1981; Spivack & Shure, 1974). Most of these measures consist of several different social dilemmas (e.g., making friends, helping a child in distress, alleviating an adult's anger). Remarkably few researchers have published the distribution of scores over the different contents. This type of analysis could provide important information on how a social-cognitive skill is integrated across social contents.

Although social-strategy repertoires have been measured across a relatively wide age range, it is rare to find any study in which the same social problem-solving test is used across age spans greater than 3 years. Therefore, an adequate data base for developmental changes in product integration does not exist. In the study described here, integration in one social-cognitive product was investigated for five different social contents in children from Grades 1, 3, and 5.

Two different methods of assessing product integration were used. First, integration was measured correlationally by examining the factor patterns that emerged from intercorrelating the social problem scores. A high degree of product integration would be reflected by a single-factor solution. Age differences would be detected through variation in the magnitude of correlations and number of factors extracted. Differences in the percentage of variance attributed to the first factor would also reveal variation in product integration level.

The second general method of assessing product integration was based on an analysis of variance model. In this approach the intraindividual variation across tasks is interpreted as task-specific variance and can be expressed as a percentage of the total variance. In addition, intraindividual task variation can be compared to variation due to stable individual differences. These indices will help to assess the relative importance of intraindividual variation, as well as developmental trends. Age differences in product integration can be tracked by differences in the percentage of variance explained by task content compared to that explained by interindividual variation.

Method

Children.   There were 88 first graders (42 boys and 46 girls), 76 third graders (38 boys and 38 girls), and 82 fifth graders (42 boys and 40 girls) who participated in a larger study of social problem solving and friendship (Krasnor, 1985).

Assessment of Social Problem Solving.   Five common social problems were selected from extant measures (Ladd & Oden, 1979; Polifka et al., 1981) and presented to individual children in randomized order. For each story, the child was asked to generate an initial social strategy and then was asked for another strategy that the story character could use if the first suggestion failed. The questioning continued until the child offered no further strategies.

Two of the five stories concerned friendship issues (making new friends, alleviating the anger of a friend after losing his or her favorite toy), two concerned object acquisitions (having a turn taking care of the class gerbil, getting a toy being pulled by another child), and one dilemma concerned defense (stopping peers from teasing). The children's responses were coded for number of social strategies. In general, strategy categories were adapted from Ladd and Oden (1979) and Polifka et al. (1981).

Reliability for strategy coding was assessed on 100 randomly selected story protocols. Percentage agreement ranged from 74% to 94% across strategy categories, with an average agreement of 87%.

Results

In the first set of analyses, correlations between the number of strategies generated for each of the five social dilemmas were calculated separately for each grade (See Table 4.1). Similar patterns emerged for the three ages. For Grade 1, correlations were positive, ranging from .15 to .38. Average correlation was .29. For the Grade 3 and 5 data, correlations were again positive, mostly significant, and of low to moderate size. The third-grade correlations ranged from .12 to .47, with a mean correlation of .31. For the fifth-grade children, the correlations averaged .31 and ranged from .18 to .46.

Principal component analyses were used to assess the factor structure at each grade level. For both first and fifth graders, a single-factor solution emerged. In Grade 1, the first unrotated factor explained 43.1% of the total variance (eigenvalue = 2.15). Similarly, the first unrotated factor in Grade 5 explained 44.6% of total variance (eigenvalue = 2.23). In Grade 3, however, two factors emerged. The first factor explained 45.2% of the variance (eigenvalue = 2.26); the second explained an additional 20.4% of total variance (eigenvalue = 1.02). A Varimax rotation revealed that the new friend, toy pull, and lost toy stories loaded most heavily on the first factor (loadings of .85, .52, and .53, respectively), whereas the gerbil and teasing stories were most closely associated with the second factor (loadings of .81 and .37, respectively). The factor analysis data, therefore, provide some support for a U-shaped developmental pattern in product integration. Note, however, that second factors for first and third graders were close to significance, with eigenvalues of .94 for both Grade 1 and Grade 5 data.

For each grade, product integration was also assessed with repeated measures

TABLE 4.1
Correlation Matrices for Total Strategies
for Five Social Problems by Grade

Grade	Social Problem	Social Problem			
		Gerbil	New Friend	Toy Pull	Lost Toy
Grade 1 (n = 88)	Gerbil				
	New friend	.38**			
	Toy pull	.26*	.19		
	Lost toy	.15	.30**	.36**	
	Teasing	.18	.38**	.36**	.32**
Grade 3 (n = 76)	Gerbil				
	New friend	.17			
	Toy pull	.39**	.46**		
	Lost toy	.35**	.47**	.40**	
	Teasing	.32**	.12	.20	.18
Grade 5 (n = 82)	Gerbil				
	New friend	.28*			
	Toy pull	.27*	.18		
	Lost toy	.36**	.36**	.22*	
	Teasing	.35**	.26*	.46**	.31**

*$p < .05$.
**$p < .01$.

ANOVAs. Variance estimates for the strength of "between-tasks" and "between-people" effects for each grade were calculated, following Vaughan and Corballis's (1969) procedures for repeated measures designs with nonadditivity assumptions. The results are displayed in Table 4.2. Across grades, individual differences explained substantially more of the total variance than did content differences. The percentage of variance attributable to individual differences appeared relatively stable across ages. There was a slightly greater percentage of variance explained by task content in Grade 3 than in Grades 1 or 5. This deviation in the Grade-3 data was consistent with the curvilinear pattern shown by the factor analysis. Most striking, however, was the relatively large percentage of variance that was not explained by either task or consistent individual differences in any of the grades studied.

Discussion

The size of social strategy repertoires was measured across five different social-problem contents in order to assess product integration over middle childhood. Task administration and format were the same for each of the social tasks, thus decreasing potential confounds due to task format.

TABLE 4.2
Variance Estimates for Social Problems and
People Effects by Grade

	Grade		
Source of Variance	Grade 1	Grade 3	Grade 5
Social problem	.029	.095	.001
	(1.5%)[a]	(4.2%)	(0.0%)
People	.546	.624	.632
	(28.1%)	(27.4%)	(29.6%)
Total	1.94	2.28	2.13

[a]Percentage of total variance.

The correlational analyses indicated moderate overlap in repertoire size across task content. This result was consistent with findings for other social-cognitive domains. The analyses thus provided some evidence for a general skill factor, as well as partial or task-specific structures for this product.

Certainly, much of the variance in scores could not be attributed to either systematic individual or task differences, as indicated by the large unexplained error variance apparent in the repeated measures ANOVAs. In this analysis, it was impossible to separate the percentages of variance due to error from that due to interaction of individual and task content (Vaughn & Corballis, 1969). Designs that can test the task-by-person interaction must include multiple assessments of the same task content for each individual; this will allow an examination of person-by-task effects, as well as increasing the measurement reliability.

Given the role of specific experience and practice in developing cognitive skill (Brown et al., 1983), it is likely that the task-by-person interaction component may explain a large proportion of overall variance. For example, individuals who have had repeated opportunities to make new friends would be expected to have a richer strategy repertoire for that content domain than their less mobile peers. They may not, however, have any superior *general* ability to produce alternate strategies. It is apparent that we need measures of specific individual experiences, apart from the global experience factors associated with age, in order to measure these effects.

An analysis of current research and theory led to three contradictory predictions for patterns in product integration. The factor analysis and ANOVA approaches both suggested a weak curvilinear pattern in which integration was stronger at the beginning and end of the concrete operational period than in the middle. Flavell (1982) predicted this pattern when he suggested that children halfway through a stage would show inconsistent application of a skill across tasks.

A second explanation for the nonmonotonic pattern may also be developmental differences in the relative salience of specific content. For example, social problems focusing on relationship issues (e.g., friendship) may be more important to children approaching adolescence; object acquisition problems may be more salient to children of preschool or kindergarten age. A priori theoretical analyses of the developmental relevance of specific social-cognitive task content is important for a systematic assessment of task variance. Further information regarding the relative importance of specific content could be obtained from children's ratings and reports by teachers or parents. In addition, naturalistic observations (e.g., Charlesworth, 1983; Krasnor & Rubin, 1983) can help to identify important social problems on the basis of relative frequency. The development of a taxonomy for classification of social tasks is an essential and immediate research need.

Evaluation of developmental trends and individual differences in product integration is difficult, because there is no basis for judging what is a "good" level of integration. Total integration would mean exact similarity in performance across content. Such lack of differentiation would seem operationally inefficient, because it would not allow an individual to develop specialized skills for frequently occurring task content. A total absence of integration would mean that performance across tasks was uncorrelated. This complete differentiation would also be an inefficient organization of the cognitive system, in which learning and development in one area would be isolated from another (Flavell, 1982). Establishing desirable levels for product integration is an important empirical question. An individual's level of product integration may, in itself, be an important individual-difference variable. The extent to which an individual shows performance similarity across tasks is likely to be due to similarities in the ways in which information is processed. In the next section, factors effecting how social-cognitive processes are integrated are explored.

PROCESS INTEGRATION

Process integration is defined as the smooth flow of activity along the steps of a social-cognitive process. Each step receives the information or "input" it requires from the processes that preceded it. Once the processing at that step is completed, it outputs information needed by the next step. The social problem-solving model presented by Krasnor and Rubin (1981; Rubin & Krasnor, 1986) can be used to illustrate this process orientation to integration.

Once a social goal is selected, task-relevant information is obtained from the environment. The effectiveness of the information gathering depends on a clear, well-specified goal, which has been "passed on" by the initial step. Similarly, the success of the strategy selection depends on the adequacy of the goal and task information, which was obtained from prior steps in the process. Such sequential dependency between successive steps is apparent throughout the social problem-solving process.

The outcome of this process will depend on the ability to accurately assess information from the environment and adaptively respond to it. A well-integrated social-cognitive process, therefore, should be characterized by: (a) efficiency (e.g., relatively short latency from start to finish, and exclusion of irrelevent activity); (b) completeness (once started, the process should proceed to completion); and (c) flexible adaptation to environmental feedback.

In poorly integrated social-cognitive processes, the flow of control or information between components of the system breaks down. Necessary steps malfunction or are not completed. The products (cognitions, behaviors, and emotions) that are outputs of the process may be based on distorted or outdated information. These outputs may stop as the process stops flowing (e.g., the individual gives up), or they may become repetitive if the system fails to respond to environmental changes. In addition, nonintegration may be reflected in mismatches in the information passed between steps (e.g., the provision of more information than the next step can process will lead to overload and possible disruption). Successful processing depends on continuing feedback from the environment. This feedback provides information about the success or failure of the process outputs. Potential causes of poor integration may be drawn from cybernetic models of feedback loops.

Feedback loops have several basic steps. First, the system senses external conditions. This is followed by a comparison between what is sensed and a reference standard. Results from this comparison are used to select appropriate action, to continue to monitor conditions, or to exit the loop entirely (Miller, Gillanter, & Pribaum, 1960). Suppose, for example, that a child has a goal of making friends with a new child in the neighborhood. From prior experience, the child has established a reference standard for " a friend" (e.g., likes you, smiles at you, shares toys, doesn't fight). The feedback loop begins with an assessment of the new child's behavior (senses conditions). This information is then compared to the reference standard. If no descrepency is detected (success), the child may exit the loop or just continue to monitor conditions. The new child is recognized as a friend. If a moderate descrepency exists, the child may act to reduce it (e.g., invite the new child to the movies) and then reassess the new child's behavior to see if it is closer to matching the reference criteria for friendship. If the descrepency is very large, the child may exit the loop (give up).

A well-integrated feedback procedure controls the actions of a system smoothly and responsively. The feedback process is vulnerable to disruption at several points, however (Carver & Scheier, 1981): (a) the absence of reference values (no goals, or goals that are poorly specified); (b) breakdown in outputs (a lack of ability or opportunity to perform the act); (c) input breakdown (feedback is nonexistent or very delayed); and (d) breakdown in the comparison process (a lack of awareness of own state). In addition, intense emotion may "short-circuit" or overwhelm the process and lead to its breakdown (Simon, 1967).

Disruptions that are not severe enough to stop the feedback process may still substantially distort it. The process would continue to operate but would be based on faulty information (Carver & Scheier, 1981). This distortion may result from the use of inappropriate standards (e.g., failing to adjust for cultural differences), from a misreading of cues (e.g., mistaking a lie for the truth), or from a false judgment of potential (e.g., believing that one's own acts will have no effect).

Well-integrated systems, therefore, should be characterized by a direct path to goal, relatively short latency, responsiveness to feedback, and flexibility. Processes may break down due to factors that either stop or distort the regulation process. The relative frequency of breakdowns, and the conditions under which they occur, will change as the social-cognitive system changes. We expect change in process integration, therefore, as a result of experience and maturation.

In general, maturing systems show increasing levels of differentiation and hierarchical structuring (Berrien, 1968). Suprastructures emerge that direct the function of lower level processes. These subprocesses become more specialized and precisely interfaced with each other. For example, role-taking processes, means–end thinking, and strategy-selection processes become well meshed and work together within a social problem-solving suprastructure. Schank and Abelson (1977) described a similar differentiated functioning for hierarchical levels of scripts (e.g., lower level plans and goals serve higher level life themes). Growth should lead to greater social-cognitive differentiation and therefore give the overall system increased flexibility, adaptiveness, and resiliency. Development is expected to lead to smoother integration between steps in the social-cognitive process and reduce potential sources of disruption.

As a child's social world expands outside the home, the child is likely to develop a wider range of appropriate social goals. In addition, older children should have more precise and detailed reference standards for social acts than younger children, because they have greater opportunities for observation and participation in social interaction. Furthermore, older children are able to access a wider range of possible social strategies. These developmental changes should make disruption of social-cognitive processes less likely in older children than in younger ones.

In addition, older children are more likely to accurately infer other people's reaction to themselves (see Maccoby, 1980). By middle childhood, children also become able to use social comparison to evaluate their own behavior (Ruble, 1983). Because older children can produce their own immediate feedback, their cognitive processes are less likely to fail due to lack of explicit feedback from others. Age-related increases in emotional control decrease the likelihood that social-cognitive processes will be disrupted. In addition, physiological maturation, increased familarity with social situations, and greater expertise in social actions should lead to enhanced capacity to process social information. With age, children are also better able to integrate multiple sources of information (Anderson, 1980). This extra capacity makes the older child less vulnerable to cognitive "overload" and subsequent disruption.

Short-term memory capacity and information-handling skills are important limiting factors in cognitive systems. In a recent review, Sternberg and Powell (1983) identified several major principles of intellectual development, including (a) growth of sophisticated control strategies, (b) more exhaustive information processing, and (c) greater flexibility in strategy and information use. In addition, Case (1978) observed developmental increases in executive strategies, greater automaticity in lower level cognitive operations, and larger working memory capacity. These age-related changes should lead to social-cognitive processes that are better integrated, and thus more adaptive, efficient, and flexible.

There have been few attempts to capture the dynamic aspects of social cognition in the developmental literature. Admittedly, measurement of internal process has been one of psychology's most difficult tasks. This assessment problem is complicated by children's response limitations. Two of the most common adult research techniques in this domain are poorly suited to young children. The ability to simultaneously perform the tasks required by "think-aloud" procedures (monitor performance, complete the task, and report ongoing actions) is likely to be beyond the processing capacity of young children (see, for example, Flavell, 1981). Similarly, young children are not yet able to consider themselves as "objects" and thus would be less able to provide accurate introspective reports. The extra processing demands that children experience with these techniques are also likely to increase the reactivity of the measures. More passive and less intrusive methods would be especially appropriate for studying social-cognitive processes in children.

In spite of these methodological limitations, some process dimensions have been examined within a social problem-solving framework. The most heavily studied aspect has been how social processing is affected by an interruption or failure. In these studies, the interruption or negative feedback was introduced experimentally (e.g., Weissberg et al., 1981) or occurred spontaneously (e.g., Krasnor & Rubin, 1983). Persistence levels (whether the child "exits the loop" or continues to try) after failure has been of considerable theoretical and applied interest. Persistence has been found to vary, for example, with peer status and sociability (e.g., Dodge, 1986; Rubin & Krasnor, 1986). Consistent failure to persist may reflect a fragile processing sequence that is easily disrupted.

Researchers have also been interested in the nature of the child's response to interruption or failure. Several different approaches to classifying strategy sequences after failure can be found in the literature. Sequencing dimensions include flexibility (Rubin & Krasnor, 1986), escalation and deescalation (Gottman, 1983; Patterson, 1979), and responsiveness to feedback (Lefebvre-Pinard et al., 1982).

Experimental manipulations of outcomes is one way to vary inputs to a process in order to understand its functioning in a more controlled context. Other manipulations may also clarify processing sequences. For example, systematic variation in the timing of social information, and observations of corresponding effects on products, should uncover aspects of social-cognitive processing (Fiske & Taylor, 1984). In addition, there is rich potential for understanding social cognition using computer models that simulate the operation and growth of cognitive processes (Anderson, 1983). Computers provide a unique context to experiment with controlled manipulations of variables (e.g., information timing or context).

In general, there has been remarkably little empirical investigation of process integration. The accumulated data describing social-cognitive products may be useful in predicting how components work together. This static product view, however, is not enough. An individual, for example, may have the "pieces" of social cognition but be unable to coordinate them in sequence. In addition, the utility and characteristics of each of the "pieces" is altered by what came before and after it. For example, the ability to produce a great quantity of potential social strategies is considered to be a sign of competence. This skill will create a processing problem, however, if the next step in the social problem-solving sequence (selection of alternatives) is unable to evaluate more than a few strategy alternatives. It is time to focus more attention on the difficult task of measuring "social-cognition-in-action."

REFERENCES

Anderson, J. (1983). *The architecture of cognition.* Cambridge, MA: Harvard University Press.

Anderson, N. (1980). Information integration theory in developmental psychology. In F. Wilkening, J. Becker, & T. Trabasso (Eds.), *Information integration by children* (pp. 1–46). Hillsdale, NJ: Lawrence Erlbaum Associates.

Berrien, F. (1968). *General and social systems.* New Brunswick, NJ: Rutgers University Press.

Brown, A., Bransford, J., Ferrara, R., & Campione, J. (1983). Learning, remembering, and understanding. In J. Flavell & E. Markman (Eds.), *Cognitive Development* (Vol. 3, pp. 77–166). New York: Wiley.

Carver, C., & Scheier, M. (1981). *Attention and self-regulation: A control-theory approach to human behavior.* New York: Springer–Verlag.

Case, R. (1978). Intellectual development from birth to adulthood: A neo-Piagetian interpretation. In R. Siegler (Ed.), *Children's thinking: What develops?* (pp. 37–71). Hillsdale, NJ: Lawrence Erlbaum Associates.

Chandler, M. (1977). Social cognition: A selective review of current research. In W. Overton (Ed.), *Knowledge and development* (pp. 94–147). New York: Plenum.

Charlesworth, W. (1983). An ethological approach to cognitive development. In C. Brainerd (Ed.),

Recent advances in cognitive-developmental research (pp. 237–258). New York: Springer-Verlag.

Damon, W. (1977). *The social world of the child.* San Francisco: Jossey-Bass.

Dodge, K. (1986). A social information processing model of social competence in children. In M. Perlmutter (Ed.), *The Minnesota symposium on child psychology* (Vol. 18, pp. 77–126). Hillsdale, NJ: Lawrence Erlbaum Associates.

Elias, M., Larcen, S., Zlotlow, S., & Chinsky, J. (1978, August). *An innovative measure of children's cognitions in problematic interpersonal situations.* Paper presented at the Annual Meeting of the American Psychological Association, Toronto.

Fiske, S., & Taylor, S. (1984). *Social cognition.* Reading, MA: Addison-Wesley.

Flavell, J. (1974). The development of inferences about others. In T. Mischel (Ed.), *Understanding other persons* (pp. 66–116). Oxford: Basil Blackwell.

Flavell, J. (1981). Monitoring social cognitive enterprises: Something else that may develop in the area of social cognition. In J. Flavell & L. Ross (Eds.), *Social cognitive development* (pp. 272–287). Cambridge, England: Cambridge University.

Flavell, J. (1982). Structures, stages, and sequences in cognitive development. In W. Collins (Ed.), *The concept of development. Minnesota symposia on child psychology* (Vol. 15, pp. 1–28). Hillsdale, NJ: Lawrence Erlbaum Associates.

Ford, M. (1982). Social cognition and social competence in adolescence. *Developmental Psychology, 18,* 323–340.

Goetz, T., & Dweck, C. (1980). Learned helplessness in social situations. *Journal of Personality and Social Psychology, 39,* 246–255.

Gottman, J. (1983). How children become friends, *Monograph of the Society for Research in Child Development, 48,* No. 201.

Hall, G. S. (1883/1972). The contents of children's minds. *Princeton Review, 11,* 249–272. In W. Dennis (Ed.), *Historical readings in developmental psychology* (pp. 119–137). New York: Appleton-Century-Crofts.

Hastie, R. (1984). Causes and effects of causal attribution. *Journal of Personality and Social Psychology, 46,* 44–56.

Humphrey, K. (1976). The social function of intellect. In P. Bateson & R. Hinde (Eds.), *Growing points in ethology* (pp. 303–318). London: Cambridge University Press.

Krasnor, L. (1982). An observational study of social problem solving in young children. In K. Rubin & H. Ross (Eds.), *Peer relationships and social skills in childhood* (pp. 113–132). New York: Springer-Verlag.

Krasnor, L. (1985, April). *Social problem solving between friends.* Paper presented at the Biennial Meeting of the Society for Research in Child Development, Toronto.

Krasnor, L., & Rubin, K. (1981). The assessment of social problem solving skills in young children. In T. Merluzzi, C. Glass, & M. Genest (Eds.), *Cognitive assessment* (pp. 452–478). New York: Guilford Press.

Krasnor, L., & Rubin, K. (1983). Preschool social problem solving: Attempts and outcomes in naturalistic interactions. *Child Development, 54,* 1545–1558.

Ladd, G., & Oden, S. (1979). The relationship between peer acceptance and children's ideas about helpfulness. *Child Development, 40,* 402–408.

Lefebvre-Pinard, M., Bufford-Bouchard, T., & Feidler, H. (1982). Social cognition and verbal requests among preschool children. *Journal of Psychology, 10,* 133–143.

Maccoby, E. (1980). *Social development.* New York: Hartcourt Brace.

Messick, S. (1983). Assessment of children. In W. Kessen (Ed.), *History, theory and methods.* In P. Mussen (Ed.), *Handbook of child psychology* (Vol. 48, pp. 477–526). New York: Wiley.

Miller, G., Galanter, E., & Pribaum, K. (1960). *Plans and the structure of behavior.* New York: Holt, Rinehart & Winston.

Nakamuri, C., & Finck, D. (1980). Relative effectiveness of socially oriented children and predictability of their behavior. *Monographs of the Society for Research in Child Development, 45,* (No. 185).

Patterson, G. (1979). A performance theory for coercive family interaction. In R. Cairns (Ed.), *The analysis of social interactions: Methods, issues and illustrations* (pp. 119–162). Hillsdale, NJ: Lawrence Erlbaum Associates.

Pellegrini, D. (1985). Social cognition and competence in middle childhood. *Child Development, 56,* 253–264.

Piaget, J., & Inhelder, B. (1969). *The psychology of the child.* New York: Basic Books.

Polikfa, J., Weissberg, R., Gesten, P., Flores de Apodaca, R., & Piccoli, L. (1981). *The open middle interview manual.* Rochester Social Problem Solving Group, Rochester, NY.

Renshaw, P., & Asher, S. (1982). Social competence and peer status: The distinction between goals and strategies. In K. Rubin & H. Ross (Eds.), *Peer relationships and social skills in childhood* (pp. 375–396). New York: Springer-Verlag.

Rubin, K. (1981). *Manual for the Social Problem Solving Test.* University of Waterloo, Ontario.

Rubin, K., & Krasnor, L. (1983). Age and gender differences in the development of social problem solving skill. *Journal of Applied Developmental Psychology, 4.*

Rubin, K., & Krasnor, L. (1986). Social-cognitive and social-behavioral perspectives on problem solving. In M. Perlmutter (Ed.), *Minnesota symposium on child psychology* (Vol. 18 pp. 1–68). Hillsdale, NJ: Lawrence Erlbaum Associates.

Ruble, D. (1983). The development of comparison processes and their role in achievement-related self-socialization. In E. T. Higgins, W. W. Hartup, & D. Ruble (Eds.), *Social cognition and social development* (pp. 134–157). New York: Cambridge University Press.

Schank, R., & Abelson, S. (1977). *Scripts, plans, goals and understanding.* Hillsdale, NJ: Lawrence Erlbaum Associates.

Selman, R. (1980). *The growth of interpersonal understanding.* New York: Academic Press.

Shantz, C. (1983). Social cognition. In J. Flavell & E. Markham (Eds.), *Cognitive development* (Vol. 4, pp. 495–555), in P. Mussen (Ed.), *Manual of child psychology.* New York: Wiley.

Simon, H. (1967). Motivation and emotional control of cognition. *Psychological Review, 74,* 29–39.

Smith, E. (1984). Model of social inference processes. *Psychological Review, 91,* 392–413.

Spivack, G., & Shure, M. (1974). *Social adjustment of young children.* San Francisco: Jossey-Bass.

Sternberg, R., & Powell, J. (1983). The development of intelligence In J. Flavell & E. Markman (Eds.), *Cognitive development* (Vol. 3, pp. 341–419). New York: Wiley.

Turiel, E. (1983). *The development of social knowledge: Morality and social convention.* Cambridge, England: Cambridge University.

Vaughn, G., & Corballis, M. (1969). Beyond test of significance: Estimating strength of effects in selected ANOVA designs. *Psychological Bulletin, 72,* 204–213.

Weissberg, R., Gesten, E., Carnrike, C., Toro, P., Rapkin, B., Davidson, E., & Cowen, E. (1981). Social problem-solving skills training: A competence-building intervention with second- to fourth-grade children. *American Journal of Community Psychology, 9,* 411–423.

Werner, H. (1948). *Comparative psychology of mental development.* New York: International Universities Press.

Play and Integration

5

James E. Johnson
Thomas D. Yawkey
The Pennsylvania State University

> *Play is a Must of the first order for individuals . . . and for mankind . . .*
> —Piers, 1972

Decades ago William James described the infant's world as one of "booming, buzzing confusion." Nowadays, one might wonder just how much clearer things can be for the preschooler growing up in modern times. From punk rock to cable video, from blended families to exploding space shuttles, the developmental task of making sense of it all has reached gargantuan proportions. Our social and technological environments have become so increasingly complicated as to stagger young and old imaginations alike.

Scholars have noted that species and cohorts across the evolutionary scale vary in the length of time it takes to reach adult status. For the more versatile and interesting species like man and other primates and mammals, a longer span of time is required to prepare for basic survival and other responsibilities that go with full maturity. This extended "incubation period" is interlinked with having a larger cerebral cortex. And, with the prolongation of immaturity also goes a heightened capacity for play. The proposition that play behavior is important in development and evolution is widely accepted (Bruner, 1972), with face validity for it existing in the simple fact that so much time is consumed at play by the young of advanced species.

The primary purpose of this chapter is to examine play as an important way by which young children not only display their developing organizational skills but also attempt to make sense of their experiences and thus achieve success in their encounters with the social and physical environment. Primary attention is given

97

to the developmental period from the beginning of early childhood to middle childhood, where research is reviewed first on the development of integrative abilities as seen *in play,* and second on the integrative functions served *by play.* The place and value of play in education and socialization during the transition from early to middle childhood are then highlighted. Finally, the phenomenon is examined from the point of view of the adult. Here is dicussed the way in which play is an important and integral feature of early childhood *and* childhood education.

Before reviewing the literature on the topics just outlined, some advantage may be served by discussing briefly the difficulties in defining play and integration and indicating how these terms are used in the present context.

DEFINITION OF TERMS

The terms play and integration, much like the terms personality and stress and other important constructs commonly employed in the social and behavioral sciences, seem easy enough to relate to or appreciate as long as they are used in a general and vague manner. However, as soon as an exact specification of meaning is required, there is much less agreement and more confusion. The writings of classical developmental theorists and the extrapolations by those contemporary researchers inspired by them are responsible for how the constructs of play and integration have generally taken on meaning in the field.

Play. Problems with classifying types of play, measuring play behaviors, and arriving at agreement over its essential defining characteristics in general have beset researchers for decades. Susanna Millar (1968) quipped that play is not a "noun" but an "adjective." Nothing is play but anything can be playful. A major research review by Rubin, Fein, and Vandenberg (1983) suggested six dispositions that seem to pertain to the phenomenon. To the extent that these are additive in applying to the same behavior, the greater is the likelihood that the behavior under consideration should be rightfully called play. These dispositions are: (a) it is intrinsically motivated; (b) it is characterized by attention to means rather than ends; (c) it is distinguished from exploratory behavior (while exploring the organism seemingly is posing the question to itself, "What is this object and how does it work?" but while playing the question becomes, "What can I do with this object?"); (d) it is characterized by nonliterality or pretense; (e) it is free from externally applied rules (in contrast to games); and (f) the participant is actively engaged (in contrast to daydreaming or idling). An earlier similar set of criteria were proposed by Ellis (1973). In this scheme, play is more likely to occur to the degree that : (a) Reality constraints can be relaxed; (b) basic needs are met; (c) the process is more important than the product; and (d) positive affect and intrinsic motivation dominate. Similarly, Krasnor and Pepler (1980) hypothesized four qualities that delimit play: flexibility, positive affect, intrinsic motivation, and nonliterality. These definitions include intrinsic motivation as a critical attribute. A recent study, however, questioned the value of this characteristic serving as a telltale sign of play. The problem seems to be that intrinsic motivation applies to so many other behaviors as well (Smith, Takhvar, Gore, & Vollstedt, 1986). Smith et al. reported that for independent judges rating 30-minute videotapes of various preschool activities, the highest consensus was achieved when the nonliterality criterion served as the working definition of play behavior (the behavior is nonliteral, i.e., it is not carried out seriously but has an "as if" or pretend quality). The hallmark of play seems to be its nonliterality or "unearnest" flavor (Johnson, Christie, & Yawkey, 1987). Make-believe play and other types of play as well can be described in this way. Play is activity under a frame of mind different from that which exists when behaviors are exhibited in actuality and governed by reality-based concerns. Characteristics of flexibility, separation of means from ends, and positive affect are also often useful correlates needed to pinpoint the behavior.

Integration.   In developmental psychology the concept of integration has taken on central importance as it has had in other disciplines such as biology and sociology. The notion is as abstract as play, but perhaps less elusive in that there is general agreement as to its meaning. According to the Oxford English Dictionary, *to integrate* is to render entire or complete, to put or bring together, and *integrative* is defined as having the quality of integrating, tending to integrate. The number of definitions for these terms is remarkably few compared to the word "play," in which the same dictionary lists 116 distinct definitions!

One example of a very broad definition of integration can be found in the developmental-organismic psychological theory of Heinz Werner (1957). For Werner the two processes of differentiation and hierarchical integration (i.e., the orthogenetic principle) are central in characterizing the process of development in its most general sense: "wherever development occurs it proceeds from a state of relative globality and lack of differentation to a state of increasing differentation, articulation, and hierarchical integration." To differentiate is to segregate elements of development; to integrate is to desegregate, to reassemble elements on a higher emergent plane. Integration meant for Werner, and for other theorists under the psychoanalytic and organic lamp (Langer, 1969) perspectives, the coordination of mental processes into an effective personality and the coordination of mental processes with the environment. According to the holistic conception of psychological experience, the environment is not conceived as an assortment of stimuli but as a more or less integrated world, and the organism is not viewed as an assemblage of faculties but as integrated (Franklin, 1983). Taking this holistic approach is necessary to infer properly the nature of the organism's experiences.

Another general definition of integration is found in the genetic epistemology of Piaget (1956, 1960). Here integration is a concept closely related to hier-archization as a criterion for cognitive stages. Integration specifies that later occurring developmental stages or levels "transform" earlier stage-related be-haviors into new structural entities. In contrast to an additive or substitutive process of replacement, prior stage-related behaviors become subordinated and subsumed within higher level functioning. This characteristic of cognitive stage progression reflects the "emergence" assumption of all organismic as opposed to mechanistic models of development (Nagel, 1957; Reese & Overton, 1970).

An example of a specific treatment of integration is found in contemporary research (Bruner, 1970; Fenson, 1984). Bruner (1970), in a study of sen-sorimotor sequences between 12 and 17 months, proposed that prior to sequenc-ing individual acts become "modularized," which means that they no longer require focal attention on the part of the child. Modularized acts, in other words, become part of the child's subsidiary awareness (Polanyi, 1966) and, as such, enable the child to concentrate more on linking behaviors to other actions. Bruner gave three types of sequences: (a) repetition with variation (analogous to Piaget's secondary and tertiary circular reactions); (b) integration where behav-iors become part of a larger whole; and (c) differentiated elaboration such that an articulated clear sequence of parts emerges from behaviors that used to be ex-pressed in a global way. The latter would be exemplified when the child goes from gross motor play (e.g., "messing around" with sand using a pale and a shovel) to being able to scoop the sand into the pale in a systematic way. Integration occurs when two separate acts are joined together into one larger performance, as illustrated by the child stirring with a spoon some real or "in-vented" substance inside a cup. Fenson (1984) has devised measures of integra-tion for investigating motor actions, speech, and symbolic play in infants, tod-dlers, and preschoolers. For Fenson, integration refers to the child's increasing ability to combine separate actions into coordinated behavior sequences. He noted, parenthetically, that information concerning integration in language also exists in a general way in data on the growth of syntax.

Both the broad and the specific meaning of integration in development are relevant in the study of early childhood and childhood play. At the risk of creating a spurious binary division, it may well be that the general sense of integration in developmental theory is emphasized more by those interested in illuminating the significance of play behavior in the grand scheme of overall developmental functioning, whereas the narrower interpretation is stressed more by those motivated to learn more about how play develops as a behavior in its own right. The former group of researchers and theorists are required to cast a wider conceptual net, entertaining in a more general way how play may be implicated in important developmental areas, whereas the latter group is preoc-cupied with various micro as opposed to macrolevel concerns in their analysis of specific play phenomenon. Research and theory from both camps is spotlighted next.

INTEGRATION IN PLAY

Integrative processes in manipulative or symbolic play have been investigated in a number of studies examining both motoric as well as symbolic patterns of behavior. As noted in the previous section, earlier work (e.g., Bruner, 1970) focusing on presymbolic sensorimotor sequences as displayed by infants have served as an example for later research investigating presymbolic and symbolic behaviors of infants, toddlers, and preschoolers. Both research procedures and measurement tools have been borrowed and modified in the process.

Increasing integration in manipulative and pretend play is but one of three different but related developmental trends. Integration, which has been operationalized in many investigations as sequential and hierarchically organized play, is the trend focused on in this chapter. The other two trends are decontextualization and decentration (McCune-Nicholich & Fenson, 1984). Decontextualization refers to the growing child's decreasing need for concrete props or environmental supports for play. For example, the child is able to pretend a role without a costume or any other realistic prop. Decentration refers to the growing child's increasing liberation from an exclusive dependence on one's own point of view or body as an anchoring point for action. For example, the child is able to turn the baby doll's head to look out a car window during a real or pretend automobile trip. Briefly, research has documented that children at first require realistic props for play and that their actions tend to be self-directed. Sometime between 12 and 18 months of age, most children extend play beyond the self (other-directed) in either an active fashion, as seen in the preceding example of the car trip where the doll is an active agent, or in a passive way, as seen in pretending to feed the baby. Here the doll is a passive recipient in the pretend episode (decentration). Eventually, the child during play becomes able to employ substitute and then invented objects to stand in for the Real McCoy (decontextualization). In the research literature on play, integration has been studied extensively, usually in conjunction with either or both decentration and decontextualization.

Nicholich (1977) and Fenson and Ramsay (1980) provided two of the first reports on the structure of play that used measures for integration. Both studies used similar procedures and coding schemes, and each owed theoretical credit to Piaget for his account of the six developmental stages within the sensorimotor period.

Nicholich (1977) was interested in describing levels of pretend games of infants in light of Piaget's stages. Nicholich (1977) observed individually five normal girls who were from 14 to 19 months at the time the study began. Each child was given a bucket of 36 toys with mother present. Children were observed once per month for one year. Over this period of time qualitative changes occurred in the symbolic play of the children. In addition to progressive decentration from self, there was increasing integration of separate behaviors into a more fluent pattern of action. Three types of integrated sequences were noted.

Single-scheme combinations, which emerged concurrently with decentered acts, occurred first. Here the same action was repeated over again but with a different recipient or implement of action. There followed *multischeme combinations* in order of appearance in this longitudinal study, first of the unordered and then of the ordered variety. *Unordered multischeme combinations* were coded whenever two unrelated actions were juxtaposed but not in any specific logical or temporal succession, whereas *ordered multischeme combinations* did possess this quality of a logical relationship of some kind; for instance, scraping a spoon across the plate before inserting it in the doll's mouth. All multischeme combinations require the ability to mentally relate two actions. However, whether planning is involved is uncertain. For example, in covering a doll with a blanket, the second action may be somehow merely automatically triggered by the first.

Fenson and Ramsay (1980) also observed children during their second year of life. These investigators were primarily interested in relating decentration with integration. This study included both a longitudinal and a cross-sequential component. It was learned that by 19 months decentered actions to objects and people occurred, at the same time that single-scheme combinations were evidenced. Virtually all of them were ordered, in contrast with Nicolich's (1977) findings that unordered ones preceded ordered multischeme combinations developmentally. Unlike in the Nicolich study, however, Fenson and Ramsay (1980) arranged play things around the room in a way that may have promoted children's completing coordinated sequences. Having a doll, a bed, and a blanket being physically near each other could facilitate the cognitive linking of them. Putting the doll to bed and covering the doll with a blanket is less difficult compared to when objects are presented all in a bucket in an unrelated way, as was the case in the Nicolich study (McCune-Nicolich & Fenson, 1984). Hence, procedural differences in the choice and presentation of the toys may explain the discrepancy in findings between the two studies.

Studies of handicapped preschoolers have also employed indices of integration in symbolic play (Ershler, 1982; Hill & McCune-Nicolich, 1981). Hill and McCune-Nicolich (1981) investigated the relationship between symbolic play and cognitive functioning (Bayley Mental Scale and Infant Behavior Record) in 30 Down's syndrome children 20–53 months of age, with mental ages ranging from 12 to 26 months. Each child was videotaped at home playing for 30 minutes with the primary caretaker present, usually the mother. Data analyses suggested four qualitative levels of play integration: (1) *presymbolic,* (2) *single pretend acts,* (3) *symbolic play sequences,* and (4) *planned pretend.* In planned pretending (another index of integration), the child announces verbally or gesturally that a pretend manuever is in the making. Searching for materials, constructing props to be used in make believe, repeating systematically a sequence of pretend actions, or performing a preparatory act prior to the pretend one are all behavioral evidence for planning. Hill and McClune-Nicolich found that degree of play integration in handicapped young children was more related to mental age than it was to chronological age. It is interesting that in this study children who failed to combine symbolic play acts also did not produce two-word (pivot-open) utterances in their oral language. Adding some validity to planning as a developmentally related indice of play integration, Field, DeStefano, and Koewler (1982) reported that 3-year-olds announced their fantasy intentions during play to a greater extent than did 2-year-olds.

Ershler (1982) investigated the play behaviors of 20 nonhandicapped and 20 handicapped preschoolers, observing each child for twenty 1-minute play episodes over a period of several weeks. Handicapped preschoolers were assessed using the Minnesota Preschool Scales (Goodenough, Mauer, & Van Wagenen, 1940), which taps various developmental domains (social, cognitive, language, motor, and self-help). Handicapped was defined as 20% delay in one or more domain using standardized, age-related norms. The Parten/Smilansky combined scales for social participation (solitary, parallel, interactive) and for cognitive content (functional, constructive, and dramatic) were used to code play behaviors following Johnson and Ershler (1981). Dramatic play was further scored for frequency and duration of transformations (person, situation, and object-real, substitute, invented), and for the overall organizational quality (*functional-* vs. *constructive-dramatic* play). Finally, the codes for integration and decentration were applied in scoring the dramatic play episodes.

Five measures of play integration were entered into the multivariate analysis. The first three were from Fenson and Ramsay (1980): (1) *single-scheme acts,* (2) *unordered multischemed combinations,* (3) *ordered multischemed combinations,* (4) *role enactment,* and (5) *constructive-dramatic play.* The fourth measure, *role enactment,* was a composite variable comprised of subvariables for *self-transformation* and the *use of no props* in pretend play. Ershler found that there was often extensive use of language when a child would elaborate a role in describing or directing the play situation. Examples of roles adopted included chairperson, customer or waiter, thief, baby, dying or dead person, and firefighter. Role enactments were verbal, not object-related behaviors.

Results showed that nonhandicapped and handicapped preschoolers did not differ significantly in the amount of pretend play behaviors exhibited. However, they did on indices of play integration with nonhandicapped children outperforming the handicapped children. For instance, examining the mean frequency data for constructive-dramatic play, nonhandicapped children had an average score of 3.52, whereas handicapped children had an average score of zero. Similar to the findings of Hill and McCune-Nicholich (1981), play scores were associated more with estimates of mental maturity than they were with chronological age.

Thus far this chapter has examined the organizational quality of manipulative or symbolic play behavior. It appears that from late infancy to the early preschool years there is a steady increase in integrative skills in action and speech during play. There is an increase in multischeme combinations, planning, and elaborate and sequenced role play. By the middle of the third year there appears to be a considerable amount of integration in the play of nonhandicapped children both in action and in speech.

Fenson (1984), in an interesting study, explored the problem of the extent to which young children relied on actions or speech to express pretense. The sample consisted of 72 middle-class children, 24 at each of three ages: 20, 26, and 31 months. After observing a model perform a play sequence, children were observed at play. Tabulations were made of the frequency of pretend actions that were accompanied or unaccompanied by language. The results indicated that at 20 months actions without language accounted for 83% of make-believe play; at 26 and 31 months the corresponding percent scores were 45 and 53%, respectively. Fenson concluded that, for both gestural and linguistic features of pretend play, there is a steady increase in integrative skills or multischeme combinations. Furthermore, language did not replace gestural modes of expression in play. The use of language and gestures sometimes were independent. However, at other times they were seen to be complementary or parallel during play behavior.

Preschool play behavior also has been investigated for its conversational coherence (Goncu & Kessel, 1984), and for its dramatic content organization (Forbes & Yablick, 1984), illustrating additional ways of examining integration in play.

From the conceptual perspective of play as communication (Garvey & Berndt, 1977; Schwartzman, 1978), Goncu and Kessel explored how 24 middle-class 4½-year-olds, familiar with one another, constructed imaginative play situations in conversation and maintained and finally terminated these situations. Various indices that were used in coding the data may be construed as tapping integration in social pretend play: *Plans, transformations, invitations,* or *object statements, negations,* and *acceptance statements.*

Children were observed and videotaped in a special room near their regular classroom. The room was arranged as a kitchen, dress-up, and block corner, each equipped with appropriate props. Children were videotaped playing in this room in 20-minute sessions for each of 2 consecutive days.

A good amount of speech occurred in the play sessions. The study further yielded evidence consistent with the hypothesis that within the play dialogues the children connected their intentions regarding ongoing activities and seemed to refer to their partners' expectation by preparing ground for the partners' next step during play. Linked utterances were significantly higher in the older than in the younger children. Goncu and Kessel concluded that any qualitative and quantitative microgenetic analyses, such as theirs, can lead to a better understanding of the meaning of integrated play and also can produce data having important potential bearing on views about social cognition during the preschool years. Interpretive-hermetic analysis of children's play was urged.

Wolf and Grollman (1982) conducted an investigation directed toward describing the narrative script organization of pretense play. These researchers provided an indepth analysis of four girls from the first cohort of five subjects from the longitudinal study of early symbolic development, Harvard Project Zero. In this project children were followed from their first birthday and were seen in weekly visits observed at play or doing other tasks such as story telling, music, movement, number use, or gestural depiction activities. Sociodramatic play was exhibited by the four girls between 1½ and 4½ years.

Data analysis focused on measuring the maturing of sociodramatic play in terms of the level of narrative organization. Narrative organization refers to the ability to enact a sequence of events in a coherent and detailed way. The levels identified were: (a) *scheme level* (single action or brief series of actions); (b) *event script level* (at least two schemes as part of the same process); and (c) *episode level* (at least two event scripts as part of the same process or aimed at achieving a particular goal. At the event and episode levels episodes are either *simple* or *contoured. Contoured events* are when the sociodramatic play performance involves at least four different schemes that are aimed at achieving a particular goal, whereas *contoured episodes* are at least two contoured events directed toward a particular objective.

Wolf and Grollman found that all four children under study displayed sociodramatic play behavior that conformed to the hypothesized sequence of levels. Their coding scheme for the level of complexity in play content provided yet another lens with which to evaluate the nature of integrative processes occurring during play.

Forbes and Yablick (1984) adopted a reality-creation paradigm in their analysis of the dramatic content of the fantasy play of 5- and 7-year-old children. Play groups of three boys and three girls at each age level met for 1 hour per day for 12 days over a 3-week period. Sessions were videotaped and behavior was coded on an utterance basis with *element categories* for character, behavior, scene, purpose, and object as well as with *ratios* (relational) *categories* for different kinds of statements children could make regarding the relationship between categories (e.g., scene-behavior ratio, "This is a church, be quiet!"). Coded behaviors appeared to be "metaplay" utterances on some occasions inasmuch as children seemingly would snap the play frame when making them.

Three kinds of analyses were reported. The first analysis examined the frequency of the five types of elements, the second emphasized the types of relationships or ratios the children referred to, and the third analysis was anecdotal in nature. The findings from the first analysis showed that there were significant age differences in the types of elements used: 5-year-olds had significantly more action statements, whereas 7-year-olds had more statements about the purposes of fantasy action (e.g., "We need to go out of the fort to be safe."). The second analysis revealed that older children mentioned how actions fit together more than did the younger children. They were seemingly more concerned with the appropriateness of the behavior for particular role-played characters. Anecdotally, from the third analysis, Forbes and Yablick stated that the 7-year-olds generally coalesced their social pretend play using a focus on the pursuit of a goal or using elaboration of character, whereas the 5-year-olds derived cohesion by anchoring to an ongoing fantasy behavior, action, or scene. In other words, the older children appeared to be more concerned about the inner coherence of their fantasy, whereas the 5-year-olds seemed more preoccupied with the concrete and external and less with abstract and psychological concerns. Five-year-olds did not focus on the character, with the result that their enactments were generally unidimensional in nature.

The reality-creation paradigm or the meaning creating perspective on imaginative play emphasizes that the transformational activities of children during social pretense provide them with opportunities to learn something about how situations are organized (Franklin, 1983). This parallels exploratory play where children learn through their own object experimentation by accommodating to the outcomes of their experiments with objects by assimilating new forms of organization into their knowledge base. Franklin (1983), following Werner (1957), sees play in this vein as nonreductionistic. In the play process children create a medium of expression involving use of bodily actions, objects made and found, space between persons and props, and language. Play, and the integrative processes occurring during play, draw on and reflect the interrelated domains of the emotional, social, and cognitive life of the child. The Wernerian, holistic approach requires conceptualizing both the dynamic interactions among aspects of the media (object use, language, use of space, gestures), and the dynamic interrelationship between the play medium and that which it incarnates or signifies.

In sum, then, integrative processes in play have been traced from late infancy through the onset of middle childhood through a survey of selected studies. Emphasis has been on identifying operational measures of integration and in describing developmental trends. Included have been studies dealing with increases in integrative skills in action and speech, in presymbolic manipulative play, and in symbolic play. Additional indices of integration that were reviewed included planning, role enactment and elaboration, and measures for conversational coherence, narrative organization of play scripts, and the dramatic content organization of social pretend play. Increases in integrative skills with age as witnessed in other play domains, such as in game-with-rules play, sports, or in performing more complex role play (Connolly, Doyle, & Ceschin, 1983), or in directing fantasy play (e.g., putting on "shows"), are also known to occur with advancing developmental status.

INTEGRATIVE FUNCTIONS OF PLAY

A considerable amount of print has been devoted to the question of the significance of play in child development. Its importance has been conceptualized as having a great deal to do with integration by many accounts. For example, Werner (1957) has conceptualized development in terms of differentiation and hierarchical integration. Piaget (1962) has maintained that the organizational and adaptational features of intelligence and development depend on the complementary processes of accommodation and assimilation. Play serves important cognitive consolidating functions, as seen in the cementing of the child's recent concept acquisitions and new learnings (Piaget), and in its assisting the child's constructing meaning from experience (Werner).

The integrative value of play is seen not only in intellectual development but also in self construction or personality formation, and in the social and emotional development and well-being of children.

Cognitive Development

According to Smilansky (1968), a chief developmental task during the preschool years is to become able to interrelate and thus comprehend events that to the child often at first seem to be disconnected. Young children, particularly from homes that are economically impoverished, are very limited in their capacity to read the various scripts of their everyday life—the sequence of events involved in going to the drug store or doctor's office, for example. Smilansky (1968) proposed that an advanced form of social pretense—sociodramatic play that is common in middle-class children—is instrumental in helping children get behind the scenes and read what is going on: "By its (sociodramatic play) very nature it demands from the child that he utilize his potential abilities and knowledge, combine his scattered experiences in a flexible way, in an almost lifelike situation" (p. 3). Sociodramatic play, in other words, helps the child integrate experiences that are separate and seem unrelated at first; through role playing emerges coherence. This is achieved in part by seeing the different character's points of view on the same event in a particular scene like grocery store. Smilansky found that sociodramatic play enhanced children's cognitive and language skills.

Saltz and Johnson (1974) and Saltz, Dixon, and Johnson (1977) tested the hypothesis that social pretense can help children connect discrete events. Preschool children who were from economically impoverished backgrounds were randomly assigned within their regular classroom to either social pretense or dimensionality training groups (Saltz & Johnson, 1974) or to sociodramatic play and thematic-fantasy play training groups (Saltz, Dixon, & Johnson, 1977). Thematic-fantasy training consisting of helping children learn to enact the plot of simple fairy tales. Other control or comparison groups were used that controlled for the effects of adult attention and language use. One important finding to emerge from this research project was that training in social pretense (sociodramatic and especially thematic-fantasy play) had a significant and positive effect on children's ability to score high on sequence and comprehension tests that required a reconstruction of the order of pictures representing a story line and an explanation of the relationship between pictures. Evidently, social pretense play fostered this type of integrative skill.

Other cognitive theorists or researchers have emphasized how play serves integrative functions through enabling children to replay and record experiences (Singer, 1973). Similar to Piaget's theory, Singer proposed that the internal activity accompanying imaginative play enables preschoolers to practice and consolidate recently acquired skills. Imaginative play enables children to assimilate new information. Although such play often reflects children's limited capacity for logical thought, nonetheless for Singer and others, it is also constructive activity, not compensatory as it is to Piaget. Play represents children's effort to comprehend and create meaning.

Bruner (1972), among others, emphasized how play promotes creativity and flexibility. Bruner pointed out that in play the means are more important than the end. Because children at play do not worry about accomplishing specific aims, they can experiment with new and unusual combinations of actions they may never have tried if attempting to achieve a specific goal. New combinations happening in play can then be used to solve real-life problems. Thus, play promotes flexibility by increasing the child's behavior options. Integration of novel and established patterns of behaviors is learned. Such divergent thinking functions are complements to the integrative functions of play during early to middle childhood. Although both components are equally important in intellectual development, in this chapter the emphasis is on the integrative functions of play.

Ego-Integrative Functions

Psychoanalytic theory of play has been most influential particularly prior to the mid-1960s. According to Freud (1961), play has an important role in emotional development due to its potential cathartic value. Negative affect related to traumatic events can be reduced through play when children, by suspending reality, are able to switch roles from being the passive recipient of traumatic experiences to being in control. Such role reversals enable the child to gain a sense of mastery and autonomy.

Repetition is another mechanism used by children to alleviate anxiety due to unpleasant events. Frustrations and conflicts of growing up can be dealt with vicariously through play. By dividing into smaller segments and repeating a bad experience over and over again, children can defuse the negative affect. Erikson (1950) has applied the psychoanalytic theory of play to normal personality development. For Erikson, children create model situations in play that assist them in mastering developmental tasks related to the stages of psychosocial development.

The pulling apart and putting back together of experiences in play is an integral feature of the construction of the self concept. For Erikson, a sense of hope in the future is of paramount importance in human development over the life course, and this hope is implicit in the child's role play enactments. Continuity of selfhood is perhaps no more reflected on, and reflected in, as it is in play behavior. However, for all play theorists with a holistic conception of development, play is not simply reducible to these various important integrative functions that they do serve. As Herron and Sutton-Smith (1971) have commented: "It has been said, for example, that play may well be, in many respects, a resemblage of thoughts and feelings from everyday life, it still has unique properties. It is a polarization with its own character" (p. 20). Generative and expressive functions of play merge together for the ego-integrative theorists more so than they do for the cognitive theorists, with the notable exception of Werner.

Socioemotional Functions

Play serves socioemotional integrative functions as well. Research on the rhesus monkey by Harry Harlow and his associates years ago indicated the critical nature of group play for normal social development (Suomi & Harlow, 1978). Evidently, play fighting is instrumental in learning how to inhibit aggressive tendencies that is necessary for group integration. Peer play also is necessary for normal sexual development. Adult monkeys who as infants lacked peer contact displayed immature sexual behaviors as adults (Suomi & Harlow, 1978).

Research on humans has also indicated the significance of play for social integration. Rough and tumble play or play fighting seems to be important for children as it is in other species (Pellegrini, in press). Furthermore, play in general fosters peer relations. Children learn to cooperate and get along with other children during play (Humphreys & Smith, in press). As discussed earlier in this chapter, cohesiveness and internal integration of play episodes depends on turn taking and role taking on the part of the children involved. In the social skill domain and in other areas, a "chicken-and-egg" dilemma persists regarding the extent to which play reflects and the extent to which play promotes the various integrative skills emerging during childhood. However, some evidence from play training studies suggest that sociodramatic play skills could lead to more positive peer relations (Rosen, 1974; Shmukler & Naveh, 1980; Smith, Dalgleish, & Herzmark, 1981).

Piaget (1962) has maintained that play is assimilatory activity. As such, the child is able to express behavior in different ways using abilities that the child already possesses. There is no fear of evaluation or risk of failure involved under these conditions. A child at play can acquire a sense of mastery, self-confidence, and calm by engaging in various expressive activities. Elkind (1981) asserted that play is an anedote to childhood stress, a kind of safety valve to let off tension due to the added demands pressuring children as they grow up in modern times.

In sum, then, in addition to integrative skills seen in play, there are integrative functions served by play. In this section a brief survey of selected studies has been made dealing with the significant integrative purposes served by play in the area of cognitive development, ego integration, and socioemotional development.

TRANSITION FROM EARLY TO MIDDLE CHILDHOOD

As noted earlier, considerable integration is evidenced in play forms that have not been discussed previously in this chapter. Specifically, games-with-rules, sports, arts and crafts, hobbies, sports and athletics, and drama, music, and the like come into their own as children move into the middle childhood years. These sundry activities, to the extent they are engaged in during middle childhood (and how well) certainly would indicate, require, and perhaps promote integrative skills in the player. It is sometimes claimed that when children reach this stage and develop these new interests that they leave behind the world of make believe, that overt "acting-out" fantasy "goes underground" as the child achieves concrete logical abilities. For instance, Piaget (1962) tied his concrete operational period of intellectual development to games-with-rules play.

Research indicates that make-believe play does not disappear once the child enters the period of middle childhood. Doyle, Bowker, and Hayvren (1985) investigated developmental changes in social and solitary pretend play during middle childhood. The subjects were 286 children in grades 1 through 6 in two elementary schools serving families of diverse ethnic and social class backgrounds. Children were systematically observed once per week for 10 weeks during their 20-minute art period when they were free to interact socially while working in groups. A 1-minute scan procedure was used and instances of pretend play were coded in terms of duration (in seconds), object use (replica, substitute, invented or animated), and role enactment (nonspecific, familial, stereotypic, character, generalized character). Conservation ability of the children was evaluated using the Goldschmidt and Bentley Concept Assessment Kit, and imaginative predispositions were assessed using Singer's Interview (Singer, 1973).

The results indicated that age differences were not significant for frequency of social pretend play and that pretend play was still present in 12-year-olds, but that in terms of duration social pretense decreased from ages 7 to 11 years and that the proportion of pretend play that involved objects also dropped. Fantasy-making tendencies declined also as tapped by the Singer Interview. However, school and gender differences in play behavior were greater than age differences in play. Furthermore, changes appeared to follow attainment of concrete operational thinking. The turning point was the achievement of conservation of discontinuous quantity. These findings are consistent with the results of Becher and Wolfgang (1977), who reported that duration and object use in social pretend play declined with increasing age and that these changes in pretend play seem to be based on cognitive factors.

Other evidence indicates that pretend play continues into middle childhood.

Piaget (1962) claimed that by age 6 or 7 symbolic play is replaced by games-with-rules. Children become more reality conscious as their thought becomes more logical and as peer group pressures for conformity increase. Children shy away from overt pretend play for fear of adult and peer ridicule. However, Hetherington, Cox, and Cox (1979) reported increases in solitary fantasy in 6- and 7-year-olds; Eifermann (1971) reported that among disadvantaged Israeli children sociodramatic play and not games-with-rules play continued to increase in the first and second grades and then dropped in the third and fourth grades. In higher social class children, on the other hand, Eifermann found that by age 6 symbolic play declined to a more or less stable level. Interest in rule-governed games jump dramatically between the first and second grade. Eifermann's project was mammoth, including 150 observers recording the 10-minute recess behavior of 14,000 Israeli children between 1964 and 1966.

The transition, then, to middle childhood is marked by a decline but not by a disappearance in dramatic play interests. The empirical base is limited, however, and a clear picture of the extent that older children engage in pretend play is not available. A safe bet seems that a fair amount of such play is done by children in private indoor home settings or neighborhood yards or street settings. Nevertheless, new play interests during middle childhood are also seen to emerge, reflecting further advances in children's integrative abilities.

THE ROLE OF THE ADULT

In stark contrast to early childhood, play has not been viewed as having an important place in education when children reach the middle childhood. Teachers and parents in general see play during the preschool years to be crucial for socialization and learning. However, on entry to formal schooling, children and education get defined differently. Priority goes to academic subject matter with strong emphasis on basic literacy and numeracy skills. Play is then usually demoted in status to the category of the trivial, sometimes finding expression in music, art, or gym class, or as learning "games" during math or language arts in the regular classroom.

Some parents and educators may need to reexamine their views on the place of play at school in light of social commentaries like the one provided by Elkind (1981). The causes, nature, and consequences of childhood stress, and how it might be ameliorated, is a topic of increasing concern. Some have advocated elevating the role of the arts in education as one remedy (*Art Education,* 1983). Others have urged a closer look at play provisions and expectations and have called for a change in attitude on the part of teachers, which can result from the acquisition of theoretical and research knowledge linked to play applications (Johnson, et al., 1987). Whatever the solution, one thing is clear: the current push for mastery at a constant or accelerated pace is leaving less and less time for childhood play and its important integrative functions. This trend may be one of the era's greatest disservices to children.

Specific Roles

There are several specific roles that the adult can perform that are critical to high-quality play and its integrating functions at early and middle childhood levels. Prior to play intervention, the adult should consider "setting the stage" for play by preparing the environment and observing the children in their play. This section provides information on various activities for adults involved in children's play. For a more detailed treatment of the adult's roles in children's play, the reader is referred to Chapter 2 in Johnson et al. (1987).

In "setting the stage" for high-quality play and its potential for integrative functions, the adult must consider four variables that influence the type and level of play: (a) time, (b) space, (c) materials, and (d) preparatory experiences. First, children need time to begin and carry out their dramatic and sociodramatic play and to develop persistence in their play routines. The amount of time will vary by age and play skills, but for the preschool and kindergarten children, from 30 to 50 minutes of massed play is generally considered necessary (Yawkey & Trostle, 1982). Second, space is a consideration for it provides "special" places in schools and homes were children can play. Space can also be partitioned into areas such as housekeeping, blocks and theme-oriented areas, for example, a post office and space command center. Partitioning space into smaller areas may actually increase the quality of sociodramatic play (compared to open, nonpartitioned space) (Walling, 1977). Third, play materials are needed for quality dramatic and sociodramatic play. Theme-related ones may include props such as old adult clothing and discarded uniforms. In addition, play materials should include construction materials such as small blocks.

Finally, preparatory experiences with various roles unfamiliar to the child are needed in order for children to understand and enact sociodramatic themes based on these characters. For example, the majority of children at early and middle childhood levels may not have had experience with roles such as job-related ones outside the home. In order to provide them with background experiences of unfamiliar roles and themes, taking field trips to novel job settings, interviewing key resource personnel about their roles, reading nonfictional stories, and using colorful magazines depicting job functions are recommended. These and other forms of preparatory experiences help clarify and provide meaning to roles and themes that are later enacted in free play.

Another consideration prior to adult involvement is observation of play. Observation assists the adult in determining what help if any is needed. Additional space, time, materials, and preparatory or extended experiences required to carry out play can be determined. Moreover, children's needs, interests, and concerns can be learned.

In the context of setting the stage and observing children at play, the adult may consider various types of involvement in children's play. Types of involvement are parallel play, coplaying, play tutoring, and spokesperson for reality (Johnson et al., 1987; Wood, McMahon, & Cranstoun, 1980).

Parallel playing, as one adult role in child's play, is where the adult positions her or himself in proximity to the child and plays with the same materials as the child. In playing with materials, the adult does not interact either verbally or nonverbally with the child but may direct comments to her or himself and about her or his own play activities, for example, "I put the tire on this wheel and it spins?" Although the adult does not directly interact with the child, the adult's presence serves to support and increase the length of play time and shows that play is a worthwhile, sanctioned activity important to both child and adult. Also, the adult's play may actually serve as models for object play that the child may imitate and use in novel ways. The role of the adult as parallel player is ideal for functional play such as shaping playdough or pushing wheel toys back and forth as well as constructional play, for example, building with blocks, or putting together pieces to make various objects.

Coplaying is another role the adult might use for involvement in child's play. As coplayer the adult joins directly in the play activity and permits the child to direct the development and course of the episode. Here, the adult may ask questions and make comments in order to extend the duration of the play episode. The adult primarily responds to the child's questions or comments. However, while coplaying the adult frequently asks for information or instructions in addition to responding to the children's actions or comments. Adults enter the play episode by assuming a complementary role, making comments that fit with the play episode, or providing play materials requested by the child.

A coplaying adult offers similar advantages to the playing child. The coplayer role helps build rapport with the child and therefore may be a stronger influence on the level of play. The adult may spark the children's imagination when the play becomes repetitious.

In play tutoring, the adult takes a more dominant role in play than the adult does in the coplayer role. The adult teaches new play behaviors showing how to become involved in adopting and carrying out roles and story lines. The adult may intervene from outside the play episode or decide to participate directly in the child's play and actually assume roles.

In addition to intervening from outside or within the play episode, the adult may use thematic-fantasy training. With this form of play tutoring, the adult helps children enact fairy tales or short stories with few characters and simple repetitive plots (Saltz & Johnson, 1974). Thematic-fantasy training is highly structured compared to the other roles in play and is more demanding than sociodramatic play. Johnson et al. (1987) suggest that adults consider play tutoring when children do not engage in make-believe play on their own, show difficulty playing with other children, or are engaging in make-believe play but the player has become repetitious or appears ready to break down.

The final role of the adult is spokesperson for reality. Here play is used by the adult as a tool for academic instruction. The adult does not directly participate in the children's play but prompts children to bridge gaps and make connections between their play and the real world. Through adults' prompting children to bridge gaps between play and real life, make believe is suspended in favor of life-like situations, events, and objects.

SUMMARY

After discussing how play and integration might be defined, this chapter reviewed selected research studies on the development of integrative skills in play from late infancy to middle childhood. Developmental trends were described and a number of measures of integration in play were identified. Researchers have employed diverse measures. The new terminology is impressive: single scheme, unordered multischeme, ordered multischeme, presymbolic acts, single pretend acts, symbolic play sequences, planned pretend role enactment, constructive-dramatic play, plans-, transformations-, invitations-, negations-, acceptance-, and negations-statements, scheme level, event script level, episode level, simple contoured events, contoured episodes, element categories, and ratio categories. The research has shown that there are dramatic changes in integrative abilities in the play of children from late infancy to middle childhood. These developing integrative abilities are seen in the action and speech used in manipulative and symbolic play and in the planning, role enactment, and elaboration of pretend play. Furthermore, developmental trends have been documented for conversational coherence, and the narrative and dramatic content organization of play and metaplay behaviors. Children become more aware of their cognitive strategies applied to play as they get older, not only expressing but also representing and directing play episodes.

The significance of play for development was discussed by reviewing selected theoretical accounts on the integrative roles of play in cognitive development, ego-integrative functioning, and socioemotional development. Cognitively, play was viewed as serving important consolidating and meaning-construction functions to go together with its divergent production functions not considered in this chapter. From a psychoanalytic perspective, play was viewed as having cathartic value enabling children to reinterpret negative experiences and concerns about growing up, and thus achieve a sense of mastery and control not possible in real life. Furthermore, play was viewed as providing an important strand in the continuity of selfhood and as helping children acquire social skills and preparation for future roles. In terms of the socioemotional functions of play, research was cited on the importance of play for group integration and stress modulation.

In conclusion, an overview of selected studies was included showing changes in play during the transition to middle childhood. Increases in integration, of course, are evidenced in the many new play interests of this developmental period: games-with-rules, sports, arts and crafts, hobbies, clubs, dramatic skits, and the like. Moreover, pretend play continues to occur during this period; but, an empirical base is lacking precluding making definitive statements about the nature or extent of this phenomenon. Finally, the chapter ended with a note on the importance of socialization agents ensuring some degree of continuity in play provisions and expectations for children during their transition from early to middle childhood, thereby reducing for them what would be today's version of the "booming, buzzing confusion" of William James' infant years ago.

REFERENCES

Art Education (1983, March) Special Issue: Art and the Mind, *36* (2).

Becher, R. M., & Wolfgang, C. H. (1977). An explanation of the relationship between symbolic representation in dramatic play and the cognitive and reading readiness levels of kindergarten children. *Psychology in the Schools, 14,* 377–381.

Bruner, J. S. (1970). The growth and structure of skills. In K. Connolly (Ed.), *Mechanisms of motor skills development* (pp. 63–94). New York: Academic Press.

Bruner, J. S. (1972). The nature and uses of immaturity. *American Psychologist, 27* 687–708.

Campbell, J. (1984). *Grammatical man: Information, entropy, language, and life.* New York: Simon & Schuster.

Connolly, J., Doyle, A. B., & Ceschin, F. (1983). Forms and functions of social fantasy play in preschoolers. In M. Liss (Ed.), *Children's play: Sex differences and the acquisition of cognitive and social skills* (pp. 71–92). New York: Academic Press.

Doyle, A., Bowker, A., & Hayvren, M. (April, 1985). *Development changes in social and solitary pretend play during middle childhood.* Society for Research in Child Development, Toronto.

Eifermann, R. (1971). Levels of children's play as expressed in group size. *British Journal of Educational Psychology, 40,* 161.

Elkind, D. (1981). *The hurried children: Growing up too fast too soon.* Reading, MA: Addison-Wesley.

Ellis, M. J. (1973). *Why people play.* Englewood Cliffs, NJ: Prentice-Hall.

Erikson, E. H. (1950). *Childhood and society.* New York: Norton.

Ershler, J. (1982). *Play behavior in nonhandicapped and handicapped preschool-aged children.* Unpublished doctoral dissertation, University of Wisconsin-Madison.

Fenson, L. (1984). Developmental trends for action and speech in pretend play. In I. Bretherton (Ed), *Symbolic play: The development of social understanding* (pp. 249–264). New York: Academic Press.

Fenson, L., & Ramsay, D. S. (1980). Decentration and integration of play in the second year of life. *Child Development, 51,* 171–178.

Field, T., DeStefano, L., & Koewler, J. (1982). Fantasy play of toddlers and preschoolers. *Developmental Psychology, 18,* 503–508.

Forbes, D., & Yablick, G. (1984). The organization of dramatic content in children's fantasy play. In F. Kessel & A. Goncu (eds.), *Analyzing children's play dialogues* (pp. 23–36). San Francisco.

Franklin, M. B. (1983). Play as the creation of imaginary situation: The role of language. In S. Wapner & B. Kaplan (Eds.), *Toward a holistic development of psychology* (pp. 197–220). Hillsdale, NJ: Lawrence Erlbaum Associates.

Freud, S. (1961). *Beyond the pleasure principle.* New York: Norton.

Garvey, C., & Berndt, R. (1977, September). *The organization of pretend play*. Paper presented at the Annual Meeting of the American Psychological Association, Chicago.

Goncu, A., & Kessel, F. (1984). Children's play: A contextual-functional perspective. In F. Kessel & A. Goncu (Eds.), *Analyzing children play dialogues* (pp. 5–22). San Francisco: Jossey-Bass.

Goodenough, F. L., Mauer, K. M., & Van Wagener, M. J. (1940). *Minnesota preschool scales*. Minneapolis: Educational Testing Bureau.

Herron, R. E., & Sutton-Smith, B. (1971). *Child's play*. New York: Wiley.

Hetherington, E. M., Cox, M., & Cox, R. (1979). Play and social interaction in children following divorce. *Journal of Social Issues, 35*, 26–49.

Hill, P., & McCune-Nicolich, L. (1981). Pretend play and patterns of cognition in Down's Syndrome children. *Child Development, 52*, 611–617.

Humphreys, A., & Smith, P. (in press). Rough-and-tumble play, friendship and dominance in schoolchildren—Evidence for continuity and change with age. *Child Development*.

Johnson, J. E., Christie, J. F., & Yawkey, T. D. (1987). *Play and early childhood development*. Evanston, IL: Scott Foresman.

Johnson, J. E., & Ershler, J. (1981). Developmental trends in preschool play as a function of classroom program and child gender. *Child Development, 52*, 995–1004.

Krasnor, L. R., & Pepler, D. J. (1980). The study of children's play: Some suggested future directions. In K. H. Rubin (Ed.), *Children's play* (pp. 85–96). San Francisco: Jossey-Bass.

Langer, J. (1969). *Theories of development*. New York: Holt, Rinehart, & Winston.

McCune-Nicholich, L., & Fenson, L. (1984). Methodological issues in studying early pretend play. In T. D. Yawkey & A. D. Pellegrini (Eds.), *Child's play: Developmental and applied* (pp. 81–104). Hillsdale, NJ: Lawrence Erlbaum Associates.

Millar, S. (1968). *Psychology of play*. Baltimore: Penguin Books.

Nagel, E. (1957). Determinism and development In D. B. Harris (Ed.), *The concept of development* (pp. 15–24). Minneapolis: University of Minnesota Press.

Nicholich, L. (1977). Beyond sensorimotor intelligence: Assessment of symbolic maturity through analysis of pretend play. *Merrill-Palmer Quarterly, 23*, 89–99.

Pellegrini, A. (in press). Elementary school children's rough-and-tumble play. *Educational Psychologist*.

Piaget, J. (1956). Les stades du development intellectual de l'enfant et l' adolescent. In P. O. Sterriety (Ed.), *Le Probleme des stades en psychologie de l'enfant* (pp. 33–42). Paris: Presses Universitaires de France.

Piaget, J. (1960). The general problems of the psychological development of the child. In J. M. Tanner & B. Inhelder (Eds.), *Discussions on child development* (Vol. 4, pp. 3–27). London: Tavistock.

Piaget, J. (1962). *Play, drama, and imitation in childhood*. New York: Norton.

Piers, M. (Ed.) (1972). *Play and development*. New York: Norton.

Polanyi, M. (1966). *The tacit dimension*. New York: Doubleday.

Reese, H. W., & Overton, W. F. (1970). Models of development and theories of development (pp. 115–145). In L. R. Goulet & P. B. Battes (Eds.), *Life-span developmental psychology: Research and theory* (pp. 116–149). New York: Academic Press.

Rosen, C. F. (1974). The effects of sociodramatic play on problem-solving behavior among culturally disadvantages preschool children. *Child Development, 45*, 920–927.

Rubin, K. H., Fein, G. G., & Vandenberg, B. (1983). In P. H. Mussen & E. M. Hetherington (Eds.), *Handbook of child psychology* (4th ed., Vol. 4, pp. 693–774) New York: Wiley.

Saltz, E., Dixon, D., & Johnson, J. (1977). Training disadvantaged preschoolers on various fantasy activities: Effects on cognitive functioning and impulse control. *Child Development, 48*, 367–380.

Saltz, E., & Johnson, J. (1974). Training for thematic-fantasy play in culturally disadvantaged children. *Journal of Educational Psychology, 66*, 623–630.

Schwartzman, H. B. (1978). *Transformations: The anthropology of children's play*. New York: Plenum.

Shmukler, D., & Naveh, I. (1980). Modification of imaginative play in preschool children through the intervention of an adult model. *South African Journal of Psychology, 10*, 99–103.

Singer, J. L. (1973). *The child's world of make-believe: Experimental studies of imaginative play*. New York: Academic Press.

Smilansky, S. (1968). *The effects of sociodramatic play on disadvantaged preschool children*. New York: Wiley.

Smith, P. K., Dalgleish, M., & Herzmark, G. (1981). A comparison of the effects of fantasy play tutoring and skills tutoring in nursery classes. *International Journal of Behavior Development, 4*, 421–441.

Smith, P. K., Takhvar, M., Gore, N., & Vollstedt, R. (1986). Play in young children's problems of definition, categorization and measurement. In P. K. Smith (Ed.), *Children's play: Research developments and practical applications* (pp. 37–54). New York: Gordon and Breach Science Publishers, 37–54

Suomi, S., & Harlow, H. (1978). Early experience and social development in rhesus monkies. In M. Lamb (Ed.), *Social and personality development* (pp. 252–271). New York: Holt, Rinehart, & Winston.

Walling, L. S. (1977). Planning an environment: A case study. In S. Kritchevsky & E. Prescott (Eds.), *Planning environments for young children: Physical space*. Washington, DC: National Association for the Education of Young Children.

Werner, H. (1957). The concept of development from a comparative and organismic point of view. In D. B. Harris (Ed.), *The concept of development* (pp. 125–148). Minneapolis: University of Minnesota Press.

Wolf, D., & Grollman, S. H. (1982). Ways of playing: Individual differences in imaginative style. In D. J. Pepler & K. H. Rubin (Eds.), *The play of children: Current theory and research* (pp. 46–63). Basel, Switzerland: Karger.

Wood, D., McMahon, L., & Cranstoun, Y. (1980). *Working with under fives*. Ypsilonti, MI: High/Scope Press.

Yawkey, T. D., & Trostle, S. L. (1982). *Learning is child's play*. Provo, UT: The Brigham Young University Press.

Interindividual Integration:
An Introduction

Thomas D. Yawkey
The Pennsylvania State University

The developing child's environment that includes everything outside the human organism is the focus of these chapters such as family, friends, the neighborhood, and those situations that govern and make decisions about a child's day-to-day living. Rulings and decisions of school boards and parent's location of employment and social/political attitudes at local, state, and national levels affect the child's development directly or indirectly. All these aspects and situations can be viewed as an "environmental press," which act on and interrelate with the child's development. Of major importance to developmental theory in the context of this volume is how the family, friends, school, and community influence and might become both the products and the causes of development?

The topics in this section deal with the family as a socialization context, with children's peer relations, with the school and the community, and they address roles or activities expected of the child and of others. Then too, each of the topics stresses among others possible links between these varied social settings and roles. It is apparent that the child's capacity to integrate roles and social settings may depend, in part, on the compatibility between social settings. Finally, the authors of the topics are in agreement that, as social settings overlap in mutual support and involvement, roles played by these settings in fostering the child's development increase.

Christopherson initially overviews several theoretical approaches within which the family as a socialization context might be considered, that is, from structural–functional, symbolic–interactive, social exchange, and sociobiological perspectives. Although each provides a distinctive and definite set of understandings, including varied assumptions and limitations, a pluralistic perspective provides greater advantages in attempting to understand the complex intricacies of role development and human interactions and interrelations within the family as socializing agent for the developing child.

Christopherson, in the context of pluralistic perspectives on the family as a socialization context, examines possible roles, behavioral styles, and values within the family that might link it with other social settings and role expectations. Furthermore, he notes that simple family functions provide numerous settings of nondeliberate and deliberate socialization of the developing child. For example, family meals are nondeliberate, interactive settings in which the developing child experiences realities of parental values and attitudes in whatever form or direction they take.

Self-discipline, freedom to make discoveries and mistakes, and trust–honesty–confidence between parent and child are fostered within the family as a socialization agent. How well the child is able to integrate roles of child and family member and child and friend, as examples, is determined in part by the amount and degree of overlap between the family as socializing agent and other social settings, such as the peer group, school and community, and indirect constructive meshing of processes within the larger social world.

Oden reviews major theories, controversies, and problems and provides alternative perspectives on children's peer relationships, all of which involve both intrapersonal and interpersonal processes. She begins her analyses by reviewing classical and more contemporary research studies on children's peer relationships, noting their limitations and potential confounds, and pointing out possible areas for future research investigations. By making significant distinctions between children's partnerships and their friendships, Oden builds a position for increased understanding of children's progressive peer relationships across age or development levels as well as within their peer relationships.

Findings of particular interest across age or developmental level suggest that 5- through 11-year-olds emphasize friends, sharing, helping, and lack of fighting (compared to acquaintances) as primary features with over-age increases for friendships in the characteristics of intimacy and loyalty. In addition, related data suggest that children's understanding of friend relations might occur in cognitive stages in accord with growth of their social perspective-taking abilities. Analyses of data on children's interaction within peer relationships among young toddlers and preschool friends showed significance of shared meanings, as well as shared role play and fantasy play.

With the lifelong importance of peer relationships, Oden proposed that more investigations should examine interrelationships, between interpersonal and intrapersonal processes.

Asp and Garbarino examine the origins, nature, and dimensions of integrative processes at school and in the community. They begin by describing Bronfenbenner's ecological perspective on human development. They use this approach as a means for analyzing the nature of ecological transitions that emphasizes the developing child's world and necessary integrative changes in roles and settings which are required as he or she moves from the family setting to other social settings. They choose the public school as a descriptive example of ecological transitions because it is an extremely pervasive socializing agent and its demands on the social cognitive actions of children are similar to and in this instance serves as a metaphor for other community settings such as religious and scouting organizations, pee-wee gymnastics, and soccer leagues. They compare and contract new social settings within which the developing child becomes involved on a number of structural dimensions or features. These features determine roles, expectations, new rewards, and sanctions that children are expected to show between and across ecological transitions. For example, as children move from family to public school (or to other community settings) and compared to previous expectations within the family, their behavioral roles in activities are purposeful, specific, task oriented, and they must learn to respond to new rewards and sanctions. Also, within the new social setting they refine their basic knowledge of their roles through structural and logistic aspects of these new settings.

Finally, and through research findings, they document that children learn these new expectations and roles but develop and use ways to manipulate these roles to satisfy their own needs and obtain rewards from adults. Children learn to make new roles and rewards and to integrate them with their existing conceptions of their social development.

The Family as a Socialization Context

Victor A. Christopherson
University of Arizona

INTRODUCTION

Few would disagree with the assertion that much of the child's early and critical socialization takes place within the family. In order to help objectify assent that might otherwise remain on an intuitive level, a brief sketch of several theoretical frameworks are presented. The theoretical approaches provide a variety of perceptual lenses that offer insights as to how and why the family socialization context is so critical.

The structural–functional approach might consider socialization in terms of such concepts as norms, family composition, social and economic status, and functional aspects of roles. This approach often takes structural elements of the family situation as "givens" and then explores the consequences as they impact on the child. What are the effects, for example, of divorce, a working mother, a lower middle-class orientation, and being the oldest child in such a family? How the various structural elements interact with one another and what the outcomes of such interactions are is a proper concern of this approach (Eshleman, 1981).

Gecas (1981) pointed out that the traditional family as a societal unit has a relatively simple structure. A father, a mother, and children are its basic elements, and variations involve the absence of one of the parents, children, or the presence of other adults such as extended kin. These and other structural elements are part of the structural basis to be taken into account in viewing the family. The change that takes place in the child as the influence from the various structural elements is brought to bear, first by the family and later by other agencies, is referred to as socialization (Inkeles, 1969).

Another approach utilized in attempting to understand how the child learns and internalizes the ways of society is through the symbolic interaction framework. This approach stresses "meanings," definitions of situations, symbolic communication, interpretations, and other symbolic processes (Schvaneveldt, 1966). The child is thought to learn the appropriate patterns of behavior through his or her interactions with significant others, particularly within the family setting (Gecas, 1981). Roles and role behavior are an important aspect of symbolic interaction, as is also the case in the structural–functional approach. In the symbolic–interaction framework, however, the emphasis is on what the child does and what others do either in response or as models. The child, in this framework, is a part of a family unit of "interacting personalities" involved in a never-ending, completed, or fixed process (Eshleman, 1981).

Another theoretical approach within which socialization is considered is the social exchange frame of reference. This orientation assumes that, in the process of learning how to participate productively in society, the child reacts to stimuli based on need, reward, and reinforcement. Rewards are generally proportional to the cost, and exchanges become instrumental in parent–child relations as well as in other dyadic relations within the family (Edwards, 1969; Nye, 1978).

A rather new and very intriguing application of exchange theory, although not often acknowledged as such, is the emerging discipline of sociobiology (Barash, 1979; Wilson, 1975). Even so basic a matter as a mother's "love" for her infant is based on the reward she experiences in the process. A parent's apparent altruism toward a child is a phylogenetically induced response predicated on the likelihood that the child will one day reproduce and thus perpetuate the genes shared by the child and parent.

Social exchange theory, perhaps more than the others, often injects an element of sobering reality into our subjective impressions. Blau (1964) and Homans (1961) are generally credited with originating the framework, although their versions differ in some respects from each other.

Finally, the developmental frame of reference as explicated by Duvall (1977) and Rodgers (1973) is useful in providing a structure for identifying, understanding, and perhaps even scheduling the benchmarks of socialization. In some respects this approach resembles both the structure–functional and the symbolic–interaction frameworks. The peculiar character of the developmental framework lies in its attempt to account for change in the family system over time as well as to account for changes in patterns of interactions over time. A strong exponent of the approach, Duvall (1977) attempted to bring together the life-cycle concepts, central in the developmental theory, and Havighurst's (1953) developmental-task concepts.

Socialization is a very complex matter, and some of its puzzles have never been solved—for example, syntax acquisition in language development. The insights that these theoretical frameworks help bring about are valuable and can be applied to advantage in the attempt to comprehend the intricacies of family dynamics. As the discussion of socialization within the family context proceeds, elements of several of the theoretical approaches are utilized. No attempt is made to stay within the bounds of a single approach, or to extoll the virtues of one perspective over the other. Before proceeding further, however. a brief overview of societal changes occurring in the family unit may be beneficial as a foundation. The demographic trends are based largely on the U.S. Census Bureau Current Population Reports, Series P-20.

Some Recent Family-Related Trends

The definition of a family, according to the U.S. Census Bureau, is a group of two or more persons related by blood, marriages, or adoption who reside together. In 1984 there were approximately 62 million family households in the United States, and there were about 23.4 million that were not family households; e.g., they were maintained by nonfamily householders.

These figures have not changed much since 1980. One rather dramatic change, however, has taken place. The drop in the number of traditional two-parent families over the 4 years from 1980 to 1985 was comparable in size to that experienced over the 10-year period between 1970 and 1980.

Married couples with children under 18 accounted for 20% of all households in 1984, whereas in 1970 the percentage was 40. Whereas the percentage of families with young children has decreased, some of this decrease is likely because of the overall growth in the number of family households in the 1980s. There has been growth, both in numbers and percentage, of the one-parent family situations during the same period. One-parent families accounted for 26% of all family groups with children under 18 in 1984, compared with 22% in 1980, and 13% in 1970.

Another indication of directionality in family trends concerns family size. An all-time low in the number of persons per household occurred in 1984 (i.e., 2.71). In 1980 the figure was 2.76, and in 1970, 3.14 (U.S. Bureau of the Census, Series P-20, No. 398, 1984).

In addition there have also been other important changes in family-related matters since the beginning of the 1970s. The median age at first marriage has risen for both men and women. The median age for women in 1984 was 23—the highest it has been since 1890. The median age at first marriage for men in both 1983 and 1984 was 25.4, the highest levels since 1900 when it reached 25.9. At the same time the age at marriage has been rising, the proportions of never married have been increasing. The proportion has doubled for both men and women in their late 20s and early 30s since 1970.

Divorce has risen steadily from 1960 to the present with a concommitant increase in single-parent families. The steepest part of the curve occurred in the 1980s. For example, between 1970 and 1984 the number of divorced persons per 1,000 married persons increased from 47 to 121, an increase of almost 40%. A logical demographic concommitant of this increase has been the increase in the number of children living in a single-parent family. Since 1970, the number has increased by nearly 6 million. At the same time, the number of those living together without being married has nearly tripled from roughly 675,000 to 1,988,000.

In spite of the recent increase in divorce, from 4% in 1970 to 9% in 1984, and the increase in the number of those who live together but have not yet married, marriage is still a popular enterprise. Eshleman (1981) pointed out that more than 85% of the men between the ages of 35 and 64 are married, as are more than 80% of the women between the ages of 30 and 54. At least 95% of both sexes are predicted to marry at some point in their lives (Bureau of the Census, Series P-20, No. 399, 1984).

At these current and projected levels of marriage, it is unlikely that the primary context of the child's socialization is in any immediate danger. At the same time, the changes that have occurred with the emerging trends suggest that adaptive adjustments may be increasingly necessary.

Even though the family has been changing in important respects, it is still the agency in which most children learn the ways of their cultures and society.

THE NUCLEAR FAMILY FORM AND SOME VARIATIONS

The form of the family most familiar to Americans is the nuclear family comprised of mother, father, and offspring. As Mace (1976) points out, the nuclear family can be extended in three ways: (1) adding blood relatives and their dependents—grandparents, brothers and sisters, nieces and nephews, with their respective relatives by marriage; (2) multiple marriage; and (3) extension through the adoption or inclusion of unrelated persons. Single-parent families are nuclear, and they are becoming much more common than a decade ago.

Another type of family is becoming more abundant, the reconstituted family. Such families, bringing together two adults and often two sets of children, not infrequently begin their existence with a number of unresolved new relationships. Typical of the relations that can be problematic and that may pose very significant adjustment difficulties are those between the children and stepparents, between the two sets of children, between the reconstituted family and the noncustody spouses, between the reconstituted family and the noncustody parents' new spouses and their children, and possibly other relationships as well. Authority, jurisdiction, respect, friendship, and allegiance are all a part of the ground rules for the nuclear family's socialization of children. Resolving issues centering around such matters is a major problem. Preparation and anticipation become very important ingredients for successful functioning of reconstituted nuclear families.

Murdock (1965) identified four basic functions that the family performs; namely, control of sexual access, control of procreation, education of children, and economic cooperation. None of these functions is absolute, and perhaps societal changes since Murdock's discussion have further modified or eroded these functions. The education, and/or socialization, of children, however, and particularly in the early years, is the function that even deliberate social engineering has been unable to modify to any appreciable extent. The kibbutzim in Israel, for example, have attempted to reassign this function to a collective mode but with only partial and perhaps short-term success. The drift from the kibbutz to the nuclear family as the primary social reality for the child is apparent. Similarly, the postrevolutionary attempt in Russia (Timasheff, 1946) was reversed, and the nuclear family seems to be increasing in contemporary China even though the regulatory hand of the state is still apparent in bold relief.

The nuclear family is often placed in the distinguished company of cultural universals. Even in those societies where the extended family may be the modal type, "extended families do not stand in contrast to nuclear families," as is often implied (Mace, 1976). Most extended families use nuclear families as building blocks. There are differences of opinion as to whether or not the nuclear family in our society is sufficiently removed in culture and form from the extended family to stand as an isolated unit. There is little question, however, that the nuclear family as it has evolved in our American society has compressed the socialization function to the point where the relationships, both positive and negative, are intense and critical (Parsons & Bales, 1955). There are often no alternatives to which a child can turn, at least not in the early years. Consequently, as a socialization context, the family is highly significant and powerful. The directions of the influence, however, can be highly variable.

The phrase "the family" suggests both too much and too little. The too much comes from the monolithic or uniform connotation of the designation. In fact, families vary by structure, composition, social class, geographical stability, size, experience, and in many other important aspects. Each of these categories has profound implications for the child. Yet, overarching all such differences, the family is an organizing principle that structures, defines, facilitates, and gives meaning, both historical and proximate, to the behavior that occurs within its bounds. In one sense, then, the family is a statistical and conceptual myth that demands sharper penetration and analysis to tease out the specific dynamics that act in concert to socialize the child. Whereas the family suggests too much in the sense of conveying an unwarranted uniformity, it suggests too little in simplifying the vast range of possible socialization outcomes that can result from any one or a combination of variations in structural elements.

Even when we know what appears to be the socialization influences at work, as Freud (1933) pointed out, it is much simpler to arrive at a postdictive conclusion than a predictive one; that is, given the elements that led to an outcome, such as divorce, unusual achievement, or delinquency, it is simpler to reconstruct the history of the outcome than it is to preduct it given the same set of elements. Lewis and Feiring (1982) provided an idea of the complexity of interpersonal relations within the family. They described how mother–infant interaction patterns are influenced by context or situation. "It is fair to assume that situations not only affect the level of individual interaction patterns but also may be nonlinear, so that Mother A may be more responsive in situation X than Mother B, but Mother B may be more responsive in situation Y than Mother A" (pp. 122–123). It seems likely also that child A, B, . . .N will respond differentially to Mothers A, B, . . .N as the child is influenced by various contextual elements.

One of the intriguing aspects of the study of socialization, particularly within the family context, is that the solutions to problems of cause and effect remain elusive. Hence, the challenge and motivation to seek answers remains strong. Socialization equations, containing variables drawn from the unique individual genotype and the protean environmental influences, are still often beyond our present abilities to solve. The delicate and often undiscerned modes of interaction between the epigenetically developing individual and the changing environment yield an array of possible outcomes that remain fugitive to our efforts to grasp. Progress is underway, however, and if we have not achieved, as yet, a complete understanding, we are moving toward that goal.

Socialization, like the family, is a cultural universal. It is the process by which the necessary continuity, roles, duties, and norms required by an ongoing society are maintained. Socialization is also the means by which individuals learn expected and appropriate behaviors within the society. Society per se, however, is too loosely structured with elements generally lacking in specific accountability to take on the responsibilities inherent in the early years of an individual's socialization. Through probable evolutionary means, both biological and social, the family has come to be what it is and to have as its most basic function the socialization of children.

One of the reasons that family socializations, with all its imperfections, is so effective as a halfway station between the individual and the culture, preparing the individual for relatively independent functioning within the larger society, is that the family can be regarded as a microcosm of the larger society. Experiences within the family may have their analogues outside the family. The same kinds of activities and emotions occur within and outside the family, ranging from peace and love to warfare and malevolence or hate. It seems logical to assume that the prevailing kinds of experiences characteristic within a family color the child's perception of and adjustment to the larger society. The socialization process is inevitable; however, the direction it takes and the outcome at any given point in time are dependent on a complex interactive assortment of factors. At the most basic level, these factors consist of principal sets of influence coming from the child's interaction with the environment across social contexts. The environment, of course, is represented by the family with its own unique individuals and the child-rearing procedures. Child-rearing practices as recommended procedures do not necessarily represent the best tried and true knowledge. They are known to change with time in a rather "fad and fashion" manner. These changes are evident in the government publication entitled *Infant Care*. Kephart (1981) called the phenomenon of changing advice, the child-rearing "pendulum." He wrote:

> In the 1920's, thumb-sucking and masturbation were looked upon as dangerous impulses that must be curbed. As late as 1938 the book (*Infant Care*) showed a steel cuff that would stop the baby from bending its arm, thus preventing thumbsucking. Yet in 1942, readers were told that masturbation and thumb-sucking were harmless. In 1951 the caution was voiced that too much pampering might result in the child's becoming a "tyrant." Now—in the 1980's—*Infant Care* takes a markedly permissive attitude toward such things as weaning, masturbation, thumb-sucking, and toilet training. And so it goes. (p. 435)

Child-rearing procedures change from time to time. Whether or not these changes have much effect on the adult personality is something about which we can only speculate.

A third cultural universal, in addition to the nuclear family, and the family's socialization of its young, is the fact that in every society of which we have ethnographic record there is a division of labor and prerogatives often times based on sex. The division varies, of course, among the various societies.

SEX-ROLE SOCIALIZATION

The learning of gender roles and sex-role orientation reflects one of the earliest and most profound focuses in the family socialization process. Eisenberg (1982) characterized gender role as "the acceptance and adoption of socially defined behaviors and attitudes associated with being either male or female" (p. 226). The review of relevant research by Honig (1983) strongly suggests that the patterns of differential socialization based on the child's sex, and as implemented by parents according to their sex, are deeply imbedded in our contemporary culture. There seems little reason to expect that these patterns will change markedly toward an androgynous model in the foreseeable future. In Sweden, fathers of newborn babies are offered a kind of paternity leave with no threat to their employment status should they choose to stay home for a time and care for the new family member (Lamb, 1982). The choice resides with the adult members of the family. The choice to stay home, however, apparently has not yet become normative. Whether such legislation, were it to be enacted in the United States, would ever transcend a de jure status, is a matter of speculation. Cultural tradition often erects barriers that render behavioral or orientational change intended by legislative processes very difficult to implement.

Lamke and Filsinger (1983) reviewed a number of studies that had investigated the relationship between parental child-rearing practices and sex-role orientation (Bem, 1974, 1977; Kelly & Worell, 1976; Orlofsky, 1979; Spence & Helmreich, 1978). These investigators concluded that the assumptions based on these studies might have derived largely from the specific data analysis utilized, and that the relationship between sex-role orientation as currently conceptualized and parental child-rearing practices remains unclear.

There is sexual dimorphism among all species both in appearance and function. It would be strange indeed, or at least strangely unique in the phylogenetic sense, were homo sapiens to be the single exception. Conceding the importance of the child's unique genotype in mediating ontogenetic influence, certain kinds of child-rearing practices, nevertheless, can be shown empirically to modify a child's behavior in generally predictable fashion. Labeling is one such influence. A paradigm of the influence of gender labels, for example, would be: label→caretakers' treatment→congruent response on the part of the child.

Will, Self, and Datan (1976) studied the effect of sex labeling ty first dressing a baby in pink and calling "her" Beth. Next, the same baby was dressed in blue and called "Adam." Adults were asked to play with the baby under both conditions. The adults acted toward the baby in ways traditional to the sex ascription implied by dress color. Such reactions, or socialization modes, are pervasive influences on the behaviors of the child. This is nowhere more poignantly revealed than in the famous case of assigned sex discussed by Money and Ehrhardt (1972). Essentially one of two genetically male twins at the time of the report was being reared successfully as a female after having been deprived of his penis through a surgical blunder during circumcision. The effects of labeling and the consequent behavior should serve as a cautionary note for committed biological determinists. Even something as basic as sex and sex role can be culturally reassigned. The effects of labeling, of course, are not confined to sex roles and/or gender identity. Nor is labeling the only, or necessarily the principal, influence in shaping sex-role behavior and genders.

The well-known tendency for children to identify with the same-sex parent also contributes in a major way to sex-role orientation. Female children, particularly when the mother is in the home most of the time, have a ready object of identification. Even when the mother works outside the home, most little girls seem to abstract and assimilate the basics of the traditional female role. Many, to be sure, will modify the role significantly later. Boys may have a bit more complicated task. Fathers tend to be away from the home more than mothers. The signs and results of identification, however, are readily apparent to the degree that few would deny the fundamental importance of the process in learning sex-typical attitudes and behavior.

Labeling in a broader sense can act as a trigger mechanism to activate the powerful self-fulfilling prophesy in many areas of life. Cooley (1927) sensed this many years ago in describing the "looking-glass self." Haimowitz and Haimowitz (1966) emphasized the crucial nature of labeling in their discussion of the topic, "Criminals are Made Not Born." The essence of labeling, whether sensed, as in the "looking-glass self," or verbalized by a significant other, is that the child will respond in a way congruent with the label. Children come to believe what they are told they are no matter how the messages are conveyed. Not only is gender identity profoundly influenced in this way, but the child also comes to an understanding of who he or she is in a broader sense and acquires a sense of self-efficacy and value. Self-efficacy refers to the extent to which the individual feels that he or she has control over circumstances—a kind of "locus of control" to use Nowicki's terminology (Nowicki, 1975). How the parent takes the child into account, i.e., the light in which the child is perceived by the parent as a capable or incapable individual, as an attractive or unattractive child, as a bright or dull individual, leaves an impression on the child in terms of which the child will tend to form self-concepts and reflect corresponding behaviors.

The Child's Contribution

Children are not passive recipients of the intentioned efforts of those around them. They are dynamic and vital forces of influence in their own right, forces that exert as well as receive impact. Socialization is a two-way process, and parents may be as profoundly affected by the child as the child is affected by the parent. As Bell (1977) pointed out, the smile and the cry are very effective means at the disposal of the infant for shaping parental behavior.

Just as the environment acts as a mediating force in the expression of the child's genotypic characteristics, the child's own unique genotype mediates environmental influence. Some child-rearing practices, for example, may be instrumental in shaping the responses of child A, and others, those of child B. It has been said that bearing a child is not unlike buying a package of mixed seeds. With seeds, you never know what they will produce until they push up through the ground and express themselves. Knowing the immediate ancestral forms, characteristics, and the laws of genetic transmission provides some degree of prophetic sophistication; however, the probabilities of significant genetic variation among siblings is such that the idiosyncratic nature of each child is a force to be reckoned with.

Temperament is one aspect of a child's nature to which genotype makes a substantial contribution. The formulations by Thomas, Chess, and Birch (1970) and extended by Buss and Plomin (1975) are informative in this regard. Thomas et al. identified three general types of temperament: difficult, slow-to-warm-up, and easy (1970). It is quite possible, and indeed often the case, to have all three temperament types within one family. Adlerians are likely to assign more explanatory value to birth order than to temperament in accounting for such characteristics. Remember, temperament differences among children, having to do with such traits as activity level, rhythmicity, approach or withdrawal, adaptability, threshold of responsiveness, intensity of reaction, quality of mood, distractability, and persistence (Thomas et al., 1970) can be observed in infants as early as the first several months of life. Buss and Plomin (1975) saw temperament in terms of four principal traits: emotionality, activity, sociability, and impulsivity. In any event, temperament in these terms that tend to characterize an individual's reactions to environmental stimuli over time may help to explain the variance among individuals and the quality of the interactive patterns that parents and children establish with each other. There are undoubtedly more basic and powerful innate genetic forces influencing the child's responses than temperament. Even so, none of them is expressed directly. Environment still mediates in important ways.

Deliberate and Nondeliberate Socialization

Deliberate socialization, as the term implies, represents the intentioned efforts of primary caretakers, parents, for example, to teach and influence the child in desired directions. Nondeliberate socialization reflects the day-by-day influence that parents and other models exert through the countless informal situations involving the model and the child in interactive or observational frameworks. Various forms of discipline, particularly those varieties the object of which is to help the child arrive at a condition of self-discipline, are of the deliberate kind. Discipline of this kind should not be considered the equivalent of punishment. Punishment is too often impulsive and/or relatively unrelated to long-range behavioral goals. Punishment, of course, can be deliberate and goal oriented. Parke (1981) has investigated punishment with regard to its effectiveness as a socializing technique. He suggested four useful effects:

1. Reestablishment of affection following emotional release;
2. Vicarious learning through observation of others being punished;
3. Reduction of guilt; and
4. Internalization of moral and behavioral standards.

Various child-rearing methods or approaches such as Parent Effectiveness Training (Gordon, 1975), Natural and Logical Consequences (Dreikurs & Soltz, 1964), Behavior Modification (Bijou & Baer, 1961) are often used in a deliberate and systematic fashion to influence the child's behavior.

The sheer volume of time, however, on the side of nondeliberate child rearing might well tip the scales toward this mode as being of the greater significance. One such important context in which both deliberate and nondeliberate child rearing take place is the family meal (Bossard & Boll, 1954). For some families, the only time they may have the opportunity to interact is when they sit down together at a meal, usually the evening meal. Bossard and Boll identify five main types. They are:

1. The hurried meals, where the members of the family act as though they were engaged in the unavoidable process of refueling.
2. Those family meals that are devoted largely to recurrent domestic warfare. Squabbling is a habit not an episode.
3. Meals where the family's critical conversation is turned outward. They are "talking about" someone all the time. Bossard states that the parents "wonder why son Jack has no friends and wants to stop school."
4. The family meals that abound in human interest talk. Members of the family tell their experiences of the day and choice bits of news are saved for mealtime.
5. The family meals that become occasions for family rituals. They tend to be characterized by order and impressive decorum. People listen to one another. Such a procedure involves self-discipline, and this bodes well for discipline in other areas of behavior (Bossard & Boll, 1954).

The family meal might well be the single occasion in the highly scheduled families of today's society when all or most of the family is together. Very little in the family's behavioral or emotional economy remains hidden. Parental values and attitudes are modeled daily, and whatever form or direction they take, the child is being influenced.

Parents who create an environment that is warm and supportive, as opposed to cold, rigid, and either constrictive or ignoring, do much to facilitate a positive learning climate. At the most simple level, if the children are basically happy, the parents are probably not doing too much that is wrong. At a more detailed level, seven propositions are offered, which seem implicitly to fall within the conventional wisdom of child-rearing and human-relations literature. They are cast in general form and can be applied in a number of ways. They are offered as propositions that students of the family and socialization might wish to put to the test for their theoretical validity. They are offered to parents as what seem practical and hopefully beneficial guidelines for the rearing of their children.

Proposition 1: Behavior and Relationships with Others Depend on the Extent to Which the Child's Basic Needs Are Met

Inasmuch as the family is the life space for the young child, it is within the family that such needs as love, recognition, achievement, security, and others are met—or frustrated. When one or more basic needs are not met, misbehavior is often the result. Parents then tend to respond to the symptoms rather than the causes, and the problem may worsen. On the other hand, the child who feels loved and secure and whose efforts to achieve are recognized by the parents or significant others within the family is emotionally free to grow and develop along constructive pathways.

Proposition 2: Parents Need to Recognize
Each Child as a Unique Individual

Considering the fact that no two children have the same genetic makeup with the exception of identical twins, and that each parent, also, is like no other, it is a relatively easy step to acknowledge that each parent–child relationship also is unique. Parents are often heard to comment about how different from one another their own children are. When gene segregation mechanisms and histories are taken into account, the real wonder centers around the similarities of siblings rather than their differences.

Offsetting the child's unique genotype and the behavior tendencies that follow, temperament, for example, is the phylogenetic capacity of the human child to adapt to a wide array of environmental elements. Lack of parental sensitivity to the child's unique temperament and constitution may be one such element. What is at stake, then, is not anything as critical as survival, but, rather, whether or not the optimal possibilities are to be realized. Adequate sensitivity on the parents' part, all other things being equal, enhances the odds. Lack of such sensitivity, diminishes them.

Proposition 3: The Faith, Honesty, Confidence,
and Affection Between the Parent and Child
Affects the Quality of the Parent–Child Relationship

The late Professor Ray Baber (1953) cited an incident in which a parent, rather hard pressed for money, had granted a child's request for a few dollars without insisting on the child's revealing the reason for the request. The child had wanted to purchase a silver thimble. That simple, but sacrificial, act of faith and confidence on the parent's part had so impressed the child that it was remembered and appreciated long after the parents were gone. Recalling our earlier discussion of labeling and the self-fulfilling prophesy, it is important to remember that a child who is trusted and highly valued will very likely be responsive to that trust. Children profit from obvious reassurance also. A child who is hugged and told how much he or she is loved, particularly at unexpected times, will usually reciprocate in like manner. Relationships—and children—prosper.

Proposition 4: Parents Should Separate
the Worth of a Child from the Behavior

These propositions are not separate and discrete. They soon begin to overlap and dovetail. For example, we all share the basic need to be valued. Basic needs are closely related to behavior as was discussed under Proposition 1. Somehow parents must convey the sense that they value and love the child even though the child's behavior is at times unacceptable. Clinical psychology and psychiatry are predicated on this principle. If an individual's sense of worth and being valued is diminished as his or her behavior is being considered, the problems may well intensify. Approval, however, once the sense of being valued is secure, may be withheld until merited by appropriate behavior. Children desire approval also, and with encouragement and direction, they will usually strive to obtain it. One way to do this is by modifying behavior to correspond with the basic values that obtain within the family. If a child's sense of worth is not separable from behavior, there is some hazard that under sufficient and long-term provocation alternative sources of value may be pursued. The outcomes may not be what either child or parent would have desired.

Proposition 5: The Child Should Be Allowed as Much Freedom as Possible to Make Mistakes and Discoveries, But to Do so with Safety, Respect for the Rights of Others, and for Social Convention

One of the greatest freedoms is the freedom to make mistakes, even to fail. A child who is afraid to make mistakes will one day be afraid to try. On the other hand, efforts and discovery must be made according to firm and acceptable conventions; that is, principally those regarding the person, property, and rights of others. Within the parameters of safety, there is still much territory to cover. Many of the domestic "taboos" that the child encounters are mainly for the convenience of the parent. It is wise to keep in mind the admonition of Plato, which, paraphrased, stipulated that pain in the short run may yield pleasure in the long run; and pleasure in the short run may lead to pain in the long run. If a child's inclinations to try to explore are blunted for the temporary comfort and convenience of the parents, the long-run consequences may be timidity, diminished curiosity, and poor self-image—none of these are qualities among those that parents would normally select for their child. Children will make mistakes, however, if they are discussed, explained, and the child is encouraged to try again or given an acceptable alternative; even mistakes can be valuable learning experiences.

Proposition 6: Parents Should Arrange the Environment to Encourage Prosocial Behavior

The family environment probably needs to be adapted in some sense of another for children at each stage of development. The first and primary consideration is safety. Beyond that, there needs to be privacy and facilities that enable a child to meet and negotiate the developmental encounters appropriate to his or her age and status. At the early stages of development, it is better to remove those objects that the child might break or destroy than to follow after the inquisitive youngster with a never-ending chorus of "No's," or "Must not touch." Later, appropriate toys can be selected that challenge but do not discourage the child. Children have a need for increasingly complex stimulation as they develop and mature. This need can usually be met within the family environment with a little thought and effort on the part of the parents. Helping children to share in social events, little by little, also enables them to develop appropriate social skills. Most adjustments are relatively simple, but easily overlooked, unless parents are sensitized to their importance to the developing child.

Proposition 7: Parents Should Be Ready to Lend Support Directly or Indirectly Through Physical or Verbal Guidance

There are many times when children will attempt something beyond their present ability. If parents come to the child's aid quickly, they could be encouraging dependency. Many parents err in the direction of too much help rather than too little. The key is to watch and wait. The chances are that when help is really needed, the child will request it. At that time, only enough assistance should be proffered to enable the child to succeed. Appropriate support is largely a matter of careful observation and thoughtful intervention. A word of encouragement from interested parents becomes a highly instrumental motivating factor. With interest, warmth, discretion, and an environment that provides for the child's developmental tendencies "to do," socialization will naturally proceed.

SUMMARY

The family is both an historic and proximate social institution whose main function is still the socialization of children. It does not always perform this function in flawless or textbook fashion, and, indeed, there are many casualties along the way. Until a variety of social engineering appears with both the necessary long-range staying power and mandated control, there is little likelihood that the situation will change. The modus operandi of the family may change, but to the extent that the past is prologue to the future, the family will continue to be the child's primary social reality. It will be the context in which the child will develop the basic armamentarium of skills, attitudes, values, and behavior to enable him or her to venture forth into society with a reasonable expectation of success.

The changing demographics and the increasing complexity of our society strongly suggests that the deliberate and thoughtful mode of socialization be called into play more frequently and with greater insight into cause and effect outcomes. Note, however, that change is not new nor is the family new to the challenges wrought by change. Children, moreover, are resilient and flexible. Whatever the family culture of the future, the odds are that it will continue to be the best initial context for the socialization of children.

Research questions and thrusts change with changing conditions. With respect to the emerging family-related trends, higher divorce rates, smaller families, older age at first marriage, increasing numbers of working mothers, and significantly greater numbers of single-parent households, research needs to be designed to deal with the impacts of these structural changes. Presumably such research will provide the needed answers before the need for them is past.

REFERENCES

Baber, R. E. (1953). *Marriage and the family*. New York: McGraw–Hill.

Barash, D. (1979). *Whisperings within: Evolution and the origins of human nature*. New York: Harper & Row.

Bell, R. Q. (1977). Socialization findings reexamined. In R. Q. Bell & L. V. Harper (Eds.), *Child effects on adults*. New York: Wiley.

Bem, S. (1974). The measurement of psychological androgyny. *Journal of Consulting and Clinical Psychology, 42*, 155–162.

Bem, S. (1977). On the utility of alternative procedures for assessing psychological androgyny. *Journal of Consulting and Clinical Psychology, 45*, 196–205.

Bijou, S., & Baer, D. N. (1961). *Child development 1: A systematic and empirical theory*. New York: Appleton–Century–Crofts.

Blau, P. (1964). *Exchange and power in social life*. New York: Wiley.

Bossard, J. H. S., & Boll, E. S. (1954). *The sociology of child development*. New York: Harper & Brothers.

Buss, A. H., & Plomin, R. (1975). *A temperament theory of personality development*. New York: Wiley.

Cooley, C. H. (1927). *Life and the student*. New York: Knopf.

Dreikurs, R., & Soltz, V. (1964). *Children the challenge*. New York: Hawthorn Books.

Duvall, E. M. (1977). *Marriage and family development* (5th ed.) (pp. 615–632). Philadelphia: J. B. Lippincott.

Edwards, J. N. (1969). Familial behavior and social exchange. *Journal of Man and the Family, 31*, 518–526.

Eisenberg, N. (1982). Social development. In C. B. Kopp & J. B. Krakow (Eds.), *The child: Development in a social context* (p. 226). Reading, MA: Addison-Wesley.

Eshleman, J. R. (1981). *The family: An introduction* (3rd ed.). Boston: Allyn & Bacon.

Freud, S. (1933). The psychogenesis of a case of homosexuality in a woman. In *Collected Papers, 11* and quoted in *A primer of Freudian psychology*. New York: Mentor Books.

Gecas, V. (1981). Contexts of socialization. In M. Rosenberg & R. H. Turner (Eds.), *Social psychology: Sociological perspectives* (pp. 171, 170–175). New York: Basic Books.

Gordon, T. (1975). *P.E.T.: Parent effectiveness training*. New York: New American Library.

Haimowitz, M. L. (1966). Criminals are made, not born. In M. L. Haimowitz & N. R. Haimowitz (Eds.), *Human development: Selected readings* (pp. 391–403). New York: Thomas Y. Crowell.

Havighurst, R. (1953). *Human development and education*. New York: Longmans, Green.

Homans, G. C. (1961). *Social behavior: Its elementary forms*. New York: Harcourt, Brace, & World.

Honig, A. S. (1983). Sex role socialization in early childhood. *Young Children, 38*, 57–70.

Inkeles, A. (1969). Social structure and socialization. In D. A. Goslin (Eds.), *Handbook of socialization theory and research* (p. 616). Chicago: Rand McNally.

Kelly, J., & Worell, L. (1976). Parent behaviors related to masculine, feminine, and androgynous sex role orientations. *Journal of Consulting and clinical psychology, 44,* 843–851.

Kephart, W. (1981). *The family, society, and the individual* (p. 435). Boston: Houghton Mifflin.

Lamb, M. E. (1982). On the familial origins of personality and social style. In C. B. Kopp & J. P. Krakow (Eds.), *The child: Development in a social context* (p. 185). Reading, MA: Addison-Wesley.

Lamke, L. K., & Filsinger, E. E. (1983). Parental antecedents of sex role orientation. *Adolescence, 70,* 429–432.

Lewis, M., & Feiring, C. (1982). Some American families at dinner. In Laosa & Sigel (Eds.), *Families as learning environments for children* (pp. 122–123). New York: Plenum Press.

Mace, D. (1976). In defense of the nuclear family. In E. Eldrige & N. Merideth (Eds.), *Environmental issues: Family impact* (p. 68). Minneapolis, MN: Burgess.

Money, J., & Ehrhardt, A. A. (1972). *Man and woman, boy and girl* (pp. 118–123). Baltimore: Johns Hopkins University Press.

Murdock, G. P. (1965). *Social structure* (p. 10). New York: The Free Press.

Nowicki, S. (1975). The effect of locus of control on peer relationships across different age groups. *Journal of Genetic Psychology, 94,* 275–280.

Nye, F. I. (1978). Is choice and exchange the key? *Journal of Marriage and the Family, 40,* 219–233.

Ogburn, W. F., & Tibbitts, C. (1934). *Recent social trends in the United States* (pp. 661–708). New York: McGraw-Hill.

Orlofsky, J. (1979). Parental antecedents of sex-role orientation in college men and women. *Sex Roles, 5,* 495–512.

Parke, R. D. (1981). Some effects of punishment on children's behavior revisited. *Contemporary readings in child psychology* (pp. 176–188). New York: McGraw-Hill.

Parsons, T., & Bales, R. F. (1955). *Family socialization and interaction process.* New York: The Free Press.

Rodgers, R. H. (1964). Toward a theory of family development. *Journal of Marriage and the Family, 26,* 262–270.

Rodgers, R. H. (1973). *Family interaction and transaction: The developmental approach.* Englewood Cliffs, NJ: Prentice Hall.

Schvaneveldt, J. D. (1966). The interactional framework in the study of the family. In I. Nye & F. Berardo (Eds.), *Emerging conceptual frameworks in family analysis* (pp. 97–123). New York: Macmillan.

Spence, J., & Helmreich, R. (1978). *Masculinity and femininity: Their psychological dimensions, correlates, and antecedents.* Austin: University of Texas Press.

Thomas, A., Chess, S., & Birch, H. G. (1970). The origin of personality. *Scientific American, 223,* 102–109.

Timasheff, N. S. (1946). *The great retreat.* New York: E. P. Dutton.

U.S. Bureau of the Census. (1985). Current Population Reports, Series P-20, No. 398, pp. 1–3, March 1984, Washington, DC: U.S. Government Printing Office.

U.S. Bureau of the Census. (1985). Current Population Reports, Series P-20, No. 399, pp. 1–2, April 1984, Washington, DC: U.S. Government Printing Office.

Will, J. A., Self, P. A., & Datan, N. (1976). Maternal behavior and perceived sex of infant. *American Journal of Orthopsychiatry, 46,* 135–139.

Wilson, E. O. (1975). *Sociobiology.* Cambridge, MA: Harvard University Press.

Alternative Perspectives on Children's Peer Relationships

7

Sherri Oden
High/Scope Educational Research Foundation
Ypsilanti, Michigan

Not that long ago, in the 1970s, keeping up on the research on peer relationships in childhood was not too difficult. This field of inquiry caught the curiousity of many empirical investigators and a considerable data base now exists. The next major challenge is to understand the common threads across studies and determine if our conceptions of peer relations are supportable by the data and can serve as bases for theories of the contributions, content, and course of peer relations in child development. In this chapter, the empirical work reviewed and critiqued in this area is organized around the major theories, concepts, controversies, and actual problems in peer relations. Throughout, the evidence concerning perspectives on children's intrapersonal and interpersonal processes are compared and contrasted.

INTRODUCTION

We have all observed an adult saying to a young preschooler, just acquainted with another youngster, "Go play with your friend!" In everyday use, there seems to be a broad application of the term friendship. How helpful, therefore, is this term for the social scientist interested in gaining knowledge of the development of children's peer relationships? Studies have often utilized children's assessments of their relationships such as friendships to determine operational definitions. Yet, our knowledge is likely to be limited, if not confounded, by the messages adults have given to children. We should expect that children will continue to acquire the cultural views on friendship, but where adults have some notions, perhaps overly simplistic of child culture as in the case of preschoolers' peer relationships, then we may underestimate or misconstrue these relationships in research and practice. There may be a tendency for children to simply reflect on what they perceive our view of their behavior to be.

Caught in such quandries, we typically employ several well-known strategies. One is to look up a term such as friendship in the dictionary, preferably a large edition. A second strategy is to plunge ahead and attempt to define such a concept as friendship on one's own, based on logic and/or deductions from observations. Third, we study what the subjects can or typically do report to us about the concept in question. Now, to social scientists, the first strategy may be considered by some to be a desperate act, especially because we have probably never known anyone who wrote any contributions to a dictionary! As for logic, most social scientists are wary of being considered too philosophical and prefer to more covertly exercise their logic, which they hope their data will verify. On more comfortable territory, behavioral observations will certainly be considered noble and respectable, although coding schemes often differ considerably from study to study regarding similiar behavior, and there are disagreements about the more appropriate reliability tests. Experimental designs are seriously limited too by such conceptual and assessment limitations as well as by ethical concerns. For example, to what extent can we justify interfering in children's peer relationships?

Cautiousness or wariness aside, all these methodological approaches, taken together, are useful. However, perhaps due to difficulties in conceptualization of a phenomenon such as "friendship," there is a lack of conceptual models in the study of children's peer relationships. Without more conceptual work, researchers in this area may find that future studies will consist largely of replications of findings and methodologies, an important activity, but not one that should dominate the area. We may run risks of getting too far afield from gaining greater knowledge of the nature, contribution, and course of peer relations. Instead, we may create a data base bereft of knowledge needed to address real-life problems in children's social experience, such as problems in social integration, loneliness, depression, cooperation versus competition in achievement, peer comformity in areas such as drug usage and delinqency, and other social and mental health issues. Thus, in the present discussion, I review conceptual as well as empirical work on children's peer relationships and propose some alternative conceptions for future empirical investigations. Throughout this discussion, the study of peer relationships involves conceptualization and assessment of both intrapersonal and interpersonal processes.

RELATIONSHIP TYPES, PROCESSES, AND PROGRESSION

Range of Types

Several basic types of peer relationships were recently proposed by Oden, Herzberger, Mangione, and Wheeler (1984). Figure 7.1 shows a summary of these types based on research data collected by various investigators and by posthoc interpretations that we made of data that we had reported in studies by

	PARTNERSHIP	NO PARTNERSHIP
FRIENDSHIP	*Close Friends* High degree of mutual liking. Unique personal characteristics of each valued. Personal information and secrets exchanged. Problems and activities shared, help exchanged. May contribute to mutual goals and projects.	*Social Friends* Minimal to high degrees of liking. Enjoyment of social activities together. Personal information and secrets may be exchanged. Problems and activities may sometimes be shared, help exchanged. May sometimes contribute to mutual activity goals and projects.
NO FRIENDSHIP	*Activity Partners* Minimal to high degrees of liking and attraction. Sharing of activity, materials, and provide task-related help and instruction. Unique personal characteristics valued as pertain to task-related skills or knowledge. Personal information infrequently exchanged and/or not intimate. Contribute to mutual activity goals and projects.	*Acquaintances* No or minimal to high degrees of attraction. No or minimal to high degrees of friendliness. Persons know each other usually in particular setting, e.g., classroom or neighborhood. Minimal or no attention to unique personal characteristics. Minimal or no interdependence for problems or projects.

FIG. 7.1.   A conceptual scheme for categorizing children's peer relationships. *Note:* From "Children's Peer Relationships: An Examination of Social Processes" by S. Oden, S. D. Herzberger, P. L. Mangione, and V. A. Wheeler, 1984, *Boundary Area in Social and Developmental Psychology* (p. 134) edited by J. C. Masters and K. Yarkin-Levin, New York: Academic Press. Reprinted by permission.

Oden et al. (1984a), Mangione (1981), and Wheeler (1981). In Fig. 7.1, two types of relationships were proposed: *friendship* and *partnership*. Relationships were considered to range from acquaintance to intimate and were defined broadly as associations between two or more persons who are in some way connected with each other. Based on previous studies, *close friendship* was considered to include critical features such as personal sharing, emotional closeness, and mutuality of liking, whereas *activity partnership* was proposed to include features such as participating with someone in a venture, occupation, or task.

From studying children's expectations of friendships, Bigelow (1977) found that ego reinforcement and sharing appear to be expected throughout childhood.

From interviewing children, Youniss (1980) found that primary school-age children reported kindness, sharing, and helping within their best friendships, whereas older children cited sharing secrets and feelings and knowing each other well. According to Huston and Burgess (1979), in adult close relationships there are high degrees of interdependency or mutual dependency with considerable sharing about each other and contributions to individual or joint endeavors.

In contrast, *social friends* as shown in Fig. 7.1 were proposed to include a range from casual friendship with infrequent contact and/or low degrees of attraction, liking, and/or sharing and helping, to friendships with more frequent contact and/or moderate to high degrees of mutual attraction, liking, and personal sharing and helping. In the social-friend relationship, the friends are not very interdependent or integral to each other's lives and endeavors as in the close friendship. According to Huston and Burgess (1979), close relationships are unique compared to other types because the commitment is based on the awareness of the participants that they have an uncommon ability to reward one another. In adulthood, Wright (1974) found that best and "good" friends provided self-affirmation, ego support, stimulation of ideas and actions, and practical resources or help. The close friendship is thus not expected to be easily repeatable or duplicated, whereas the social friendship has more repeatable characteristics in that many persons may serve the same functions for each other. It was thus proposed that, whereas close friendships will also include partnership characteristics, there are also partnerships in which there exist no or few friendship features, as shown in Fig. 7.1. Finally, *acquaintances* are peers known to each other to a minimal degree who occasionally do interact in a given setting or circumstance in which they happen to be together.

The basic argument underlying the Oden et al. proposal is that childhood peers, in a large body of research, have been viewed in terms of their sociometric status and social interaction or participation, often overlooking the history or type of various kinds of relationships such as friendships that may be in operation. Also, peer relationships in childhood have usually been viewed too simplistically, that is, without sufficient regard to possible differences such as close friends versus other types of relationships. Researchers have often simply contrasted friends with strangers or created a "dump" category, for comparison purposes, of nonfriends that might include nodding acquaintances along with strong enemies and play or work mates or partners. We have argued that this ran the risk of oversimplifying the peer context. Other investigators have also called attention to this issue (e.g., Berndt, 1981; Furman, 1984).

Until recently, the majority of studies that had actually investigated different types of relationships had not directly studied the content of children's relationships but had focused on children's knowledge and reasoning development regarding friendships and nonfriendships, largely through interview and questionnaire methods. Such research is important, but more study of actual relationships utilizing a range of methods is needed. A large data base does exist based on sociometric methods including roster and rating techniques in which children rate each other on some basis such as play and work or nominate their close or best friends (Asher & Hymel, 1981). Correlational analyses of these data have consistently indicated that children do differentiate between best friends, friends, and other relations, e.g., for play, for work (Oden & Asher, 1977), or for talking with (Oden & Tesch, 1987), and can specify those whom they dislike (Dodge, 1983).

Hallinan and Tuma (1978) employed a sociometric instrument in 19 upper elementary school classrooms in which children indicated their "best friends," "friends," and "nonfriends." The friend category yielded 49% of children's choices; the other half of the choices were roughly divided between best friends and nonfriends. In Little League baseball, Fine (1981) found that 18% of pre-adolescents were rated as close friends, 31% as friends, 2% disliked, and 47% were neither liked nor disliked. The sociometric data that has been collected is typically used to examine children's peer status or rank by gaining the peers' assessments and then to examine the correlations of peer status with behavior and personal characteristics (e.g., race, sex, ability). This research area is more fully discussed in the second part of this chapter. It is interesting, however, to point out that we have thus collected considerable data indicating that children do see their peer relationships to be differentiated.

Left quite unexplored is the nature of the "other" peer relationships, the nonfriends and nonenemies. Oden et al. (1984a) proposed that this ignored dimension of peer relations included relationships among peer "play" or "work" activity partnerships. Cooper and Marquis (1983) and Mangione (1981) conducted research in school situations and found that children often do act as collaborators in activities or tasks in these situations by providing information, instruction, and evaluation to each other. In the Oden et al. study, 5-, 6-, and 7-year-old dyads of the same sex and same age who were previously unacquainted played on 5 subsequent days for brief play sessions that were videotaped from behind a one-way mirror. Overall, nearly 60% of all verbal messages were activity related in content, although the activity focus was highly interactive. Over the sessions, increases were found for verbal messages coded as Demand–Command, Structuring–Directing, Prosocial Behavior (the majority of which consisted of instruction and help), reference to Self and Partner, and all activity-related messages. As the dyads interacted across the sessions, they became increasingly more direct in their communications as indicated by the Demand–Command and Structure–Direct codes. Although children exchanged personal information both initially and throughout their interactions, they appeared to quickly and increasingly take on what we came to view as an activity mode. This was likely to be partly a function of the imposed situation.

The children's apparent perception of the interactional context appeared to be realistic. Although an opportunity had been constructed for dyads to get to know each other, there was no plan to create future opportunities. The situation's limitations were considered, however, to be analogous to other situations where children are simply put together for an activity or activities, as in school and playground situations. Children have also been observed in many experimental studies of school situations that were designed to encourage cooperation or competition to behave as activity partners in peer groups (e.g., Johnson, Maruyama, Johnson, Nelson, & Skon, 1981). The degree to which such activity partnerships actually has a significant frequency of occurrence and some continuity in natural settings needs exploration.

In the Oden et al. (1984a) study, data from 6-year-old dyads in one session with a more structured art task situation were also compared with 6-year-old classmates who were either mutual friends or best friends from a session in which the same task was employed previously in a study by Wheeler (1981). Compared to the newly acquainted dyads, classmate friends overall were more direct, made more comments about their own and their partner's activity, switched turns more frequently, and had disputes of briefer duration. Although this data supports the idea that acquaintances differ from friends, it is unclear how more familiar acquaintances would behave, or whether friends are more responsive partners than activity partners would be. The friend dyads appeared to interact efficiently, but also with more responsiveness to each other.

In interpreting such differences in process, conceptualizations by Clark and colleagues (1984) on adult relationships are relevant. Clark (1984) proposed that adult relationships may be distinguished in terms of whether members feel a special obligation to be responsive to each other's needs (as in kin, romantic partners, and friends). Clark referred to these as communal relationsips that are contrasted to what has been called exchange types of relationships between people, as in business, where members are reponsible for benefitting each other in response to specific benefits that they expect will be reciprocated. Clark proposed that this distinction had relevance for child relationships as well. In the model presented by Oden et al. (1984a), communal relationships would be analogous to friends, especially close friendships, and exchange relationships would be analogous to activity partnerships.

Berndt (1982) adapted Lerner's model of roles and relationships in various contexts (cited in Berndt, 1982). In this view, children and adults may be thought of as coworkers reacting to each other not as personalities but in terms of the social roles of the context. They may also see themselves as teammates or comrades, given memberships in certain activities or if finding themselves on different teams, as competitors or opponents. In the proposal herein when activity roles persist for given dyads, they are activity partners, or when working together in an ongoing project, they are collaborators. Research by Stone and Selman (1982) indicates that levels of negotiation strategies increase in interpersonal understanding within grades and across grades. Therefore, we might expect that as children develop they will increase in the complexity of their ability to operate in both close friendships and activity partnerships.

Although the general model we proposed for research on children's peer relationships shown in Fig. 7.1 is helpful in making the point that children are likely to construct and engage in diverse relationships, it is a rigid depiction even if the horizontal and vertical lines in the matrix are considered as continua, as originally proposed, to allow for change and progress in relationships and intermediate levels and combinations of relationships. This rigidity is a serious shortcoming given that data that does exist on the content and course of children's peer relationships (e.g., Brenner & Mueller, 1982; Furman & Bierman, 1984; and Gottman, 1983) indicates that children's peer relationships differ across ages and also across the phases of relationships. The following general model is thus proposed as an alternative (see Fig. 7.2).

Here, as peers begin to become acquainted, given the context and particular personality mix, they would be expected to progress at first toward the friendship or partnership dimensions. Having initiated one dimension of the relationship's potential, a given dyad or group of peers may thus progress horizontally along the continuum in degree of the dimension, stay at the same point, progress vertically, or diagonally to the other dimension. Thus, a given dyad A/B, for example, initially become acquainted and begin to pursue a relationship along the friendship dimension while sometimes exploring the activity partner dimension. This model of relationship types and progression allows for a given type to take on another dimension for a time or ultimately remain a mix of two. A given dyad might be propelled along one dimension or the other dependent on a variety of factors regarding members of the dyad or peer group, including situational factors as in different types of classrooms (e.g., Goldman, 1981; Hallinan, 1976), personality characteristics (e.g., Hansell, 1981), cultural attitudes toward diverse racial or ethnic groups and sex typing (Hartup, 1983; Singeton & Asher,

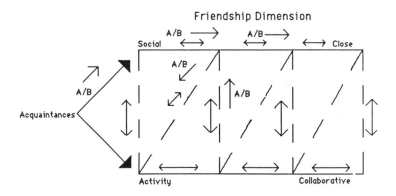

FIG. 7.2. A model of progression within types of children's peer relationships.

1979), physical size (e.g., Graziano, 1984), and peer goals and social skills (Renshaw & Asher, 1982). The model also allows for some disengagement or receding along the continua but does not allow for complete disengagement or an enemy type of arrangement. At present there is a paucity of data on the dissolution of peer relationships in childhood.

The nature of the partnership dimension needs further research to establish its frequency of occurrence and place in age or developmental level as well as its progression or course within relationships. More investigation, however, has been conducted regarding the friendship dimension.

CHILDREN'S FRIENDSHIPS

Developmental Changes in Children's Conceptions

It is interesting to consider, if we had assumed young children to be developing relationships along the partnership dimension, whether the answer to our questions and the interactions that we observe would be any different than what we have found in investigating children's friendships. Or, perhaps as indicated earlier, younger children simply interpret our questions about friendship to be equivalent, that is, they think we are referring to activity partnerships, because when children are engaged in mutual activity, we frequently refer to them as friends. We do know, however, that children behave differently with peers whom they have called friends, compared to how they behave with peers that they are unfamiliar with. Still, it is not clear how much the differences are due to simple familiarity, as pointed out by Doyle (1982).

Foot, Chapman, and Smith (1977) studied 7- and 8-year-old children who were either friend or stranger pairs as they watched a comedy film. The children who were strangers were generally more constrained in their behavior and toward each other than the friends. Newcomb, Brady, and Hartup (1979) found that in both competitive and cooperative tasks first- and third-grade children, paired with either a friend or nonfriend classmate, were more lively in the friend pairs. Even younger children evidence such differences as indicated by Gottman and Parkhurst's (1980) data with 2 through 6-year-olds' paired either with best friends or strangers. Here, friends were more likely to participate in conversation rather than a collective monologue and to engage in fantasy play. Such observations have made us curious about children's ideas, feelings, and values about friendship. What do they consider to be the basis of friendship?

Several investigators (e.g., Damon, 1979; Selman, 1981; Youniss & Volpe, 1978) have studied children's conceptions of friendship and have found, in general, that children younger than 9 years old say friends are those with whom they play and share things, whereas 9- and 10-year-old children say friends are those who like and help each other. Preadolescents say friends are those who understand each other and share personal thoughts, feelings, and secrets. Youniss and Volpe (1978) gathered data on how children 6 through 14 years of age perceive that their friendships are formed, maintained, threatened, repaired, and terminated. With development, children's understanding of a friend relationship, particularly a close one, changes from one based on the sharing of physical activities, through the sharing of resources and being kind or nice to one another, especially when in need, toward basing friendships on personality characteristics. Bigelow's (1977) data, derived from essays children wrote on their expectations for friendships, indicated that ego reinforcement and sharing across elementary school ages continued to be important expectations. Help, common activity, propinquity, acceptance, and reinforcement were important to younger children (grades 2–4), whereas preadolescents were more likely to mention honesty, intimacy, and common interests.

In research by Smollar or Youniss (1982) children of several ages were first interviewed (6–7 years, 9–10 years, and 12–13 years) to determine their views of how people become friends. Then, children of 10–11 years and 14–16 years, and adults of 18–19 and 22–24 years were asked questions aimed at gaining descriptions of processes and conceptions inherent in close friendships. Based largely on their results, they proposed three levels of types of conceptions of friendships that are summarized here as follows:

1. Positive Interaction; Cooperative Activity and Reciprocity (6–7 years)
2. Discovery of Personalities, Similarity, and Equality (Early Adolescence)
3. Self Disclosure, Sharing, and Appreciation of Individuality (Adolescence)

From interview data, Berndt (1981) found that kindergarten through sixth-grade children emphasized sharing and helping and lack of fighting in friends as compared to acquaintances, with over-age increases in intimacy and loyalty mentioned for friendships. This is also consistent with Youniss and his colleagues' findings (Smollar & Youniss, 1982; Youniss, 1980; Youniss & Volpe, 1978). In Berndt's (1981) study, he asked children questions such as "How do you know that someone is your best friend?" and "What would make you decide not to be friends with someone anymore?" Standard probes were used to explore further children's conceptions. In Study 1, working-class and middle-class children were interviewed and in Study 2, middle to upper middle-class children were interviewed. In each study, 18 male and 18 female kindergartners, third-graders, and sixth-graders were subjects. Responses were categorized as indicated in Table 7.1 and then coded separately for each of the two major friendship questions. For each content category, a child's response was coded as (1) present or (0) absent, and then scores were summed for the two questions. Mean scores for the groups are shown in Table 7.1. These data provide a very good overall picture of the general developmental findings in the research literature on children's conceptions of friendships.

TABLE 7.1
Mean Scores at Each Grade for
Categories of Friendship Conceptions

Category	Study 1			Study 2		
	Kindergarten	Third	Sixth	Kindergarten	Third	Sixth
Defining features	.97	1.06	.59	.72	.35	.25
Attributes	.16	.06	.34	.19	.17	.25
Play or association	1.31	1.47	1.22	.90	1.08	.97
Prosocial behavior	.38	.88	.91	.22	.44	.81
Aggresive behavior	.56	1.00	1.00	.75	1.06	1.06
Intimacy or trust	.03	.03	.69	.00	.24	.50
Loyal support	.03	.19	.94	.03	.03	.34
Faithfulness	.31	.16	.44	.00	.25	.28

Note: From "Relations Between Social Cognition, Nonsocial Cognition, and Social Behavior: The Case of Friendship" by T. J. Berndt. Edited by J. H. Flavell and L. Ross, 1981, Social Cognitive Development (p. 178), New York; Cambridge University Press. Reprinted by permission.

Selman and colleagues (Cooney & Selman, 1978; Jurkovic & Selman, 1980; Selman & Jaquette, 1978) have collected interview data indicating that children's conceptions of friend relationships occur in stages across developmental levels in accordance with the development of their social perspective-taking ability. In the early stages, young children are aware of the physical properties of peers and the momentary aspects of play and later become aware of feelings and intentions but expect their peers to simply please them. In middle childhood, children progress from cooperativeness without conflicts or differences being taken into account toward relationships where there can be direct and complementary reciprocity. One difficulty with the model at this point is that the age ranges when children appear to reach each stage vary so greatly, e.g., in Stage 1, *One-way Assistance,* from 4 years, 6 months to approximately 12 years, and from nearly 7 years to 15 years in Stage 2, *"Fair-weather" Cooperation.* Although the sequence appears to be invariant, in general, only cross-sectional designs have been employed. Because there is so much variability as to when a child might reach the next stage, assessment of the same subjects over time is needed to verify the stage progression. Furthermore, the wide variance among individual developmental levels depicted in this model also makes it difficult to imagine the consequences for same-age or nearly same-age interactions in school situations, in particular.

Overall, however, in this model, which roughly corresponds to Piaget's cognitive theory, the stages indicate that not until concrete operational ability (about Stage 2) are children likely to decenter from their own perspectives as would be important in Stage 3, *Intimate-mutual Sharing* and Stage 4, *Autonomous Independence.*

Selman and colleagues also proposed that children appear to develop in their *intrapersonal* and *interpersonal* understanding in parallel patterns, again in relation to their social perspective-taking ability. As children's perspective-taking ability develops, they become more aware of their own intentions and feelings and later develop greater awareness of their own and others' internal processes and their own individual personality. It is also hypothesized that relations with the peer group and with parents follow a progression that corresponds to and is similar to that of perspective-taking and intrapersonal processes.

What is unclear in interpretations of the child's perspective gleaned from interviews is whether children are able to accurately reflect on their behavior. Jurkovic and Selman and other colleagues have also been investigating the "thought into action" of children who are emotionally disturbed. These children seem to follow the same general developmental sequences as normal children. However, some appear to lag behind in their social behavioral and cognitive ability, whereas others have the cognitive ability but have difficulty putting it into effective interaction. This does seem to be in contrast, however, to normal children, whose behavior appears to be more sophisticated than their understanding or ability to reflect about it. The ability to sort out a difficulty, however, and then select and carry out the solution is a type of problem solving that does not come into more full shape until middle to later childhood.

Most studies of children's conceptions of their relationships assess children's ability to respond to fictional stories, dilemmas, or general constructs of friendship. In contrast, in a study by Ladd and Emerson (1984) interviews were conducted with first- and fourth-grade children regarding their *actual* friends. The friends were asked to give characteristics of self and partner (on separate occasions). Decline in friend similarity was found in older children. Friendships that were mutual as opposed to unilateral (one way "friends"), as would be expected, were more alike at each grade level and more accurate at predicting characteristics that were common to both partners. It should be pointed out that the nonmutual "friends" would probably not really have friendship relationships, but perhaps the potential given that the measure involves the non-reciprocated selection by one child of the other, indicating perhaps liking or attraction. Responses from fourth-grade mutual friends suggested that friends at this level do develop a reciprocal awareness of their partner's differences from self. First graders seldom knew things about friends that they did not include in their descriptions of themselves. Older mutual children were more aware of each other's unique characteristics. At each grade level, friends displayed patterns of shared knowledge for partners' concrete, observable characteristics as well as more abstract psychological attributes.

In the Ladd and Emerson study, children here were required to recognize rather than produce characteristics of their friends as in other studies. It may be that children have an ability to operate from the levels of awareness, as Ladd and Emerson pointed out, but may not have the cognitive ability to produce these characteristics in the more explorative or clinically structured interview formats used in other studies. It has often been argued that the development of thought lags behind that of action or behavioral ability, so we should expect to find a different picture of children's relationships from peer interaction data compared to data that essentially represents children's growth in their ability to conceptualize and describe or discuss their peer relationship experiences.

Children's Interaction within Peer Relationships

Observational evidence of interactions among young toddler and preschool friends also indicates the importance of "shared meaning" (Brenner & Mueller, 1982; Howes, 1983) and shared role play and fantasy play (Gottman, 1983). Indeed, Gottman's research indicates that even preschoolers are capable of close friendships that have characteristics that other data might suggest only older children were capable of experiencing. Still, it is difficult to assess growth in friendship without some external, consistent type of criteria.

Hinde, Titmus, Easton, and Tamplin (1985) prefer "strong associates" for those young peers who interact with each other 30% or more of the time. This conceptualization makes few assumptions about very young "friend" relationships and allows for the differentiations of these children from the "preferred" associates who may be friends or activity partners, as discussed earlier. It also allows comparisons across the duration of the relationships in order to gain a better understanding of the nature and progression in terms of friendship and partnership dimensions (see Fig. 7.1). Hinde et al. found that 74%–80% of 49 preschoolers observed had a preferred friend and that over an 8-month period, strong associates played together with increasing duration. Because this conceptualization allows for fewer assumptions about young children's relationships, strong associates could be compared across ages as well as used to reveal frequency and content of various types of relationships that exist or simply become more complex, unique, or intimate. Raupp (1983) also pointed to the difficulty in classifying early children's peer relationships. Using different methods and criteria of assessment, including sociometric instruments, observational measures, and teacher assessments, all methods often used in studying children's friendships, Raupp found that various numbers of mutual best and other friends emerged, and with profiles that failed to provide consistent differentiations. Only "support" behavior was consistent across the various profiles generated. Again, the lack of clarity regarding conceptualizations of peer relationships will tend to result in the use of diverse methods of assessment, often without a rationale.

In a study of general popularity, individually selected friends, and social interaction among 94 four- and five-year-old preschoolers, Masters and Furman (1981) found that popularity (as determined by nomination of 3 best and 3 least liked peers) and sending and receiving reinforcing and neutral acts were correlated. It was interesting that liking for a specific peer was not related to that peer's overall behavior, but to his or her behavior in peer–peer interactions. Specifically, high rates of reinforcing and neutral acts with the selected or preferred child were related to how that child rated him or her. From these data, it appears that children do respond to the specific behavior of the children with whom they interact, not to their overall impression. This may be especially true of younger peers, given their lower levels of social-cognitive ability and experience.

The "patterns" of children's relationships were examined by Howes (1983) with infants (5–14 months), toddlers (16–23 months), and preschoolers (35–49 months) to trace differences across age. Howes defined "friendship" operationally as mutual preference for interaction, as indicated by observable skill at complementary and reciprocal play, sharing, and affect. Friendships were thus thought to be affective and mutually engaging. Among infants, interactions consisted largely in sharing of objects, and there was a limited number of stable partners. Toddlers exhibited more verbal exchanges and tended, at first, to develop a limited number of stable partners. Later, they developed more than one partnership that was developing along the friendship dimension along with a greater number of "sporadic" relationships. Preschoolers continued to increase in verbal exchanges and several short-term "sporadic" friendships, as well as some "maintained" friends. From this data, there appears to be a progression in early development of children's relationships toward friendships, but the basic affective features seem to exist in some pairs quite early in development.

Gottman (1983) and colleagues studied preschool to 6-year-old friends whose interactions they had audio recorded as the children played in close friend pairs as determined by information provided by parents. These data were then compared with that of the same children when they played with a "stranger" partner. Several phases in friendship development were proposed based on this data and on mothers' answers to a questionnaire on the progression of the children's interactions. Further analyses and additional data by Gottman (1983) indicated that dyads would "hit it off" or limit or check or escalate the level of their relationships at various points in the process of their relationship development.

According to Gottman (1983), "Children who 'hit it off' interact in the first meeting in a connected fashion in which they exchange information successfully, manage conflict and establish common ground activity" (p. 73). These processes become increasingly important as the relationship progresses to develop the degree and direction of its development: communication clarity, information exchange, establishment of common ground activity, exploration of similarity and differences, resolution of conflicts, and self-disclosure or sharing of self. Utilizing an antecedent–consequent code system and analyses, Gottman was able to demonstrate "state" transitions, i.e., Amity (positive or easy tone) and Conflictual, which peer dyads demonstrated with three major types of social processes involved in the progression of the relationship's development: Play, Self-Exploration, and Repair.

The ability to develop and maintain a relationship has received attention from researchers of adult relationships (e.g., Huston & Burgess, 1979). In particular, the factors most relevant for children's relationship progression appear to include opportunity for proximity and frequency of interaction and for the peer partners, positive affect, communication ease, emotional and/or task support. Indeed, Gottman's data indicate that these interactional processes are important contributors to creating and maintaining states of amity and reducing and resolving conflictual states in childhood relationships. It is difficult, however, from this data to discern whether children who "hit it off" behave differently with each other due to factors such as a mutual liking reaction, or similarity and complementarity of personalities or values, or because their skills or interactional styles mesh well. Given the empirical model presented by Gottman, more research will certainly be forthcoming on the bases of the formation, development, maintenance, and dissolution of various peer-relationship dimensions.

Determinants of Peer-Relationship Selections

In adult relationships, persons are attracted to each other when they see high degrees of similarity, particularly in areas of race, cultural background, education, and values. Also important, although to different extents, dependent on stage of life and situational factors, is the ability of each person to provide resources, help, and personal support (Tesch, 1983). Different types of reciprocity have also been noted in children as they develop (see Oden et al., 1984a for a review). As pointed out by Graziano (1984), however, children face not only the constraints of cognitive level but also constraints presented by older peers and adults who can have some control over children's social situations, experiences, and outcomes of their peer relationships.

Contexts, activities, and situations in which children find themselves in schools and neighborhoods, in general, reinforce selection of peer activity partners and friends based on similarity of age (see Hartup, 1983), gender (Lockheed & Harris, 1984; Sagar, Schofield, & Snyder, 1983), race (Ramsey, 1985; Singleton & Asher, 1979; Taylor & Singleton, 1983), and physical size and appearance (Graziano, 1984; Hartup, 1983). Pairing based on personality needs for similarity and complementarity has rarely been explored in research with children. Sullivan (1953) pointed to the importance, however, in later childhood of a "chum" relationship in which children learn to be more sensitive and intimate as each comes to understand the other as an individual person. This would be an interesting direction for future studies.

As we consider the diversity of peer relationships and the social and cognitive abilities important to forming and maintaining different kinds of relationships, it becomes clear that peer relationships contribute significantly to children's overall development. An important focus for research, therefore, is with children who have persistent difficulty in developing peer relationships. One way to evaluate a child's social development with peers is to consider the extent to which a child participates in a range of peer relationships or is limited in his or her experience.

CHILDREN WITH PROBLEMS IN DEVELOPING PEER RELATIONSHIPS

Teachers and parents of young children, that is, preschoolers and toddlers, usually find themselves structuring occasions and situations for children to interact with each other. They will act as guides, coaches, and sometimes referees. Some children seem to need extra efforts from adults to initiate peer interaction or learn to share a toy or accommodate to the entry of a third peer in an activity. For most children, by the time they are first-graders. they are socially well accepted by peers similar to them and have some preferred activity partners or friendships. But some children seem to have gone "off track" or perhaps they never really were "on track" with their peers. A range of routes or patterns are becoming clear to researchers, including social neglect and withdrawal (e.g., Gottman, 1977) and peer rejection and agonistic relations (Dodge, 1983; Ladd, 1983). Peer assessment from sociometric data indicates that these patterns of behavior are found in low peer-status ranks and that low peer status, especially for rejected peers, has considerable stability. The origins of poor peer relations in childhood has been one focus of study; the consequences, another. Strategies of prevention and intervention has been an area of growing research activity. Overall, this area of research makes basic contributions to our conceptions of peer relationships and applied contributions to parenting and education, as well as to clinical efforts in promoting and intervening for children's mental health and developmental growth. Of particular concern here is both the internal, or intrapersonal and external, or interpersonal perspectives on children's peer status.

Incidence and Consequences of Peer-Relationship Problems

In a national survey of 7–to 11–year-old children in the United States (see Zill, in press), 8% of children responding indicated that they were very lonely. In a study by Asher, Hymel, and Renshaw (1984), approximately 500 third through sixth graders from 20 classrooms in two schools were given a questionnaire to assess their feelings of loneliness and social dissatisfaction. Sociometric questionnaires were later administered. Approximately 11% of the children indicated that they were lonely always or most of the time, and 17% felt left out of things always or most of the time. Children who received the lowest peer sociometric status also reported significantly greater degrees of loneliness and social dissatisfaction compared to other peers. Furthermore, children with more friends had reported a lower incidence of loneliness. Children with only one or no friends were also found to be considerably more lonely. Hymel et al. (1983) found that children's loneliness scores on the same questionnaires were moderately stable over a year's time. Asher and Wheeler (1985) found similar results to Asher et al. (1984) with another sample of 200 third through sixth graders with a slightly modified version of the same questionnaire developed previously. When children's low peer status was further differentiated according to neglected, rejected, controversial, or popular, the neglected children were found to not be significantly more lonely than other peers. Rejected peers reported the greatest incidence of loneliness.

There has been mounting evidence that persistent poor peer relations, especially for "rejected" peers, has debilitating consequences in mental and social adjustment for children and adolescents (see Ladd & Asher, 1985, for a review) and may contribute to or be indicative of psychopathology (Hartup, 1983; Jurkovic & Selman, 1980). Furthermore, being able to gain support from others appears to have lifelong importance for adults' emotional and physical well-being (see House, Robbins, & Metzner, 1984; Rathbone-McCuan & Hashimi, 1982; and Tesch, 1983).

Intrapersonal and Interpersonal Factors

Studying children who have problems in peer relationships also presents a particularly interesting case for the study of both internal, or intrapersonal and external, or interpersonal perspectives on children's peer status. Investigators need to consider children's perceptions of themselves and of their peers, their perception of their peer's evaluation of them, and the peers' actual evaluation of them. The interactive nature of peer relationships makes it especially problematic for investigators when trying to sort out the areas of "breakdown" in social processes in the child with persistent peer interaction difficulties.

In general, children who are neglected and interact less with peers may be less troublesome from a societal point of view. However, further investigation of their internal perspectives is needed to distinguish children who are socially capable of activity partnerships in school but are generally interested in individual pursuits such as reading and are not really withdrawn or lonely. From consulting with parents, I know that many "quiet" children do feel uncomfortable at school, but this may be difficult to detect. Some evidence does exist that indicates that, in general, these children become more socially involved in future social circumstances in early and/or later adolescence (Coie & Dodge, 1983).

Modest direct correlations have been found between self-esteem measures and peer acceptance (see Hartup, 1983). Although this is an area needing further investigation, Wheeler and Ladd (1982) developed the *Children's Self Efficacy for Peer Relationships Scale* to assess children's beliefs about their ability to be persuasive and found significant correlations between feelings of self-efficacy and peer status. Goetz and Dweck (1980) investigated children's beliefs about failure in social situations. They found that low-accepted children, compared to populars, tended to attribute rejection to their own personal incompetence rather than to peer compatibility or rejector traits. Intuitively, it might well be expected that a child's internal explanations for peer difficulties could become problematic if a child perceives herself or himself to be ineffectual in certain situations or types of relationships and believes that this is due to uncontrollabe factors such as appearance, interests, or inherent ability.

In our observations and interviews with children, a range of "dead-end" self-reflections have been found. One child might say of his peers "They're mean." "They make fun of me." "They call me names." Whereas such events may all be true, they also indicate a lack of insight into the reciprocal nature of interaction that Youniss (1978) pointed to as a critical social-cognitive awareness in social development. These children appear to accept their peers' dislike or rejection as unchangeable and see little relation between their peers' assessment and their own actions. Other children reflect on their own attributions for their peer problems with boastful unrealism, defensively: "I'm too smart. "They're dumb" "They're silly anyway." "She's just jealous." Children with such beliefs probably do not apply their social-cognitive abilities to resolve peer difficulties but instead view negative or rejecting encounters as further evidence to confirm their beliefs. Other children who lack social-cognitive capability (and younger children) may simply feel confused, or reflect on their affective reactions: "Nobody likes me." "I don't have any friends."

The ability to evaluate one's behavior with some realism seems to involve several social-cognitive dimensions. As children develop, they have been found to increase in their ability to understand other persons (Livesley & Bromley, 1973; Rogers, 1978). Knowledge of "social self" refers to impressions and misimpressions one perceives that others have towards oneself. Throughout childhood and adolescence, knowledge of one's social self becomes less superficial and involves a greater use of inference (Herzberger, Dix, Erlebacher, & Ginsberg, 1981; Montemayer & Eisen, 1977). Children have been found to increase in their ability to utilize more sources of information and to accurately attribute causes for a social event or action (DiVitto & McArthur, 1978) and to examine the underlying traits or motives of self and others (Maas, Marecek, & Travers, 1978). Moral judgment that is in stride with peer levels is important to friendships so that peers can make fair judgments about sharing materials and resources (Berndt, 1982; Damon, 1979). It also is important to be aware of peer norms and expectations for appropriate behavior in common situations or peer roles such as how and when to be helpful. Ladd and Oden (1979) found that children with lower peer status were less knowledgeable about appropriate ways to be helpful to peers in situations of need.

In many ways, as Piaget (1932) originally pointed out, the ability to see a situation from the other person's point of view with some accuracy seems central to social and cognitive development. This ability must go hand in hand with interpersonal skill (as illustrated in Selman's model presented earlier) to enable a child to check on his or her beliefs or assumptions about another's perspective through behavioral or conversational strategies. For example, a child may assume that another child does not like to be with him or her based on some incident, but he or she needs to test this assumption by inviting that child to play or by doing something positive toward the the child and await the outcome. One's ability to gather information to confirm or negate one's assumptions and thereby evaluate one's relationships allows for growth in social perspective taking and presumably social problem solving. Selman and colleagues (e.g., Jurkovic & Selman, 1980) have shown that with emotionally disturbed children this social-evaluation ability is critical for growth.

In recent research by Dodge and colleagues (Dodge & Frame, 1982; Dodge & Newman, 1981), aggressive low peer-status children were found to make considerable errors in interpreting peers' behavior toward them in that they perceived peers to be hostile whenever the peers' intentions were ambiguous. Thus, these children perceived that peers had hostile motives toward them and then were also found to react in kind with aggression. Oden, Wheeler, and Herzberger (1984), in studying children's disputes during a conflict of interest situation, found a greater use of confrontive, combative, conversational strategies among dyads with greater numbers and duration of disputes. It may well be that rejected peers simply are generalizing from their early family experience in that they have been rejected a great deal and/or are often responded to with hostility and have thereby come to expect this kind of response in general. Patterson (1984) reported on data indicating that aggressive children do come from families with high degrees of aggression. An important direction in this area as aggressive, rejected children are the focus of considerable research (Dodge, Schlundt, Schocken, & Delugach, 1983; French & Waas, 1985; Ladd, 1983) is to distinguish those children with serious family problems that might require clinical intervention from those children who lack positive socialization that school settings could effectively enhance in school and/or in consultation with parents.

As indicated previously, the relationship between intra and interpersonal behavior is especially interesting in considering the case of children with problematic peer relationships. These children seem to misinterpret peers' responses to their own behavior, fail to sufficiently evaluate their own behavior, and respond to peers in ways that are self-perpetuating and self-fulfilling of their negative expectations. Although social-skills training and problem-solving training (e.g., Ladd, 1981; Oden & Asher, 1977) have included social evaluation as a part of their methods, more research is needed to determine the origins of such developmental difficulties, compared to children whose socialization has resulted in their knowing how to behave effectively and resolve peer difficulties.

General Explanations for Problematic Peer Status

Several diverse views on the origins of peer-relationship difficulty have been proposed. It seems likely that each represents a major factor contributing to problems, in general, although individual cases may be due to particular sources of variation. One view points to evidence of early tempermental differences in that some children have more difficult temperments whereas others are more situationally cautious and may become avoidant given the right set of circumstances (Coll, Kagan, & Reznick, 1984).

Another view points to early family experiences. Scarr (1985) presented data that indicates that the mother's discipline strategies can account for more of the variance in children's social adjustment than the children's behavior in peer situations. It would thus seem critical to focus more on parental behavior in future studies of children's peer-relationships problems, particularly for preventive aims. This is also important in that children's values and goal directions are typically influenced by parental values and goals. Investigators of children's fairness and conflicts over resources have pointed out that some peers appear simply to value "winning" more than positive peer response or fairness (Asher & Renshaw, 1981; Berndt, 1982; Oden et al., 1984b). Asher and Renshaw presented data that indicates that children's goals for given situations and relationships may be critical determinants of the interpersonal strategies they enact.

Situational factors in the school and in the home may tend to enhance or detract from a child's ability to participate fully in peer relationships or may enhance the tendency for conflict (see Oden, 1982b for a review). Social ability, including social-cognitive and interpersonal skills, are viewed as major causes of ongoing peer-relationship difficulties (Ladd & Asher, 1985; Rubin, 1982) and may constitute original causes as well, in that some children lack appropriate socialization and thereby have social ability deficits. In consulting with parents about a child who has peer difficulty, I have encountered considerable anecdotal evidence that in many families there is one parent who also has interpersonal problems or that the family has few or no friends. Some parents appear to simply accept their children's problematic peer relationships or lack of peer relationships as evidence of an unchangeable personality trait. These parents reported that they seldom really tried talking with their children to help them to learn to evaluate their peer experiences. These children seem to be limited in their resources for unraveling negative cycles of poor peer relationships and gaining greater social ability.

It is also important to consider that some children may lack ability to process or interpret their social experiences. Austin and Draper (1984) found that above-average school achievers tended to be rated as popular or amiable whereas below-average achievers tended to be rejected by others. Quay and Jarrett (1984) found that mental ability was the best predictor of peer acceptance and positive peer interaction enhanced the correlation. The relation between cognitive ability and social functioning needs more thorough study, but some some skills interventions with children with achievement problems and poor peer relationships have found gains in peer acceptance and achievement (e.g., Coie & Krehbiel, 1984). Overall, the general explanations of problematic peer relatioships indicate that there are a number of directions to pursue in attempting to determine the origins of difficulty. Research designs that examine children's development earlier and over time are especially needed.

Intervention Research with Low Peer-Status Children

The major intervention research has shown that, in general, children who have problematic peer relationships or lack peer relationships can improve their appropriate social behavior and peer acceptance (see reviews by Conger & Keane, 1981; Ladd & Mize, 1983; Osberg, 1982). Most methods have included a combination of experiences designed to enhance social-cognitive and behavioral skills and motivation as well as to provide positive peer experiences. Ladd and Mize (1983) illustrated ways to compare the components of these intervention methods. Some interventions stress coaching social skills (Covill-Servo, 1982; Ladd, 1981; Oden & Asher, 1977) or problem-solving instruction (Shure & Spivack, 1978). Others have used modeling, through videotape or role play (Evers & Schwartz, 1973; Gresham & Nagel, 1980) or behavioral shaping (Finch & Hops, 1982), or combinations of all these methods (La Greca & Santogrossi, 1980). Combination methods appear to be especially useful in clinical or special-needs populations (Oden, 1982a).

As recommended by Ladd and Mize (1983), future studies need to focus on ways to compare more specific components of intervention studies even within types, e.g., social-skills training methods. Furthermore, it is not clear why social-skills instruction, for example, is effective. Methods employed by Oden and Asher (1977) and Ladd (1981) and others appeared to foster social knowledge, behavioral enactment, and rehearsal of social strategies appropriate to peer norms and expectations. Social-skills training studies using these methods, sometimes referred to as "coaching" social skills, have generally been found to be effective with children in the middle childhood years (e.g., Coie & Krehbiel, 1984; Ladd, 1981; Oden & Asher, 1977) and preadolesents (Bierman, 1983; Bierman & Furman, 1984), although there are examples of positive outcomes with younger children from modified coaching methods (Factor & Schilmoeller, 1983) and "co-play" with an adult and peer (Scarlett, in press). These methods appear to foster social judgment as children are asked to evaluate their behavior in terms of its consequences for self and partner. Renshaw and Asher (1982) also pointed out that children's social goals in Oden and Asher may have been influenced by asking children to consider the goal of "having fun" or making the game "enjoyable" for both peers to play.

There has been considerable attention to the basis for selecting peers to receive social-skill training, for example, the degree of isolation or rejection. In practical applications, there probably should be consultation with the child and parents before beginning interventions. However, this is not recommended when some children's lack of peer acceptance is mainly a function of inadequate curriculum planning that places too much stress on competition or does not allow time for peer interaction in academic activities (see Oden, 1982b for a review). For children who lack social ability, social-skills training methods developed from research present appropriate intervention approaches that could be adapted to various settings (see Cartledge & Milburn, 1986).

Another research consideration is the specific content of the social-skills interventions employed for research purposes. The preceding studies have found gains in social behavior and peer acceptance for various social skills; sometimes a wide range is covered and other times quite specific ones are the focus (e.g., Ladd, 1981). Research by Gottman and colleagues on low-interacting behaviors and inappropriate conversational strategies (Gottman, 1977; Putallaz & Gottman, 1981) and by Dodge (1983) and Coie, Dodge, and Coppotelli (1982) on aggressive behavior in children indicates that some social-skills training studies might be tailored to individual profiles as orginally suggested by Hymel and Asher (1977). It would be interesting to compare interventions with more generalized formats to those with individualized formats to evaluate the role of specific content versus the role of generalized social-cognitive content. Because peer group norms and expectations vary with age, cultural, and situational factors, it may be difficult to tailor social-skills training. Future studies should also consider various kinds of social skills enacted in diverse types of relationship contexts as discussed earlier in the chapter, e.g., close friendships, social friendships, and activity partners, in particular.

Also intriguing is the data that suggest that the frequency or appropriateness of various social behaviors of unaccepted peers may not be extremely discrepant from that of accepted peers (e.g., Coie & Kupersmidt, 1983; Rubin & Borwick, 1984). Instead, in group contexts in particular, there may be a *threshold for acceptance* by peers in typical situations and relationships and perhaps even for specific types of social behavior, for example, type of aggressive behavior, frequency of interaction. The thresholds would vary from group to group and situation to situation. Behavior that frequently deviates from the norm or violates peer expectations could fall short or exceed the threshold of acceptance, resulting in negative peer response or neglect. It may be that social-skills training is effective, not because it transforms children into very different beings, and not because they leap to higher cognitive developmental levels. Instead, social-skills training may help children to change their behavior only to a degree by lowering, heightening, or redirecting the behavior to the point where it falls within the threshold of acceptance and peers begin to respond positively. At that point, a more positive cycle may have been initiated. Or, even better, social-skills training may help children to learn to judge when they are beyond or short of the peer threshold.

A social-skills training study by Covill-Servo (1982) is relevant here. In this study, low-accepted children who were given social-skills training with peers in their classroom were compared with low-accepted chldren given social-skills training with children from other classrooms. The results pointed to the importance of considering the social psychological nature of low-peer status in that children in the group that received training with classroom peers improved the most in peer acceptance in their own classrooms. Studies by Coie and Kupersmidt (1983) by Putallaz (1983) showed that individual children with poor peer relations tend to initiate the same negative or isolating cycle with a new peer group, indicating that some children do have persistent difficulty in their peer relations and need some type of intervention. It appears that interventions that include peers with whom the children have the most continued contact may be the more powerful interventions, although more investigation is needed. The extent to which learning from social-skills training interventions with one peer group may generalize to new peer groups is somewhat supported by the follow-up study of children from the Oden and Asher (1977) research. One year later, the children who had earlier received social-skills training, many of whom were found to be in new classrooms, had continued to improve in peer acceptance.

How perceptive and receptive peers are toward a given child with problematic interpersonal behavior is important to assess when evaluating the idea of a threshold of peer acceptance. Coie and Pennington (1976) interviewed first-, fourth-, seventh-, and eleventh-grade children and asked them to identify children whom they considered to be "deviant" from most peers regarding antisocial behavior and distorted social perceptions. First graders considered children they disliked or who had different interests from theirs as deviant. Older children considered those who violated social norms to be deviant. Maas et al. (1978) interviewed second, fourth, and sixth graders using vignettes that described characters who were withdrawn, antisocial, or self-punitive (e.g., overly blameful of self). Younger children saw internal factors (e.g., "born that way") as the major causes of the disordered behavior, especially withdrawn children. In contrast, older children, especially sixth graders, considered more social environmental factors to be causal (e.g., treatment from peers, family, teachers). Especially relevant was the finding that children of all ages said that the child's behavior could change (range was from 75%–100%, $M = 89\%$, across vignettes); withdrawn children's behavior viewed as somewhat less changeable. In an experimental study by Singleton (1981), children were given negative impressions of particular videotaped children, but they did tend to alter their evaluations of a child if the child was later shown to change his behavior. As adults, we can all think of individuals we know to whom we would be more receptive, if only they would talk just a little less or help out sometimes.

The idea of the threshold of peer acceptance needs further examination in empirical investigations to determine if it is an appropriate conceptualization of the social-psychological processes in operation when children's behavior is altered from social-skills training.

Conclusion

Future study of children's peer relationships will require more theoretical analysis both to integrate and direct the course of further empirical work. To date, empirical investigations in this area have been hampered by assumptions about children's peer relationships and a lack of definition of the friendship dimension in peer relationships. Furthermore, there has been an emphasis on friendship almost to the exclusion of other likely dimensions in children's peer relationships. Given the lifelong importance of partnership and friendship dimensions in peer relationships, problematic peer relations should remain a major area of study. This research area also needs more conceptual work, particularly on the interrelationship of the intrapersonal and interpersonal processes that contribute to persistent difficulties such as peer isolation and rejection. More focus is also needed on the involvement of the family and school context. Finally, intervention research with children who lack positive peer relationships is important for parenting and education, both to enhance our understanding of the processes involved and to present models that can provide a foundation for parental, educational, and clinical applications.

REFERENCES

Asher, S. R., & Hymel, S. (1981). Children's social competence in peer relations: Sociometric and behavioral assessment. In J. D. Wine & M. D. Smye (Eds.), *Social competence,* (pp. 125–157). New York: Guilford Press.

Asher, S. R., Hymel, S., & Renshaw, P. D. (1984). Loneliness in children. *Child Development, 55,* 1457–1464.

Asher, S. R., & Renshaw, P. D. (1981). Children without friends: Social knowledge and social skill training. In S. R. Asher & J. M. Gottman (Eds.), *The development of children's friendships* (pp. 273–296). New York: Cambridge University Press.

Asher, S. R., & Wheeler, V. A. (1985). Children's loneliness: A comparison of rejected and neglected peer status. *Journal of Consulting and Clinical Psychology, 53,* 500–505.

Austin, A. M., & Draper, D. C. (1984). The relationship among peer acceptance, social impact, and academic achievement in middle childhood. *American Educational Research Journal, 21,* 597–604.

Berndt, T. J. (1981). Relations between social cognition, nonsocial cognition, and social behavior: The case of friendship. In J. H. Flavell & L. Ross (Eds.), *Social cognitive development* (pp. 176–189). New York: Cambridge University Press.

Berndt, T. J. (1982). Fairness and friendship. In K. H. Rubin & H. S. Ross (Eds.), *Peer relationships and social skills in childhood* (pp. 253–278). New York: Springer–Verlag.

Bierman, K. L. (1983). *The effects of social skills training on the interactions of unpopular and popular peers engaged in cooperative tasks.* Paper presented at the biennial meeting of the Society for Research in Child Development, Detroit.

Bierman, K. L., & Furman, W. (1984). The effects of social skills training and peer involvement on the social adjustment of preadolescents. *Child Development, 55,* 151–162.

Bigelow, B. L. (1977). Children's friendship expectations: A cognitive-developmental study. *Child Development, 48,* 246–253.

Brenner, J., & Mueller, E. (1982). Shared meaning in boy toddlers' peer relations. *Child Development, 53,* 380–391.

Cartledge, G., & Milburn, J. (Eds.). (1986). *Teaching social skills to children: Innovative approaches* (2nd ed., pp. 117–161). Elmsford, NY: Pergamon Press.

Clark, M. S. (1984). A distinction between two types of relationships and its implications for development. In J. C. Masters & K. Yarkin-Levin (Eds.), *Boundary areas in social and developmental psychology* (pp. 241–270). New York: Academic Press.

Coie, J. D., & Dodge, K. A. (1983). Continuities and changes in children's social status: A five-year longitudinal study. *Merrill-Palmer Quarterly, 29,* 261–262.

Coie, J. D., Dodge, K. A., & Coppotelli, H. (1982). Dimensions and types of social status: A cross-age perspective. *Developmental Psychology, 18,* 557–570.

Coie, J. D., & Krehbiel, G. (1984). Effects of academic tutoring on the social status of low-achieving, socially rejected children. *Child Development, 55.* 1465–1478.

Coie, J. D., & Kupersmidt, J. B. (1983). A behavioral analysis of emerging social status in boys' groups. *Child Development, 54,* 1400–1416.

Coie, J. D., & Pennington, B. F. (1976). Children's perceptions of deviance and disorder. *Child Development, 47,* 407–413.

Coll, C. G., Kagan, J., & Reznick, J. S. (1984). Behavioral inhibition in young children. *Child Development, 55,* 1005–1019.

Conger, J. C., & Keane, S. P. (1981). Social skills intervention in the treatment of isolated or withdrawn children. *Psychology Bulletin, 90,* 478–495.

Cooney, E. W., & Selman, R. L. (1978). Children's use of social conceptions: Towards a dynamic model of social cognition. In W. Damon (ed.), *New directions for child development: Social cognition* (No. 1, pp. 23–44). San Francisco: Jossey-Bass.

Cooper, C. R., & Marquis, A. (1983). *Conceptualizing children's classroom discourse and its consequences.* Paper presented at the biennial meetings of the Society for Research in Child Development, Detroit.

Covill-Servo, J. (1982). *A modification of low peer status from a socio-psychological perspective.* An unpublished doctoral dissertation, University of Rochester, NY.

Damon, W. (1979). *The social world of the child.* San Francisco: Jossey-Bass.

DiVitto, B., & McArthur, L. Z. (1978). Developmental differences in the use of distinctiveness, consensus, and consistency information for making causal attributions. *Developmental Psychology, 14,* 474–482.

Dodge, K. A. (1983). Behavioral antecedents of peer social status. *Child Development, 54,* 1386–1399.

Dodge, K. A., & Frame, C. L. (1982). Social cognitive biases and deficits in aggressive boys. *Child Development, 53,* 620–635.

Dodge, K. A., & Newman, J. P. (1981). Biased decision-making processes in aggressive boys. *Journal of Abnormal Psychology, 90,* 375–379.

Dodge, K. A., Schlundt, D. C., Schocken, I., & Delugach, J. D. (1983). Social competence and children's sociometric status: The role of peer group entry strategies. *Merrill–Palmer Quarterly, 29,* 309–336.

Doyle, A. (1982). Friends, acquaintances, and strangers: The influence of familiarity and ethnolinquistic background on social interaction. In K. H. Rubin & H. S. Ross (Eds.), *Peer relationships and social skills in childhood* (pp. 229–252). New York: Springer-Verlag.

Evers, W., & Schwartz, S. A. (1973). Modifying social withdrawal in preschoolers: The effects of filmed modeling and teacher praise. *Journal of Abnormal Psychology, 1,* 248–256.

Factor, D. C., & Schilmoeller, G. L. (1983). Social skill training of preschool children. *Child Study Journal, 13,* 41–55.

Finch, M., & Hops, H. (1982). Remediation of social withdrawal in young children: Considerations for the practitioner. *Child and Youth Services, 5,* 29–42.

Fine, G. A. (1981). Friends, impression management, and preadolescent behavior. In S. R. Asher & J. M. Gottman (Eds.), *The development of children's friendships* (pp. 29–52). New York: Cambridge University Press.

Foot, H. C., Chapman, A. J., & Smith, J. R. (1977). Friendship and social responsiveness in boys and girls. *Journal of Personality and Social Psychology, 35,* 401–411.

French, D. C., & Waas, G. A. (1985). Behavior problems of peer-neglected and peer-rejected elementary-age children: Parent and teacher perspectives. *Child Development, 56,* 246–252.

Furman, W. (1984). Some observations on the study of personal relationships. In J. C. Masters & K. Yarkin-Levin (Eds.), *Boundary areas in social and developmental psychology.* New York: Academic Press.

Furman, W., & Bierman, K. L. (1984). Children's conceptions of friendships: A multimethod study of developmental changes. *Development Psychology, 20,* 925–931.

Goetz, T. E., & Dweck, C. S. (1980). Learned helplessness in social situations. *Journal of Personality and Social Psychology, 39,* 246–255.

Goldman, J. A. (1981). The social interaction of preschool children in same age versus mixed age grouping. *Child Development, 52,* 644–670.

Gottman, J. M. (1977). Toward a definition of social isolation in children. *Child Development, 48,* 513–517.

Gottman, J. M. (1983). How children become friends. *Monographs of the Society for Research in Child Development, 44*(3, Whole No. 201).

Gottman, J. M., & Parkhurst, J. T. (1980). A developmental theory of friendship and acquaintanceship process. In W. A. Collins (Eds.), *Minnesota symposia on child psychology* (Vol. 13, pp. 197–253). Hillsdale, NJ: Lawrence Erlbaum Associates.

Graziano, W. G. (1984). A developmental approach to social exchange processes. In J. C. Masters & K. Yarkin-Levin (Eds.), *Boundary areas in social and developmental psychology* (pp. 161–193). New York: Academic Press.

Gresham, F. M., & Nagle, R. J. (1980). Social skills training with children: Responsiveness to modeling and coaching as a function of peer orientation. *Journal of Consulting and Clinical Psychology, 18,* 718–729.

Hallinan, M. T. (1976). Friendship patterns in open and traditional classrooms. *Sociology of Education, 49,* 254–265.

Hallinan, M. T. (1981). Recent advances in sociometry. In S. R. Asher & J. M. Gottman (Eds.), *The development of children's friendships* (pp. 91–115). New York: Cambridge University Press.

Hallinan, M. T., & Tuma, N. B. (1978). Classroom effects on change in children's friendships. *Sociology of Education, 51,* 270–282.

Hansell, S. (1981). Ego development and peer friendship networks. *Sociology of Education, 54,* 51–63.

Hartup, W. W. (1983). Peer relations. In E. M. Hetherington (Ed.), *Handbook of child psychology: Vol. 4. Socialization, personality, and social development* (pp. 103–196). New York: Wiley.

Herzberger, S. D., Dix, T., Erlebacher, A., & Ginsberg, M. (1981). A developmental study of social self-conceptions in adolescence: Impressions and misimpressions. *Merrill-Palmer Quarterly, 27,* 15–29.

Hinde, R. A., Titmus, G., Easton, D., & Tamplin, A. (1985). Incidence of "friendship" and behavior toward strong asociates versus nonassociates in preschoolers. *Child Development, 56,* 234–245.

House, J., Robbins, C., & Metzner, H. (1984, August). Social support. *Institute for Social Research Newsletter, 12* (2), University of Michigan, Ann Arbor.

Howes, C. (1983). Patterns of friendship. *Child Development, 54,* 1044–1053.

Huston, T. L., & Burgess, R. L. (1979). Social exchange in developing relationships: An overview. In R. L. Burgess & T. L. Huston (Eds.), *Social exchange in developing relationships* (pp. 3–28). New York: Academic Press.

Hymel, S., & Asher, S. R. (1977). *Assessment and training of isolated children's social skills.* A paper presented at the biennial meetings of the Society for Research in Child Development, New Orleans.

Hymel, S., Friegang, R., Franke, S., Both, L., Bream, L., & Borys, S. (1983). Children's attributions for social situations: Variations as a function of social status and self-perception variables. In M. Sobol & B. Earn (Co-Chairs.), *Children's attributions for social experiences.* Symposium conducted at the annual meeting of the Canadian Psychological Association. Winnipeg, Canada.

Johnson, D. W., Maruyama, G., Johnson, R. T., Nelson, D., & Skon, L. (1981). Effects of cooperative, competitive, and individualistic goals structures on achievement: A meta-analyses. *Psychology Bulletin, 89,* 47–62.

Jurkovic, G. J., & Selman, R. L. (1980). A developmental analysis of intrapsychic understanding: Treating emotional disturbances in children. In R. L. Selman & R. Yando (Eds.), *New directions for child development. No. 7. Clinical-developmental psychology* (pp. 91–112). San Francisco: Jossey Bass.

Ladd, G. W. (1981). Effectiveness of a social learning method for enhancing children's social interaction and peer acceptance. *Child Development, 52,* 171–178.

Ladd, G. W. (1983). Social networks of popular, average, and rejected children in school settings. *Merrill-Palmer Quarterly, 29,* 283–307.

Ladd, G. W., & Asher, S. R. (1985). Social skill training and children's peer relations: Current issues in research and practice. In L'Abate & M. A. Milan (Eds.), *Handbook of social skills training and research* (pp. 219–244). New York: Wiley.

Ladd, G. W., & Emerson, E. S. (1984). Shared knowledge in children's friendships. *Developmental Psychology, 20,* 932–940.

Ladd, G. W., & Mize, J. (1983). A cognitive-social learning model of social skill training. *Psychology Review, 90,* 127–157.

Ladd, G. W., & Oden, S. (1979). The relationship between peer acceptance and children's ideas about helpfulness. *Child Development, 50,* 402–408.

LaGreca, A. M., & Santogrossi, D. A. (1980). Social skills training with elementary school students: A behavioral group approach. *Journal of Consulting and Clinical Psychology, 48,* 220–227.

Livesley, W. J., & Bromley, D. B. (1973). *Person perception in childhood and adolescence.* London: Wiley.

Lockheed, M. E., & Harris, A. M. (1984). Cross-sex collaborative learning. *American Educational Research Journal, 21,* 275–294.

Maas, E., Marecek, J., & Travers, J. R. (1978). Children's conceptions of disordered behavior. *Child Development, 49,* 146–154.

Mangione, P. L. (1981). *Children's mixed- and same-age dyadic interaction.* A paper presented at the biennial meetings of the Society for Research in Child Development, Boston.

Masters, J. C., & Furman, W. (1981). *Developmental Psychology, 17,* 344–350.

Montemayer, R., & Eisen, M. (1977). The development of self-conceptions from childhood to adolescence. *Developmental Psychology, 13,* 314–319.

Newcomb, A. F., Brady, J. E., & Hartup, W. W. (1979). Friendship and incentive condition as determinants of children's task-oriented behavior. *Child Development, 50,* 878–881.

Oden, S. (1982a). The applicability of social skills training research. *Child and Youth Services, 5,* 75–89.

Oden, S. (1982b). Peer relationship development in childhood. In L. G. Katz (Ed.), *Current topics in early childhood education* (pp. 87–117, Vol. 4). Norwood, NJ: Ablex.

Oden, S., & Tesch, S. (1987). *The contribution of referential communication skill to children's peer status.* Manuscript submitted for publication.

Oden, S., & Asher, S. R. (1977). Coaching children in social skills for friendship making. *Child Development, 48,* 495–506.

Oden, S., Herzberger, S. D., Mangione, P. L., & Wheeler, Y. A. (1984a). Children's peer relationships: An examination of social processes. In J. C. Masters & K. Yarkin-Levin (Eds.), *Boundary area in social and developmental psychology* (pp. 131–160). New York: Academic Press.

Oden, S., Wheeler, Y. A., & Herzberger, S. D. (1984b). Children's conversations within a conflict-of-interest situation. In H. E. Sypher & J. L. Applegate (Eds.), *Communication by children and adults. Social cognitive and strategic processes* (pp. 129–151). Beverly Hills, CA: Sage Press.

Osberg, T. (1982). Social skills training with children: An update. *Child Study Journal, 12,* 57–75.

Patterson, G. R. (1984). Microsocial process: A view from the boundary. In J. C. Masters & K. Yarkin-Levin (Eds.), *Boundary areas in social and developmental psychology* (pp. 43–66). New York: Academic Press.

Piaget, J. (1932). *The moral judgment of the child.* London: Routledge & Kegan Paul.

Putallaz, M. (1983). Predicting children's sociometric status from their behavior. *Child Development, 54,* 1417–1426.

Putallaz, M., & Gottman, J. M. (1981). Social skills and group acceptance. In S. R. Asher & J. M. Gottman (Eds.), *The development of children's friendships* (pp. 116–149). New York: Cambridge University Press.

Quay, L. C., & Jarrett, O. S. (1984). Predictors of social acceptance in preschool children. *Developmental Psychology, 20,* 793–796.

Ramsey, P. G. (1985). *Early ethnic socialization in a mono-racial community.* A paper presented at the biennial meetings of the Society for Research in Child Development, Toronto.

Rathbone-McCuan, E., & Hashimi, J. (1982). *Isolated elders. Health and social intervention.* Rockville, MD: Aspen.

Raupp, C. D. (1983). *Classifying early peer relationships using convergent measures.* A paper presented at the biennial meeting of the Society for Research in Child Development, Detroit.

Renshaw, P. D., & Asher, S. R. (1982). Social competence and peer status: A distinction between goals and strategies. In K. H. Rubin & H. S. Ross (Eds.), *Peer relationships and social skills in childhood* (pp. 375–395). New York: Springer-Verlag.

Rogers, C. (1978). The child's perception of other people. In H. McGurk (Ed.), *Issues in childhood social development* (pp. 107–129). London: Metheun.

Rubin, K. H. (1982). Social and social cognitive developmental characteristics of young isolate, normal and sociable children. In K. H. Rubin & H. S. Ross (Eds.), *Peer relationships and social skills in childhood* (pp. 353–374). New York: Springer-Verlag.

Rubin, K. H., & Borwick, D. (1984). Communicative skills and sociability. In H. E. Sypher & J. L. Applegate (Eds.), *Communication by children and adults. Social cognitive and strategic processes* (pp. 152–170). Beverly Hills, CA: Sage Press.

Sagar, H. A., Schofield, J. W., & Snyder, H. N. (1983). Race and gender barriers: Preadolescent peer behavior in academic classrooms. *Child Development, 54,* 1032–1040.

Scarlett, W. G. (in press). Social isolation from agemates among nursery school children. *Journal of Child Psychology and Psychiatry, 21,* 231–240.

Scarr, S. (1985). Constructing psychololgy. Making facts and fables of our times. *American Psychologist, 40,* 499–512.

Selman, R. L. (1981). The child as a friendship philosopher. In S. R. Asher & J. M. Gottman (Eds.), *The development of children's friendships* (pp. 242–272). New York: Cambridge University Press.

Selman, R. L., & Jaquette, D. (1978). Stability and oscillation in interpersonal awareness: A clinical-developmental appraoch. In C. B. Keasy (Ed.), *Twenty-fifth Nebraska symposium on motivation* (pp. 261–304). Lincoln: University of Nebraska Press.

Shure, M. B., & Spivack, G. (1978). *Problem-solving techniques in childrearing.* San Francisco: Jossey Bass.

Singleton, L. C. (1981). *The influence of reputation on children's perception of behavioral change.* A paper presented at the annual meetings of the American Psychological Association, Los Angeles.

Singleton, L. C., & Asher, S. R. (1979). Social integration and children's peer preferences: An investigation of developmental and cohort differences. *Child Development, 50,* 936–941.

Smollar, J., & Youniss, J. (1982). Social development through friendship. In K. H. Rubin & H. S. Ross (Eds.), *Peer relationships and social skills in childhood* (pp. 279–298). New York: Springer-Verlag.

Stone, C. R., & Selman, C. R. (1982). A structural approach to research on the development of interpersonal behavior among grade school children. In K. H. Rubin & H. S. Ross (Eds.), *Peer relationships and social skills in childhood* (pp. 163–183). New York: Springer-Verlag.

Sullivan, H. S. (1953). *The interpersonal theory of psychiatry.* New York: Norton.

Taylor, A. R., & Singleton, L. C. (1983). *Acceptance versus friendship: A developmental study of social relationships in desegregated schools.* A paper presented at the biennial meetings of the Society for Research in Child Development, Detroit.

Tesch, S. A. (1983). Review of friendship development across the life-span. *Human Development, 26,* 266–276.

Wheeler, V. A. (1981). *Reciprocity between first-grade friend and nonfriend classmates in a conflict-of-interest situation.* An unpublished doctoral dissertation, University of Rochester, New York.

Wheeler, V. A., & Ladd, G. W. (1982). Assessment of children's self-efficacy for social interactions with peers. *Developmental Psychology, 18,* 795–805.

Wright, P. H. (1974). The delineation and measurement of some key variables in the study of friendship. *Representative Research in Social Psychology, 5,* 93–96.

Youniss, J. (1978). The nature of social development: A conceptual discussion of cognition. In H. McGurk (Ed.), *Issues in childhood social development* (pp. 203–227). London: Methuen.

Youniss, J. (1980). *Parents and peers in social development.* Chicago: The University of Chicago Press.

Youniss, J., & Yolpe, J. (1978). A relational analysis of children's friendship. In W. Damon (Ed.), *New directions for child development. Social cognition.* (No. 1 pp. 1–22). San Francisco: Jossey-Bass.

Zill, N. (in press). *Happy, healthy, and insecure: The state of the American child.* New York: Cambridge University Press.

Integrative Processes at School and in the Community

Elliott Asp
Academy School District #20
Colorado Springs, Colorado

James Garbarino
Erikson Institute for Advanced Study in Child Development

When children reach school age, they begin the process of socialization to adulthood in earnest, for the school and other community institutions not only educate in an intellectual sense; they also train them to be adults (Cornbleth, 1984; Getzels, 1974; Hamilton, 1983). When children become involved with institutions outside the family, they begin the "work" of childhood and leave play at home (LeCompte, 1980). And those who subscribe to the notion that childhood is now "hurried" (Elkind, 1981), "endangered" (Packard, 1983), "eroded" (Suransky, 1982), or "disappearing" (Winn, 1982) would argue that recent decades have seen an acceleration of this process. In facing this pressure, children have to integrate their personal characteristics and behaviors with those called for by the role of student, athlete, or church member. They must also integrate their conception of themselves as family members with these new roles. Children must come to understand what these institutions are asking of them and learn to behave appropriately in a variety of settings.

Our purpose is to examine the manner in which this process takes place. What is the nature of the interpersonal integration required of children as they move into the community? What are the new roles that children must master in these institutions. How do those differ from the role of a family member? What are the means by which youngsters come to know and understand these new expectations for their behavior? What are the risks and opportunities that children face as they attempt to integrate their own view of the world with the demands and needs of these institutions? These are the questions that guide our analysis.

167

THE SOCIAL COGNITION OF ECOLOGICAL TRANSITIONS

As children "leave the family" and enter the community, they encounter a new social environment. The ecological perspective on human development proposed by Bronfenbrenner (1979) provides a means for analyzing the nature of this transition that emphasizes the youngster's understanding of the social world (Garbarino, 1982).

The ecology of human development is the study of the developing individual within a network of social systems, based on the idea that human beings are raised, directly and indirectly, by the entire society in which they live (Garbarino & Abramowitz, 1982). Although the developing person interacts directly only with the immediate social and physical environment, what goes on in larger social contexts affects the quality and content of that interaction.

It is this interaction between person and environment that is the key to understanding the ecology of human development (Garbarino & Abramowitz, 1982). As Bronfenbrenner (1979) pointed out: "Lying at the very core of an ecological orientation and distinguishing it most sharply from prevailing approaches to the study of human development is the concern with the progressive accommodation between a growing human organism and its immediate environment, *and* the way in which this relation is mediated by forces emanating from more remote regions in the larger physical and social milieu" (p. 13).

An ever-widening human environment acts on, and in turn is acted on, by the developing individual. For the infant, the social world is limited to a few caretakers (who themselves are influenced by the baby's feeding and sleeping behaviors). A child's world is larger and can include family, friends, relatives, and others close by. Increasing cognitive and physical abilities mean that over time the child will have a greater influence on the larger environment as well. Through childhood and adolescence, the individual begins to learn about, and play apart in, the entire social world through direct experience and acculturation.

Development is a process that results in the individual having a more active, complex, and effective relation to the environment. For a baby, development is demonstrated by learning to sit up, walk, and talk, all manifestations of the baby's increased mastery of his or her surroundings. For a child the social world is more complex, but development can still be recognized in such achievements as establishing friendships and succeeding in school. For both the infant and the schoolchild, the outcome of development is a greater capacity to understand, interact with, and exert one's will on the social world. Development is a lifelong interaction between a person and the social environment, resulting in a changed relationship between them, a relationship that exists phenomenologically and thus draws heavily on integrative processes. Indeed, it is the inextricably social process of constructing one's understanding of the world (which is largely a

168

matter of creating and discovering one's role in the world) that *is* development in this ecological perspective.

Following from Bronfenbrenner's concern with both the immediate context of experience and the more distant social world, his framework allows the consideration of the entire social environment. There are four related levels in his scheme—beyond the individual organism, which is, of course, a system in its own right. Together they encompass the world of the developing human being.

The Microsystem

The most basic ecological component is the microsystem. A microsystem is a social setting in which human interaction occurs and human relations develop. It is a psychological place, a "home" of ongoing interaction and interlocking roles. For the school-age child, microsystems will likely include the family, school, and peer group. Microsystems are created and altered over time as people move through life. Some microsystems, like the family, may last many years. Others, like the peer group, may be quite fluid. Most people are members of multiple microsystems, a fact that permits the existence of mesosystems.

The Mesosystem

The mesosystem is the network of links between microsystems. For a youngster in early to middle childhood, mesosystems will mainly include relations between the family and school. It is precisely because people inhabit more than one microsystem that the mesosystem is so important. As microsystems overlap on the basis of involvement and mutual support, it becomes more likely that they will fulfill their respective roles in fostering development. For example, a child's mesosystem will be strong and constructive when his or her parents know their child's teachers. On the other hand, the connections may be weak or divisive when parents know little, or disapprove, of their child's activities in school. A mesosystem can be a network of mutually supporting settings, or a series of barriers, depending on the compatibility of the microsystems and the support of the larger social world in which microsystems and mesosystems are nested. A mesosystem dominated by hostility between component microsystems is a serious integrative challenge for the child.

The Exosystem

The exosystem is the complex of forces and institutions that influences the life and development of microsystems. Exosystems are power sources that indirectly affect people and, depending on the nature of the force, foster or hinder development. For example, children are affected by the local school board's decision to close a neighborhood school or shut down a nearby playground, although the individuals affected are not in direct contact with the institutions making those decisions. Exosystems do much to define a child's place in the world on the basis of power. Perceived powerlessness is an integrative challenge.

The Macrosystem

The macrosystem is not a tangible social system or institution. It is, rather, a cultural collectivity, an underlying consensus about how society does, and should, operate. Our basic assumptions and standards about people, roles, and society itself form the macrosystem. Bronfenbrenner (1979) refered to it as a "blueprint," a programmed set of shared ideas about how the world works. For children, a powerful source of status in society follows from our culture's *ideas* about childhood, child rearing, and schooling. The child must operate in the world as it exists culturally.

Central to Bronfenbrenner's approach to human development is the process by which people pass into and out of ecosystems, which he calls "ecological transitions." Ecological transitions are changes in role or setting that effectively alter an individual's ecosystem. Such changes occur across the entire life course, but one of the most critical of these is the child's entry into school.

In Bronfenbrenner's terms, "a setting is a place where people can readily engage in face-to-face interaction" (p. 22). He sees a role as a "set of activities and relations expected of a person occupying a particular position in society, and of others in relation to that person" (p. 85).

CHANGES IN SETTING AND ROLE

The new settings and role expectations that children experience when they venture into the community reflect the nature of the institutions that youngsters encounter. The school is a good example for discussion because it is the most pervasive socializing institution (outside of the family) in the lives of children, and the demands it makes on them are similar, in large part, to those of other institutions. Therefore, although we briefly examine the roles that other settings in the community place on the developing child, the school is our primary focus.

Schools (particularly public schools) are what Carlson (1964) calls "domesticated organizations." They do not struggle for survival. They have a steady and predictable flow of clients and their financial well-being is not tied to performance. However, they must accept all comers. They are characterized by a high population density with a small number of adults in charge of a large number of children. As a result of the large population of people who must safely and productively share a small amount of space, the great number of involuntary clients, and the relatively small amount of staff, control is a critical issue in schools (Willower, 1971). Moreover, because the performance of the staff in meeting the stated goal of the institution (education of children) is not easily measured and performance is (at best) only indirectly related to survival, goal displacement often occurs, leading to an ever-greater emphasis on control; that is, whereas some degree of order and stability is undoubtedly necessary if the schools are to do their job, control may become an end in itself, because it is easily "measured" and makes life easier for those in charge. There is no doubt that the behavioral expectations for students will reflect this characteristic of the school as an organization. And, the emphasis on control is likely to be much greater in the school than in the family.

Schools (and other community institutions) and families differ on a number of structural dimensions that have implications for the kinds of behaviors and attitudes that children must integrate if they are to behave appropriately in both settings. First, the number of individuals in the primary social unit of the elementary school (i.e., the classroom) is much larger than the family. Also, the social relationships within schools are typically of shorter duration (Dreeben, 1968). Third, the adult-to-child ratio is much larger in schools. In addition, the social composition of the nonadults in the classroom is much more heterogeneous than that of the nuclear family (although age is one exception). Also, the characteristics of the adults that children encounter in the school are more heterogeneous than those they previously experienced (Dreeben, 1968). Finally, classrooms have more features of a public place than do most of the settings the child experiences prior to entering school; that is, many of a youngster's in-school activities are carried on in front of a large number of people, and public evaluation of performance is often involved. This invokes many indirect ways of eliciting and concealing information to meet personal needs, what Goffman (1969) called "strategic interactions." Elkind (1980) has shown how the development of the capacity and inclination to engage in these strategic interactions reaches a crescendo in adolescence. As children move into and through elementary school, they learn to play this game. For one thing, they construct "personal fables" and "imaginary audiences." Both indicate an effort to define self as "special" and have a strong social component.

The structural features of the school are also typical of many of the other community institutions with which the school-aged youngster is often involved. For instance, if children participate in athletic or recreational programs in their neighborhood, they are likely to be part of a relatively large social group (as compared with the family), characterized by a high degree of social heterogeneity among the nonadults and a large adult-to-child ratio. And, their activities and performances may be even more public than in the school.

The structural features of the school setting are reflected in the components of the student role. (Again, the school serves as a general example of the role expectations for children held by a number of institutions.) Using Bronfenbrenner's conception of role, we turn first to the activity component and then to the relationships that characterize "being a student." First, as compared to previous expectations, the activity of the schoolchild is expected to be purposeful. Students are expected to learn or develop certain cognitive skills. Activity in the classroom is more specific and task oriented than outside of school (Dreeben, 1968), and the degree to which children master these skills is evaluated.

In addition, children are expected to acquire certain interactional or social skills; to behave according to a set of rules—the so-called "hidden curriculum" of the school (Hamilton, 1983; Jackson, 1968). They are to work at their lessons, be friendly and kind to their peers, remain relatively quiet, pay attention to the teacher, and so on. However, there are some settings in school where only some of these "rules" apply, for example, in physical education class or on the playground.

Besides these new expectations for behavior, there are also new rewards and sanctions to which children must learn to respond (Dreeben, 1968; Hamilton, 1983). The rewards and sanctions in the family usually center on the relationship between parents and children and are concrete in nature. Rewards in school are more abstract and have to be learned, particularly those that accompany the mastery of cognitive skills (Dreeben, 1968). Children ultimately have to come to view good grades as rewarding and poor grades as punishing. They also have to learn that admonishments or criticisms from the teacher are punishment and must develop ways to avoid them. In "learning the ropes" some children have the advantage of a basic consistency between home and school, whereas others face basic discontinuities.

School success requires that the significant adults in the child's home and immediate environs maintain the motivation to develop competence as defined situationally in and by the school. We can call this complex of attitudes, values, and behaviors the *academic culture* (Garbarino & Asp, 1981). As used here, *culture* is a definition of social reality through values and behavior. Mastery of this academic culture is perhaps the single most important factor in school success. This is a problem because the degree of consistency between family and school varies across our society. The quality of the school–home mesosystem is variable both across and within socioeconomic and ethnic groups.

We may now turn to an analysis of "process" variables linked to school success. These characteristics, which are both affective and cognitive, are the basis of competence as defined situationally by the schools. In Getzels's terms, they include both *value codes* and *language codes*. A list of these characteristics includes the following (Garbarino & Asp, 1981):

1. Fluency in conceptual language;
2. A hypothesis-oriented style of personal inquiry;
3. Positive orientation to written materials;
4. Willingness and ability to delay gratification based on the authority of adult requests;

5. Ease in manipulating symbols.

The absence of these characteristics constitutes what some have called a *cultural deficit*. A more precise and more rigorous analysis suggests the term *cultural difference* as a more appropriate label for the phenomenon (Tulkin, 1972). There are other cultural patterns that, although not as effective in the social and intellectual context of the school, are nonetheless anthropologically legitimate.

The academic culture tends to be rooted in the value codes of adults as a function of their position in the socioeconomic order. Thus, there is a positive relationship between social class and the academic culture. This relationship is not invariant, however. This is the starting point for the assertion of Tulkin (1972) and others that this is primarily a cultural or ideological matter rather than simply an appendage to social class (Ogbu, 1979).

The relationship component of the student role differs from that of the family also. Before becoming a student, the child's relationship with adults is (relatively speaking) close, warm, dependent, and playful. In school, however, relations with adults are more detached or impersonal, more independent in nature, and have an attitude of seriousness about them (Getzels, 1974; LeCompte, 1980). Relations in school are universalistic (based on *what* one does), whereas relations in the home are more particularistic (based on *who* one is; Getzels, 1974). This is typically the case in other institutions (compared to the family) as well. This means the youngsters must learn to distinguish between various qualities or labels that may be attached to relationships or behaviors. For example, what is fair at home may not be at school. As Getzels (1974) pointed out:

> relationships in the family and the school may very well be distinguished with respect to what is considered fair or more generally with respect to the idea of equity. In the family it is fair—it is equity—that the children be given special treatment as compared to children not in the family; departure from equal treatment for all children is not considered favoritism. In the school it is fair—it is equity— that all children be given equal treatment; departure from equal treatment for all children is considered favoritism and is condemned.
>
> *The child must learn the definitions of fairness and equity in the family and in the school.* He must learn that the special status he enjoyed in the family by ascription, by merely being a member of that particular group, does not carry over to the school. If there are special statuses in the school, as in fact there are, they are open to competition equally to all children and are not to be assumed by ascription but earned through achievement, as is presumably the case in most institutions other than the family. (p. 220)

Even the reasons for the development of affection and the timing of its expression vary from home to school. Affection and warmth and its expression are expected between family members (even if that is not always the case). In school, however, "matter-of-factness" is more the rule (Dreeben, 1968). Teachers and students are expected to be friendly, but open and intense displays of affection (either physical or verbal) are discouraged (Dreeben, 1968): "classrooms are settings in which teachers are expected to avoid establishing enduring relationships with pupils premised on affection . . . both the adult and nonadult members of a classroom are expected to help and like one another because they are engaged in performing a multitude of individual and collective tasks, and not because they love one another" (p. 30).

UNDERSTANDING ECOLOGICAL TRANSITIONS

We have seen that the demands that community settings place on children differ fundamentally from the behavioral patterns that youngsters have learned in the home. How do children come to an understanding of what is expected of them in school, on the athletic field, or in some community activity?; that is, how do they come to view these situations as different from the family and integrate their own conception of themselves into the roles proscribed for them by these institutions? It seems that some of this occurs before the youngster participates in any of these settings.

LeCompte (1980) examined young children's views of school *before* they entered kindergarten and after they had completed almost a year of school. Among other things, she was interested in how children described their own role in school and the role of the teacher; the activities they would engage in and the responsibilities they would have in school; and the rules and regulations for behavior. Children were interviewed in their homes in July before entering school and in the school itself the following April. Despite some sampling problems and the inherent difficulties in reducing and coding children's responses into adult-devised (and oriented) categories, LeCompte's results are interesting.

Generally, she found that "before school" children were better able to describe what teachers did than they could their own role. Basically, the children in the study thought teachers were supposed to teach them to read, write, and do arithmetic. Most of the respondents indicated that teachers would work closely with them, but they emphasized work; that is, teachers would help them learn, or teach them, but there was no mention of play. These youngsters clearly saw school as a place to "work" (at least in terms of interactions with the teacher in the classroom). These children also believed that teachers would help them gain some nonacademic skills, which the youngsters seemed to think were important in school; for example, how to be "good," make friends, and get on the bus.

The children also thought that teachers would manage and discipline them; that is, teachers let children do things (go to the bathroom or to gym class), show them how to be orderly (line up for activities or lunch), and punish them when they "get in trouble" or are "bad." Interestingly enough, before they entered school the children in this study felt that teachers would respond to misbehavior with punitive measures such as spanking or isolation. In April, they said a teacher would most likely "scold" or "talk to" a youngster who was misbehaving.

As for the children's views of their own role, for the most part, they looked on school "as a place where they did what other people wanted them to do" (LeCompte, 1980, p. 112). And, as one might guess, these youngsters indicated that they thought students spent most of their time engaged in cognitive activities. However, the youngsters also predicted that they would spend a lot of time playing. This is particularly interesting given the fact that they had indicated (as we mentioned earlier) that school was not "play-time" (at least in terms of student–teacher interaction).

The children distinguished between "work" and "play" on the basis of location, materials, mood, and the presence of an adult. Work was done at a desk, with paper, pencils, glue, scissors, and so forth, without laughing, and with the teacher nearby or helping.

LeCompte's findings seem to indicate that children have integrated some portion of the "student role" before they enter school. At least they have some idea of what to expect and can generally distinguish between appropriate and inappropriate behavior in that setting. This information probably comes from several sources. Obviously, parents or older siblings may tell children what school is like and how "you have to act." Also, television shows may be another source of information about school. In addition, many youngsters have been involved in day care and preschool programs and have learned about public school in that setting (both from the structure of the programs themselves and deliberate efforts by the staff to help youngsters make a smooth transition to school). However, it appears that initially they know much more about the cognitive dimensions of the institution than they do about its behavioral requirements.

How do children refine their basic knowledge of the student role and learn the "finer points" of being a student? The structural and logistic aspects of the classroom undoubtedly play a part (Meehan, 1980). In school, the individual child is truly "one among many." As a result, it is physically impossible for him or her to have the same kind of relationship with the adults in this setting that he or she has experienced in his or her family. Also, the teacher's attitude towards the child is likely to be more impersonal and task oriented than those of the adults at home. Furthermore, many of the behaviors that brought approval and positive attention from adults at home may be ignored or may even result in adult or peer criticism and rejection in school.

Children also learn how to be a student, a scout, a church member, or a team member by observing and interacting with other children in these settings. As we mentioned earlier, these contexts are more universalistic in nature than the family. Youngsters are treated by adults and peers in a less special and more uniform manner, as is the norm in these social systems. As a result, a child who "demands" special attention from the adults in these settings is likely to be criticized harshly by his or her peers for this behavior (and judged negatively by adults as well). In school, for instance, he or she may be labeled *teacher's pet, a baby,* or with other, less polite terms by peers and as *attention seeking, overly dependent,* or *socially incompetent* by adults. The demands for more universalistic treatment and greater emotional distance from adults than is characteristic of most families may be even stronger in other community institutions (such as organized athletics). By observing older children and those in his or her own age group, the youngster learns the reward system of his or her social group. He or she learns what it takes to be accepted in these settings and how one must act in order to have positive relationships with peers.

It is important to note that, when the child first enters these new settings, the "code" of behavior for person–other interaction that he or she must master may not vary much from adults to peers. However, by the time the child is 9 or 10, a separate peer culture with its own norms and values has begun to develop. This is particularly true in the school (Willower, 1971). Thus, children begin to develop an "us–them" orientation with the adults in these settings, with them and their peers often at odds with those in charge. Although we are not quite sure why and when this emotional division occurs, the beginnings of it are evident in preschool children. For instance, in the study by LeCompte we mentioned earlier, even before coming to school, children described it as a place where you "do what others want you to do, not what you want." Also, after less than 9 months of kindergarten, many of the children in that study indicated that they would avoid work if they could.

Even in kindergarten and first grade, it appears that some youngsters are already adept at carrying out their own agendas and dealing with adult demands at the same time (Meehan, 1980); that is, they have already become somewhat skilled at strategic interaction. Meehan's (1980) ethnographic analysis of the interaction of a group of youngsters and their teacher is a good example. The purpose of the study was to examine the social behavior of youngsters in a classroom. The study demonstrates that children not only learn the role of a student; they may also develop ways to maipulate that role so that they can satisfy their own needs and obtain rewards from adults at the same time. Being able to do this may be one means for youngsters to deal with the new behavioral expectations that result from ecological transitions. Part of competence in these new settings may be the ability to manipulate adults in order to get what you want. To be competent, one may need to know how to be "incompetent." Meehan (1980) stated:

> When the fact that students' have agendas they want to accomplish is incorporated into the analysis, it casts students' errors in a new light. Before accepting the

conclusion that students' errors stem from a lack of competence, it is necessary to determine the part that the behavior in question plays in the students' scheme of things. Not all wrong answers stem from a lack of academic knowledge, not all disruptions stem from a lack of interactional competence. Instead of being an incompetent move in a teacher's game, the behavior in question may be a very sophisticated move in a student's game, a move calculated to manipulate the teacher's normative arrangements to accomplish items on the student's agenda. (p. 146)

It appears that youngsters learn "the ropes" in various settings by watching others, both those who succeed and those who fail, and by direct experience. In fact, some of what is often termed incompetence by adults on the playground or in the classroom (or in church or the Boy Scout meeting) may be attempts by children to integrate both their own wants and desires with the roles demanded by these institutional settings.

RISKS AND OPPORTUNITIES

For almost all children there are some environmental features that hinder the incorporation of new norms and behaviors and the learning of contexts where these are appropriate. For some groups of children, however, the environment functions to erect even more barriers than is inherently the case. From an ecological perspective, these environmental characteristics may be referred to as sociocultural risks and opportunities. By "opportunities for development" we mean relationships in which children and adolescents find material, emotional, and social encouragement compatible with their needs and capacities as they exist at a specific point in their developing lives. The best fit between individual and environment must be worked out through experience for each individual within some very broad guidelines of basic human needs and then renegotiated again as development proceeds and situations change.

Risks to development can come both from direct threats and from the absence of normal, expectable opportunities. Besides such obvious biological risks as malnutrition or injury, there are sociocultural risks that threaten development. Sociocultural risk refers to impoverishing the developing individual's world of essential experiences and relationships; sociocultural opportunity is the opposite. For example, orphans may suffer from their lack of family ties whereas other children may have many and diverse role models as part of a large close-knit family. Similarly, adolescents graduating from high school into the low point of an economic depression are likely to have fewer job opportunities than those graduating during a booming economy. Understanding these sociocultural risks and opportunities is a central concern of human ecology.

In this final section of the chapter we examine the general problems that all children face in understanding ecological transitions. Also, we utilize Bronfenbrenner's (1979) ecological framework that we outlined earlier to analyze the unique risks and opportunities posed by the environmental characteristics encountered by some children.

Getzels (1974) described the general discontinuities between home and community institutions that hinder all children in making the psychological and social transitions required at school age as the affectivity and scope of the relationships in the two basic settings (home versus community, although Getzels refered mainly to school). As we described earlier, the affectivity of the relationships between children and adults in the home are particularistic, whereas in community institutions they are universalistic. Adult–child relations in the home are functionally diffuse in scope, whereas they are more functionally specific in most community institutions. In other words, although parents and families have some general goals for their children (in regard to the outcomes of socialization), schools (and other institutions in the community) socialize the child for specific characteristics that are (or are supposed to be) needed in adult society. Thus, children must learn a new set of relationships, tasks, and rewards and integrate that with their existing conception of their social environment. They must learn to work, as opposed to play (to what others tell them, rather than what they want); be treated by adults in the same manner as their peers (no "special treatment"); and accept punishment for behavior that was rewarded for in another setting. Thus, the nature of the family and of childhood itself may hinder children's understanding of ecological transitions.

In addition, some youngsters may have learned to use language in certain ways, have developed language codes, or have learned or adopted values that are not useful or in accordance with those demanded by the school or other institutions (Bernstein, 1961; Hamilton, 1983; Ogbu, 1981; Wright, 1983). In particular, the modes and utilization of language, and the values regarding the future and the utility of schooling displayed by some minority children and many lower SES youngsters, are more at odds with that demanded by community institutions than those of their middle- and upper class counterparts. Some have labeled these systematic discontinuities as deficits (e.g., Hess & Shipman, 1973), whereas others have referred to them as differences (e.g., Passow, 1970). The question is not one of deficit or difference but of understanding how the language and values of some children hinder them in successfully integrating the demands of community institutions.

We must recognize that children not only learn a language; they learn how to use it to get what they want and to fit in with a particular social group. In other words, language usage is a means of understanding "the reality common to the group and in constructing and maintaining it" (Wright, 1983). The child who learns to use a "different" language or uses language in a different way in the home than is demanded in the school is at a "disadvantage" compared to those youngsters for whom that is not the case. It is not so much that lower SES children do not have the language skills that they need as that they apply language or use it for different ends than those required in institutions outside of their families (Wright, 1983). Schools, for example, require a representational function of language that calls on the child to adopt a somewhat detached and analytical perspective on information as a cognitive object. This places a heavy demand on the language user, especially the young child.

In regard to values, many institutions in the community require that the child adopt an achievement ethic (Getzels, 1974). This requires placing a great deal of value on the future, the ability to defer gratification, and the willingness to accept symbolic representations of success. Getzels (1974) said:

> (the school) assumes that every child has had an opportunity to acquire beliefs that anyone can get to the top and that if he tries he too can reach the top. The future, not the present, is what counts; one must use the present to prepare for the future. It is expected that the pupil will be able to defer immediate gratification for greater gratification through symbolic commitment to success . . . Not only are these the values of the school; they are also the values of the families in which many children are socialized or, shall we say, educated before coming to school.
>
> In contrast to this, other children have experienced primarily a survival or subsistence rather than an achievement ethic, with consequent high valuation on the present rather than the future, on immediate rather than deferred gratification, on concrete rather than symbolic commitment. These children, in contrast to other children, face severe discontinuities in values when they come to school—discontinuities often having a profound effect on their behavior toward school and the school's behavior toward them. (p. 219)

Not all writers agree with Getzels's explanation of the differences in values between the school and home that some children experience. For instance, Ogbu (1981) felt that lower SES parents (like most parents) want their children to succeed in life; to be competent. They do not train their children to fail or instill the values in them that Getzels described. Rather, in his view the systematic difficulties that lower SES children (particularly blacks), as a group, experience in meeting the cognitive and behavioral demands of school and other institutions stem from other regions in the child's immediate and distal social environment.

For example, a youngster's parents may recognize (or at least believe) that success in school is the key to personal and economic success in adulthood and encourage the child to do well in school. However, the child herself is likely to realize early on that those who are the most economically successful in his or her community are not necessarily those who did well in school. In fact, just the opposite may be the case; the most materially successful may be those who "hustle the best." Those who do well in school may do no better in the marketplace than their less academically successful peers because of prejudice in hiring and the poor economic conditions and lack of employment opportunities characteristic of many lower SES environments. (And "objective" data on the income-enhancing effects of education for blacks have tended to confirm the validity of this perception; Garbarino & Asp, 1981). In addition, the school may be perceived by parents and children as unsympathetic to their needs or even to be openly hostile, because school personnel are typically from white, middle-class backgrounds and have little understanding of the needs and desires of lower SES and minority children and their families (Garbarino & Asp, 1981; Ogbu, 1981). Thus, even well-meaning school officials often act at odds with the needs of their clients, while ignoring the sound advice and rational requests of those whose input is potentially highly valuable, the parents of their students.

The general and specific discontinuities between home and community (whatever their origin) are described by Bronfenbrenner as poorly developed meso-systems.

Mesosystems play an important role in an individual's success or lack of it in dealing with (understanding or the social cognition of) ecological transitions. The more powerful the mesosystem, the more likely it is that a youngster will be successful in the new setting (behave appropriately), and the more likely it is that he or she will successfully integrate this new role with his or her existing conceptions of self and others.

There are four kinds of interconnections between microsystems.

1. *Multisetting Participation.*   This is the most basic link between settings, and at least one such cross-setting participation is required to meet the definition of a mesosystem. In the case of the child and community institutions, the meso-system forms when the focal person makes the ecological transition into the institution. This makes that individual the primary link. Thus, for example, when a youngster joins the local chapter of the Girl Scouts, the child is the primary link, and all the others who participate in both settings are supplementary links.

2. *Indirect Linkage.*   When the focal person does not participate in both settings but has a relationship with someone who does, that person becomes an intermediate link between the two settings, *vis-a-vis the focal person.* A child may learn about school or some community activity through an older sibling or a friend who participates in a community recreation program.

3. *Intersetting Communications.*   This refers to the messages that are sent to and from each setting involved in the mesosystem. For example, the child's teacher may call or meet with the youngster's parents or the parents may attend a school function or ask for a meeting with school personnel.

4. *Intersetting Knowledge.*   This refers to the information that each setting has about the other. For example, parents may ask their friends for information about a specific teacher before or after their child goes to school. A teacher may know something about the family and a child because of his or her experiences with another youngster from the same home or children from the same neighborhood.

These four kinds of links add up to a mesosystem that exists on a continuum of "linkage strength." At one end is the weakly linked mesosystem in which only indirect links exist beyond the single primary link. At the other end is the strongly linked mesosystem in which more than one person participates in both settings, and all the other links are active. In general, the more strongly linked a mesosystem, the greater its power for catalyzing development (Bronfenbrenner, 1979). Note that one of the most powerful mesosystem effects comes from situations in which a *relationship* (e.g., the parent–child dyad) participates in two microsystems and thus forms a mesosystem. Thus, for example, a teacher or school that views school–family cooperation and interaction as part of its educational program represents a more powerful socialization agent than the same educational program without such a strong mecosystem. The same would apply to a child's attendance at church and Sunday school when the parents attend as well. It is *cross-contextual* relationships that are more powerful. Bronfenbrenner (1979) offered several hypotheses that speak to this point: "the developmental potential of a setting in a mesosystem is enhanced if the person's initial transition into that setting is not made alone, that is, if he enters the setting in the company of one or more persons with whom he has participated in prior settings" (p. 212).

This tells us that the ecological transitions faced by the school-age child, especially that of becoming a student, have great significance. It suggests that the involvement of the family may have far-reaching effects on the ultimate outcome of the socialization process. It also suggests that the developmental status of the child bears importantly on the transition.

Again, we note the importance of family involvement, particularly in regard to the transition to school. *Unless it is the family itself* (its dynamics, patterns, values, etc.) *that is the problem,* the institution should seek to replicate the family insofar as that is possible. The justification is that by establishing such a coherent and consistent mesosystem, the institution is in a better position *both* to accurately access the child's functioning *and* to produce changes well matched to the enduring realities outside the institution. This also means, however, that where the family is identified as problematic, intervention in the family is imperative. The mesosystem can be made coherent and consistent through family change as well as by institutional accommodation.

An ecological perspective also alerts us to the importance of geographic and social factors in the development of mesosystems. Mesosystems are more likely to arise when community institutions are small and geographically within reach of families. Small schools are less universalistic than larger ones and encourage the staff and students to interact with each in multiple roles. Neighborhood schools and recreational programs encourage parent support and involvement. When families are involved, the institution is more likely to reflect the needs of children and provide the support and guidance required for the successful incorporation of new values and behaviors.

The key to reducing the risks faced by some children in the ecological transitions we have described seems to be the building of a pluralistic mesosystem. By this we mean a mesosystem that harmonizes or balances the universalistic orientation and the particularistic orientation; that is, for example, teaching families to understand the expectations of community institutions and encouraging them to train their youngsters to deal with the discontinuities between these settings. On the other hand, this also involves encouraging community institutions to become more sensitive to the specific needs of their clients by listening to them and involving them in the operation of the institution. Also, various community institutions could benefit each other and the youngsters they serve by building up the mesosystems between themselves. This would help children to understand the differences in roles among these institutions and help them to integrate these often conflicting roles in their conception of themselves. It is the integration of new modes of interacting with the environment that is the definition of development (Bronfenbrenner, 1979).

REFERENCES

Bernstein, B. (1961). Social class and lingistic development: A theory of social theory. In A. Halsey, J. Floud, & C. Anderson (Eds.), *Education, economy, and society* (pp. 87–101). New York: Free Press.

Bronfenbrenner, U. (1979). *The ecology of human development*. Cambridge, MA: Harvard University Press.

Carlson, R. (1964). Environmental constraints and organizational consequences: The public school and its clients. In D. Griffiths (Ed.), *Behavioral science and educational administration* (pp. 127–139). Sixty-third Yearbook of the National Society for the Study of Education. Chicago: University of Chicago Press.

Cornbleth, C. (1984). Beyond the hidden curriculum. *Journal of Curriculum Studies, 16,* 29–36.

Dreeben, R. (1968). *On what is learned in school*. Reading, MA: Addison-Wesley.

Elkind, D. (1980). Strategic interactions in early adolescence. In J. Adelson (Ed.), *Handbook of adolescent psychology* (pp. 432–444). New York: Wiley.

Elkind, D. (1981). *The hurried child*. Boston: Addison-Wesley.

Garbarino, J. (Ed.) (1982). *Children and families in the social environment*. New York: Aldine.

Garbarino, J., & Abramowitz, R. (1982). The ecology of human development. In J. Garbarino (Ed.), *Children and families in the social environment* (pp. 11–30). New York: Aldine.

Garbarino, J., & Asp, C. E. (1981). *Successful schools and competent students*. Lexington, MA: Lexington Books, D. C. Heath.

Getzels, J. (1974). Socialization and education: A note on discontinuities. *Teachers College Record, 76,* 218–225.

Goffman, E. (1969). *Strategic interaction*. Philadelphia: University of Pennsylvania Press.

Gold, M. (1973). *Status forces in delinquent boys*. Ann Arbor, MI: University of Michigan Press.

Gross, M. (1967). *Learning readiness in two Jewish groups*. New York: Center for Urban Education.

Hamilton, S. (1983). Socialization for learning: Insights from ecological reserach in classrooms. *The Reading Teacher, 37,* 150–157.

Hess, R., & Shipman, V. (1973). Early experience and the socialization of cognitive modes in children. *Child Development, 36,* 869–886.

Jackson, P. (1968). *Life in classrooms*. New York: Holt, Rinehart & Winston.

LeCompte, M. (1980). The civilizing of young children: How young children become students. *Journal of Thought, 15,* 105–127.

Mehan, H. (1980). The competent student. *Anthropology and Education Quarterly, 11,* 131–152.

Ogbu, J. (1979). Social stratification and the socialization of competence. *Anthropology and Education Quarterly, 10,* 3–20.

Ogbu, J. (1981). Origins of human competence: A cultural-ecological perspective. *Child Development, 52,* 413–429.

Packard, V. (1983). *Our endangered children.* Boston: Little, Brown.

Passow, A. (1970). Deprivation and disadvantage: Nature and manifestations. Hamburg, Germany: UNESCO Institute for Education.

Suransky, V. (1982). *The erosion of childhood.* Chicago: University of Chicago Press.

Tulkin, S. (1972). An analysis of the concept of cultural deprivation. *Developmental Psychology, 6,* 236–239.

Willower, D. (1971). Social control in schools. In L. Leighton (Ed.), *Encyclopedia of Education: Vol. 8.* New York: Macmillan and Free Press.

Winn, M. (1983). Children without childhood. New York: Penguin Books.

Wright, R. (1983). Functional language, socialization, and academic achievement. *The Journal of Negro Education, 52,* 3–14.

Intra and Interindividual Integration: An Introduction

James E. Johnson
Thomas D. Yawkey
The Pennsylvania State University

Any comprehensive understanding of human development requires conceptualizations on many levels. Two ways the term *integration* has been used in this volume have been: (a) *intraindividual integration* or the interrelationships of various capacities within the developing child; (b) *interindividual integration,* the interrelationships between children and socialization agents. To bring these strains together, however, will require additional integrations of a different kind. For example, Goldman recommends integration in the form of a multidisciplinary focus combining biological and social-behavioral phenomenon, Levine and Mueller discuss the integration of social and affective elements in attempting to come to terms with the development of communicative abilities in social contexts, and Emmerich presents an original integration of moderate and strong stances regarding the role of individual differences in socialization. The authors' treatment of the assortment of topics presented in this section spans from the molecular to the molar, from the concrete–empirical to the abstract–theoretical. Either implicitly or explicitly, however, each is concerned with relating the two types of integration.

Goldman begins by pointing out that a great deal of research has been conducted attempting to explicate the role of the family, the peer group, and cognitive processes (social cognition) in social development. In comparison, little is known about the role of biological and biochemical processes in social development. Thus, her intent is to overview four areas of research in the field of food-behavior relations. Calling on work in biochemistry, genetics, nutrition, and neuroscience, she examines current behavioral research on malnutrition, food dyes, sugar, and food sensitivities.

In each of the preceding areas, Goldman examines the results of evaluative intervention or experimental research and offers her conclusions and reservations based on an analysis of the methodological shortcomings and the confounding variables in the studies reviewed. Furthermore, she notes the implications of diet not only for social behavior but also for the social systems in which the child develops. For example, she points out that marginal malnutrition is related to reduced social responsiveness and activity and reduced cognitive functioning. However, the added demands from adults as the child manifests these behaviors are implicated in the developmental outcomes. Synchronous and reciprocal patterns develop in the case of food dyes and sugars also, as seen in changes in family interaction when a special problem exists and a remedy is directed to the target child. Interdisciplinary research is needed to illuminate the relations of these intraindividual and interindividual processes. The area has been neglected for the most part by researchers.

LeVine and Mueller pose the questions, "What is important for the development of communication?" They begin first by reviewing the literature for views of the infant and the environment, and second for various theoretical frameworks that one can adopt when approaching this topic. After making some important conceptual distinctions (e.g., interaction versus communication, LAD versus LASS), they proceed to describe the intra and interpersonal landscape of the developing child.

A major concept for LeVine and Mueller is that of "shared meaning" between child and socialization agents. They emphasize that the early interaction pattern between caregiver and infant must convey a sense of being understood by showing response contingency predictability. This becomes the basis of attachment as well as being a social prototype with a strong affective component serving for all future interpersonal communications. They propose a continuum from incidental communication to interaction to reciprocal communication and adopt a homologue model in which caregiver–neonate harmony is a prerequisite or necessary precursor to preverbal communication, which in turn is a prerequisite to verbal communication. They trace the elaboration and expansion of the communication system through the toddler and preschooler years and into the middle childhood years. The chapter repeats the need to conceptualize communicational development in terms of both affective-social and cognitive factors. Reference is made to the importance of shared meaning between participants as seen in adult scaffolding or in mutual respect between peers. In closing, the authors speculate about the extent to which later occurring communication patterns attempt to recapture an element of the "complete unified harmony of the infant–caregiver dyadic world." From infancy to middle childhood, past and present intra and interpersonal processes seemingly interact as the child achieves greater social and communicative competence.

Emmerich in his chapter discusses how the study of individual differences can contribute to an understanding of the socialization process and, furthermore, can generate hypotheses on the role of intraindividual integrative processes in socialization. Reviewing briefly the first of three theoretical positions on the role of individual differences in socialization (the "weak stance" or radical situationalism), Emmerich discusses "moderate" and "strong" stances concerning how much of the explanatory burden should fall on underlying biological factors in attempting to understand individual differences and socialization. After noting that there is a trend among researchers to dip down to earlier and earlier ages to try to pinpoint exactly when individual differences stabilize or can be detected, he distinguishes cognitive developmentalists from differentialists by discussing the latter group's greater reliance on quantitative assumptions.

Emmerich proposes that McCall's two-phase scheme of intellectual development (first phase: canalization; second phase: malleability) may provide a framework for joining the moderate and strong stances on the role of individual differences in socialization. Again, measurement issues enter the picture in that during the first phase maturational factors are said to dominate in determining individual differences in rate of attainment (discontinuous or qualitative change), whereas in the second phase there is emphasis on quantitative attributes, continuous variation, and individual differences in levels of attainment. Thresholds between phases depend on measurement reliability. Emmerich discusses integration in the sense of components becoming integrated in phase one (stage integration) and then with attributes stabilizing and forming broader constructs during phase two. Citing his own research on the personal-social behaviors of preschoolers, he views the concepts of dimensionality and adaptivity as important for understanding intra and interindividual integration.

Diet and Behavior:
A Consideration of Recent
Research

Jane A. Goldman
University of Connecticut

Over the last decade there has been a rapid increase in the number of studies investigating the social development of young children. This growth reflects increased interest in a wide variety of phenomena now recognized as impacting on social development. For example, research on family influences that had focused on dyadic interactions has expanded to view the family unit as an interacting system (Belsky, 1981; Bronfenbrenner, 1979; Walsh, 1982). There also has been rapid expansion in the number and variety of studies investigating the impact of peers on social development (Hartup, 1983; Rubin & Ross, 1982), as well as in the number and variety of studies investigating the role of cognitive processes (Shantz, 1983). Increased attention also has been focused on ways in which social institutions, such as schools and television, and social policies influence development (Stevenson & Siegel, 1984).

In contrast to the increased attention that developmental psychologists have given to these topics, comparatively little attention has been focused on the physiological and biochemical factors that influence social development and social interactions. Yet, any attempt to understand social behaviors also must take into account recent advances in the areas of biochemistry, genetics, nutrition, and the neurosciences. One of the areas in which there is a growing body of information linking physiological factors and behavior concerns ways in which foods and specific nutrients influence behavior (Brozek & Schurch, 1984; Galler, 1984; Kniker & Rodriguez, 1986; Miller, 1981; Wurtman, 1982). This chapter provides an overview of four areas of research in which links between dietary factors and the social behaviors of children have been identified. These include research dealing with malnutrition, food dyes, dietary sugars, and food sensitivities.

MALNUTRITION

Malnutrition is defined as a state in which cells of the body do not receive sufficient nutrients and/or calories to provide an adequate substrate for optimal functioning (Margen, 1984). Among children, the vast majority of cases of malnutrition are due to deficits in the intake of energy (calories) and/or protein (McLaren, 1984). In cases of severe malnutrition, in which the child's weight is less than 60% of median body weight for children of the same age, all aspects of growth and development are severely impaired, and unless there is immediate intervention the child will not survive. In cases of mild to moderate malnutrition, in which the child's weight is 60% to 80% of the median weight for children of the same age, there is growth retardation and some biochemical imbalances are likely to be present. However, extreme clinical signs such as wasting (reduced weight for height) and edema (excess of extracellular fluid) and skin problems are not present (McLaren, 1984). In addition, the problems associated with malnutrition often are compounded by the synergistic relationship between malnutrition and infection. Malnourished children are especially susceptible to infection; infection leads to an increased need for nutrients; and this increased need, in turn, leads to a worsening of the malnourished state (Zeskind, Goff, & Huntington, 1984).

Research on the behavioral effects of malnutrition has focused on children with mild to moderate malnutrition—often referred to as marginal malnutrition. A majority of these studies have investigated the impact of malnutrition on health and physical growth or on cognitive development (Pollitt, Garza, & Leibel, 1984; Pollitt & Thomson, 1977). Yet, recent studies indicate that marginal malnutrition also has a significant effect on the social and emotional functioning of children (Brozek & Schurch, 1984; Galler, 1984; Levitsky, 1979). Based on a comprehensive review of the literature on malnutrition, Barrett (1984) reports consistent findings linking malnutrition with reduced social responsiveness, lowered activity level, apathy, and reduced interest in environmental stimuli. He suggests that these early deficits in social functioning, particularly the deficit in social responsiveness, may serve as major factors contributing to the deficits in cognitive functioning that have been found in children suffering from chronic malnutrition.

Two longitudinal studies, one involving infants and toddlers (Chavez & Martinez, 1982), and one involving young school-aged children (Barrett, Radke-Yarrow, & Klein, 1982) provide examples of the effects of marginal malnutrition on social and emotional functioning. In the first study, Chavez and Martinez monitored the development from birth through the second year of life of children raised in a poor agricultural village in Mexico. For the 20 children in their experimental group, food supplements were provided to the mothers from the sixth week of pregnancy through lactation. Children received supplementation beginning at 3 months of age. A matched control group consisted of 20 children who did not receive supplementation.

Chavez and Martinez noted significant differences in the behaviors of children in the two groups from early infancy. Supplemented children were much more active; they slept less, spent less time in their cribs, and spent more time outside. These children made more demands on the adults in their environment, and they were more successful in eliciting responses from the adults. They also received more stimulation from adults, including verbal stimulation, coddling, instruction, and positive reinforcement. The supplemented children also began to play at an earlier age, dedicated more time to play, and were more advanced in their level of play, including play with animals, other children, and objects. In contrast, the nonsupplemented children consistently were described as timid, withdrawn, insecure, apathetic, and dependent. Particularly notable in these children was their flat affect. They expressed neither positive nor negative emotion.

Barrett et al. (1982) investigated the effects of early caloric supplementation on the behavior of young school-aged children living in villages in a chronically malnourished region of Guatemala. The study included 138 children, 6 to 8 years of age, who were part of the INCAP (Institute of Nutrition of Central America and Panama) longitudinal study of chronic malnutrition (Klein, Irwin, Engle, & Yarbrough, 1977). Half the children had received high levels of nutritional supplementation during early childhood, including both maternal supplementation during pregnancy and child supplementation from birth to 4 years. The remaining children had not received supplementation on a regular basis. Barrett et al. found significant differences in the social functioning of the children in these two groups. Children who had received high levels of supplementation showed higher levels of social responsiveness, were more involved with peers, demonstrated more appropriate expression of affect (including both positive and negative emotions), were less often anxious, and more often exhibited moderate (as opposed to low) activity levels. They also were more able to cope with moderately stressful situations.

The literature on malnutriton clearly documents that a primary response to low caloric intake is a reduction in energy expenditure. Both Chavez and Martinez (1982) and Barrett et al. (1982) postulate that it is this reduction in energy level that leads to a reduction in responsiveness to people and to environmental stimuli. This reduced responsiveness, in turn, leads to deficits in social functioning. Based on their own work and on the findings of Lester (1979) and Rossetti-Ferreira (1978), Barrett et al. (1982) hypothesized this sequence of events as follows: Early malnutrition depletes energy resources. This in turn stresses the central nervous system of the organism. Under these conditions the child is poorly equipped to stimulate the caregiver, respond to the caregiver's social initiations, or develop a normal (i.e., synchronous and reciprocal) pattern of interaction with the caregiver. In turn, this failure to learn how to interact with persons in the first few years of life inhibits the development of interpersonal skills and thus influences the course of social and emotional development in later childhood.

As indicated previously, studies of malnutrition document a definite link between early malnutrition and deficits in social development. In interpreting the results of supplementation studies, however, keep in mind that a number of factors in addition to caloric intake per se distinguish between malnourished and supplemented children. For example, supplemented children tend to be healthier, suffering less from infection and other health-related problems (Chavez & Martinez, 1982). Also, it is likely that the mothers of supplemented babies, who also receive supplementation, are in better health and are more responsive to their children than are the mothers of children who do not receive supplementation. In addition, because of the designs of the supplementation studies, children in supplemented groups often have more contact with persons outside the immediate family. However, even keeping these limitations in mind, it is clear that the nutritional status of a child has a significant effect on the child's social and emotional functioning.

FOOD DYES

Within the field of food-behavior relationships, the topic that has received the most publicity concerns the possibility that certain foods, particularly food dyes and sugar, may have an effect on behavior. Controversy on this topic began in the mid 1970s when Dr. Ben Feingold, a pediatrician and Chief of the Department of Allergy at the Kaiser–Permanente Medical Center in San Francisco, reported that through dietary manipulation he was able to reduce the activity level of approximately half the hyperactive children seen is his clinic (Feingold, 1975a, b). This diet, which Feingold labeled the Kaiser–Permanente (K–P) diet, but which popularly is referred to as the Feingold Diet, requires that children eliminate all artificial colors and flavors and all foods containing salicylates.

Based on observations of the success of this diet, Feingold became an ardent spokesperson concerning the negative effects of synthetic food additives. His ideas, particularly the suggestion of a link between additives and hyperactivity, attracted a good deal of attention from the press and the lay public and even from members of Congress (Lipton, Nemeroff, & Mailman, 1979). However, within the scientific community much controversy insued concerning the validity of his claims. Critics stressed, for example, that Feingold's conclusions were based on clinical observations rather than on rigorous experimental evidence. They also suggested that the success of the diet could be related to the changes in family interactions that usually took place in families using the diet (e.g., more attention given to the target child), rather than to the content of the diet per se (Lipton et al., 1979; Stare, Whelan, & Sheridan, 1980).

In response to the controversies surrounding Feingold's claims, many agencies, including the department of Health, Education, and Welfare, established advisory committees to develop guidelines for further research investigating the relationship between diet and hyperactivity (Lipton et al., 1979). Experimental studies employing the rigorous controls recommended by these panels can be divided into two groups: those that evaluated the behaviors of hyperactive children while on the Feingold diet as compared to a placebo diet, and those that investigated responses to food dye challenges.

Studies of the Feingold Diet.   Studies investigating the effect of the Feingold diet per se require that two comparable dietary regimens be established, and that the child be maintained on each diet for a number of weeks. However, researchers working in this area have found that it is difficult to insure compliance with the Feingold diet (which, among other limitations, eliminates all processed foods), and that it is difficult to develop an equivalent placebo diet. Thus, it is not surprising that only two comprehensive studies of the Feingold diet have been reported.

In a very elaborately controlled study of the Feingold diet, Harley, Ray, Tomasi, Eichman, Matthews, Chun, Cleeland, & Traisman (1978) monitored the behavior of 36 hyperactive school-age boys and 10 hyperactive 3- to 5-year-old boys. Each child was maintained on the Feingold diet for 3 or 4 weeks and on a control diet for the same number of weeks. In order to maximize compliance, the experimenters provided all food for the child *and* for all members of his family for the duration of the study. Order of diets was counterbalanced across the children, and all persons working directly with the children and their families were blind as to the experimental conditions.

For the school-age boys, Harley et al. reported equivocal results. Parent ratings indicated that some of the boys were more manageable when on the Feingold diet. However, differences in teacher ratings and in classroom observations and laboratory measures were minimal. In contrast, much more pronounced behavioral differences were found for the preschool boys. All 10 of the mothers and 4 of the 7 participating fathers of these preschoolers rated their sons as more manageable when they were on the Feingold diet. Again, no differences were found on laboratory measures. (Teacher ratings and classroom observations were not available for this age group.)

In the second dietary study, Conners and associates (Conners, Goyette, Southwick, Lees, & Andrulonis, 1976) monitored the behaviors of 15 hyperactive children, 6 to 12 years of age, who were maintained on the Feingold diet for 4 weeks and on a placebo diet (similar to the Feingold diet in balance of nutrients, difficulty of preparation, attractiveness, etc.) for 4 weeks. Order of the diets was counterbalanced across the children. Parent ratings indicated that some of the children were more manageable when on the Feingold diet, and teacher ratings indicated significant improvements in behavior when children were on this diet. However, Conners et al. noted that the differences they observed could be attributed to 4 of the 15 children in their sample who appeared to be responders. Given these individual differences in responsiveness, they cautioned against generalizing as to the appropriateness of the Feingold diet for the majority of hyperactive children.

Examination of the data from the Harley et al. and Conners' et al. studies indicates that effects of the Feingold diet are less dramatic and less predictable than would be expected based on Feingold's claims. However, although the Feingold diet may not have as strong an effect as predicted, or have an impact on as many children as predicted, both studies indicate that *some* children are helped by the diet. In both studies, a few children were identified who demonstrated a dramatic reduction in hyperactive symptoms when following the Feingold diet.

Food Dye Studies.   In contrast to the Conners et al. (1976) and Harley et al. (1978) studies that incorporated the Feingold diet versus a placebo diet as their independent variable, most researchers interested in evaluating the controversy sparked by Feingold have limited their investigations to studying the effects of food dyes on behavior. In order to maintain double-blind conditions, these studies have involved the use of specially prepared foods, often chocolate cookies prepared by the Nutrition Foundation, designed to be identical in every way (taste, texture, appearance, etc.) except that some contain a mixture of food dyes ("challenge" condition) and some do not (placebo). In general, these studies have involved the following procedures: (a) The child is maintained on an additive-free diet for a period of time before the beginning of the study and is continued on the diet for the duration of the study; (b) using double-blind, crossover procedures, the child is given the experimental food (e.g., cookies) once or twice a day over a period of days; (c) on each day the behavior of the child is monitored following ingestion of the food; (d) at the end of the study, after all coding is completed, the experimenter is "unblinded" as to the days on which children received food dye challenges versus the placebo; and (e) behaviors under the two conditions are compared.

Although the design for these studies is straightforword and many such studies have been conducted (for example, Goyette, Conners, Petti, & Curtis, 1978; Harley, Matthews, & Eichman, 1978; Swanson & Kinsbourne, 1980; Weiss, Williams, Margen, Abrams, Caan, Citron, Cox, McKibben, Ogar, & Schultz, 1980; Williams, Cram, Tausig, & Webster, 1978), there still is much controversy concerning the relationship between food dyes and hyperactivity. Debates concerning interpretation of the findings of these studies have been extremely heated and there still is no consensus on the issues. (For examples of reviews and debates see Conners, 1980, 1984; Lipton et al., 1979; Rimland, 1983; Stare et al., 1980; Swanson & Kinsbourne, 1979; Wender, 1980).

Part of this controversy stems from reviewers approaching the data from two different perspectives. Some reviewers focus on mean scores aggregated across subjects for the food dye versus placebo conditions. Others focus on the ways in which individual children respond across the two conditions, approaching the results as a series of N of one studies. Those who focus on group scores (i.e., data aggregated over subjects) conclude that there is no relationship between food dyes and hyperactivity.

In contrast, those who look at the data in terms of individual differences focus on the reactions of individual children in order to assess whether or not there are specific cases in which hyperactivity is exacerbated by the ingestion of food dyes. Given that the term *hyperactivity* is applied to a heterogeneous group of children representing multiple etiologies, these researchers argue that it is not appropriate to expect that *all* hyperactive children would be sensitive to food dyes. Rather, they are interested in finding out if there might be a *subset* of hyperactive children who show a sensitivity to these dyes. In keeping with this perspective, researchers interested in individual differences interpret the results of the food dye studies as indicating that there are some children for whom there is a link between food dyes and hyperactivity (Weiss et al., 1980).

In addition to these different approaches to interpreting the findings of the studies on food dyes and hyperactivity, many methodological problems also contribute to the difficulties in reaching definitive conclusions. One of the major methodological problems concerns the very small quantity of food dye that has been used in the food challenges. Recent reports from the FDA indicate that average food dye consumption is 59 mg/day for children ages 1 to 5 (90th centile = 121 mg/day) and 76 mg for children ages 6 to 12 years old (90th centile = 146 mg/day) (Rimland, 1983; Swanson & Kinsbourne, 1980). Yet, in a majority of studies the challenge involved only 26 mg of food dye, and often this was divided into smaller doses. It is quite possible that the amount of food dye contained in these "challenges" was below the threshold needed to stimulate a response (Rimland, 1983; Swanson & Kinsbourne, 1980). The findings of Swanson and Kinsbourne (1980), who reported significant effects when using a food dye challenge of 100 mg, support the argument that many of these negative findings may have been an artifact of the small doses that were used.

Another methodological problem related to administration of the food dye challenges concerns the fact that in some studies the challenge was administered on randomly selected days, often with many days elapsing between challenge doses (e.g., Weiss et al., 1980). Based on findings of increased responsiveness to food dye challenges over a series of days, Conners (1980) suggested that the effects of these dyes probably are cumulative. According to Conners, it is "as if the children were 'loaded' by the first day of the challenge and showed their worsened behavior thereafter" (p. 64). This loading phenomena suggests that the intermittent administration of a food challenge is not an appropriate model for testing the effects of foods such as food dyes that in the "typical" diet are consumed on a daily basis. The literature on food allergies also suggests that reactions to an occasional challenge will not mimic reactions found as a result of constant exposure to an offending agent.

A third confounding factor involves the fact that some children had to be dropped from the studies because of reactions to the placebo cookies (for example, some were thought to be sensitive to the chocolate in the cookies). This selective elimination of sensitive subjects suggests that, in studies in which such subjects were dropped, the final samples may have been biased against finding significant differences. A final methodological problem involves the fact that dietary infractions took place while children were on the additive-free diet. In many of the studies there is no mention of eliminating data from placebo trials that took place on days on which there was a dietary infraction. Yet, it is possible that the behaviors observed on these days were more accurate reflections of the "challenge" condition than of the placebo condition.

Conclusions.   In conclusion, it is clear that researchers have not yet reached consensus concerning the relationships between the Feingold diet and/or food dyes and hyperactivity. However, a review of the related literature indicates that there are *some* children whose hyperactivity is exacerbated by the ingestion of food dyes, and that there are *some* children who are helped by the Feingold diet. There also are repeated indications that preschool children, as compared to school-age children, might be more sensitive to dyes and might respond more favorably to the Feingold diet (Harley et al., 1978; Lipton et al., 1979). Conclusions identifying a relationship between food dyes and behavior also are supported by data from animal studies that have identified a link between food dyes and central nervous system functioning (Goldenring et al., 1980; Logan & Swanson, 1979; Silbergeld, 1981).

In assessing this body of literature it also is important to note that the results of studies that have been limited to evaluations of the effects of food dyes on behavior should not be interpreted as providing evaluations of the Feingold diet. Although many researchers and reviewers have made such interpretations, keep in mind that the Feingold diet eliminates many substances in addition to food dyes. As Rimland (1983) and others have pointed out, food dyes account for only 10 of the over 3,000 additives that are eliminated from the diets of children following the Feingold diet. Also, because the Feingold diet eliminates almost all processed foods, diets of children following the Feingold regimen differ from the "typical" American diet in many ways in addition to the elimination of additives. For example, children on the Feingold diet often consume lower quantities of refined sugars (Prinz, Roberts, & Hantman, 1980).

These distinctions between the restrictions imposed by the Feingold diet as opposed to the restrictions involved in the elimination only of food dyes help to explain the finding that the percentage of children who are helped by the Feingold diet appears to be considerably higher than the percentage who appear to be sensitive to food dyes. Thus, it is likely that many of the children who respond favorably while on the Feingold diet might be responding to aspects of the diet other than, or in addition to, the elimination of food dyes.

In emphasizing this distinction, it also is interesting to note that although the results of many of the studies evaluating the effects of food dyes have been interpreted as indicating that the Feingold diet does not work, within many of these studies a major criterion for selection of subjects was that each child show marked improvement on the Feingold diet.

SUGAR AND BEHAVIOR

As described previously, research investigating food-behavior relationships in children began with studies designed to evaluate Feingold's hypotheses concerning food additives and hyperactivity. Although controversy regarding the effects of additives continues, questions also are being raised concerning links between dietary sugars, particularly sucrose (table sugar), and behavior.

The possibility that sugar consumption may affect behavior is especially relevant given the increasing amount of sugar in the diets of children (Conners, 1984; U.S. Senate Select Committee on Nutrition and Human Needs, 1977). It is estimated that, on the average, each child in the United States consumes close to 2 pounds of dietary sugars each week. Approximately 70% of this sugar is in the form of sucrose (Morgan & Zabik, 1981; Riddle & Prinz, 1984).

Relationships between sugar consumption and a variety of health problems such as dental caries (tooth decay) and obesity have been well documented (Warren, 1975). Relationships between sugar consumption and hyperactivity and other behavioral problems also have been noted. For the most part, however, these reports have been anecdotal, such as reports of parents and teachers that children are particularly difficult to manage after high sugar snacks, or have involved case studies (Crook, 1975; O'Banion, Armstrong, Cummings, & Stange, 1978; Phlegar & Phlegar, 1979; Rapp, 1978). Given all the speculation concerning the relationship between sugar and behavior, and all the press coverage that this topic has received, it is surprising that very few rigorous, controlled studies dealing with the behavioral effects of sugar are available.

In their pioneering study investigating the relationship between sugar and behavior, Prinz, Roberts, and Hantman (1980) reported a positive correlation between sugar consumption, as measured through 7-day dietary records, and activity level for a sample of "normal," healthy preschool and younger school-age children. They also found a positive correlation between sugar intake and destructive–aggressive behaviors for a sample of hyperactive preschoolers.

In a second correlational study Lester, Thatcher, and Monroe-Lord (1982) investigated the relationship between some dietary factors and school achievement. Results indicated a significant negative correlation between the proportion of refined carbohydrates (foods high in sugar) in the diet and school achievement (i.e., children with higher levels of sugar in their diet did less well in school). Although results of both the Prinz et al. and Lester et al. studies support the possibility of a sugar–behavior relationship. neither study was able to address the issue of causality.

In order to address this issue of causality, four groups of researchers have used double-blind crossover designs to experimentally investigate the effect of sugar on behavior. Conners, Wells, Horn, Blouin, Beerbohm, O'Donnell, Seidel, & Shaw (in press) investigated the effect of sugar intake on school-age children hospitalized for psychiatric problems. Over a series of experimental days, the children were given either a challenge drink that was sweetened with sugar or a placebo that was sweetened to an equal degree with an artificial sweetener. Systematic behavioral observations conducted during the first 2 hours following the drinks indicated that the children exhibited more movement and engaged in more inappropriate behaviors on the days on which they had received the sugar challenge. However, behavioral ratings that were based on observations occurring over longer periods of time following the drinks failed to detect any behavioral differences.

Behar, Rapoport, Adams, Berg, and Cornblath (1984) investigated the effects of a sugar challenge in 21 school-age boys, all of whom were reported by their parents to have adverse behavioral reactions to sugar. A majority also had histories of behavioral problems, including a number of cases of hyperactivity. Each boy was observed for 5 hours after receiving a sugar drink and for 5 hours after receiving a placebo. Results indicated no differences in behavior following the two drinks.

Focusing specifically on a hyperactive sample, Wolraich, Milich, Stumbo, and Schultz (1985) investigated the effects of a sucrose challenge in 32 hyperactive school-age boys. These boys were observed for 3 hours following a sucrose challenge and for 3 hours following a placebo. Results again indicated no significant behavioral effects associated with the sucrose challenge.

Working with a sample of younger children, Goldman, Lerman, Contois, and Udall (1984, 1986) investigated the effect of sucrose consumption on the behavior of 8 normal, healthy preschool children. Each child was observed for 90 minutes following a sugar drink and for 90 minutes following a placebo. During these observations the child alternated between 15-minute sessions of work on structured tasks and 15-minute sessions of free play. Following the sucrose drink the children showed a decrement in performance in the structured testing situation, and they were more active and less task oriented during the free-play sessions.

It is obvious that the results of these few studies that are available are far from consistent. However, a comparison of the subjects included in each of the studies and of the types of procedures used suggests a number of factors that might help to explain these inconsistencies. Such a comparison suggests, for example, that younger children, especially preschoolers, may be more sensitive than older children to the effects of sucrose. Such a comparison also suggests that changes in activity level following a sucrose challenge may be more evident in non-hyperactive children than in hyperactive children. In contrast, the reactions of hyperactive children might be reflected in changes in the form of their activity (such as increased aggression) rather than in the amount of activity per se. Consideration of time parameters suggests that behavioral reactions to sucrose may vary depending on the amount of time elapsed between sucrose ingestion and the behavioral assessment. Responses may be relatively short term, with maximum reactions occurring somewhere between 30 minutes and 2 hours following ingestion of a sucrose challenge. Other factors that might influence behavioral reactions to sucrose include the amount of sugar used in the challenge condition, the behaviors chosen as the dependent variables, possible behavioral effects of the substances used as placebos, dietary history of the subjects, the research setting, and the invasiveness of procedures used.

Although the results of these studies are far from consistent and a great many questions remain concerning both the conditions under which sugar might influence behavior and the types of behaviors most likely to be effected, it is possible to draw a few tentative conclusions. The first is that to date there is no systematic evidence indicating that sucrose consumption "causes" hyperactivity. Rather, the data suggest that the behavioral effects of sucrose, if they do exist, may be relatively subtle, and that these effects may differ for hyperactive versus nonhyperactive children. Also, whereas the available data do not indicate a systematic, causative relationship between sugar and hyperactivity, these results do not rule out the possibility that there may be a small subgroup of children in whom, possibly due to metabolic abnormalities, sucrose does have adverse behavioral effects (Egger, Carter, Wilson, Turner, & Soothill, 1983; O'Banion et al., 1978).

FOOD SENSITIVITIES

When investigating food-behavior relationships, one approach is to identify a specific food or food additive as an independent variable and to evaluate evidence concerning the behavioral effects of that food. As described earlier, such procedures have been used by researchers interested in the effects of food dyes and sugar. A second approach, which involves much more individualized procedures for working with children, involves the identification of food sensitivities. Although there is some debate regarding the definition of such sensitivities (National Dairy Council, 1983), in general, a child is defined as having a food sensitivity if he or she exhibits an "abnormal" response to a food that for most people causes no adverse effect.[1] Both professionals and the general public are well aware of links between a number of physical symptoms, such as hives, rashes, stomach cramps, and runny noses, and food sensitivities. However,

---

[1]The term food sensitivity is used to refer to any unusual reaction to a food, making no assumptions regarding the mechanisms underlying this reaction. In contrast, the term food allergy is reserved to describe those adverse reactions to foods that have a demonstrated immunological basis.

comparatively few individuals are aware of the links between foods sensitivities and behavioral disturbances. Although reports describing such relationships have been available for many years (e.g., Randolph, 1947), it is only recently that the topic of food sensitivities is receiving attention from researchers interested in child behavior.

The approach used by researchers interested in food sensitivities differs in a number of ways from the approach of those investigating the effects of particular foods. For example, whereas researchers investigating food dyes and sugars have focused on hyperactivity as their dependent variable, clinicians and researchers investigating food sensitivities have identified a wide range of behaviors that, in particular individuals, appear to be linked to such sensitivities. These include behaviors associated with fatigue, such as lethargy and depression, and as well as behaviors associated with irritability, distractibility, excitability and impulsiveness, and hyperactivity (Ilg, Ames, & Baker, 1981; Kniker & Rodriguez, 1986).

In addition, researchers interested in food sensitivities do not focus on a particular food as their independent variable. Rather, using extensive interviews, observations, and testing, they work individually with each child and his or her parents in order to identify the foods, if any, to which the child might be sensitive. Here it is important to note that researchers and clinicians interested in food sensitivities do not focus on "junk" foods as opposed to "healthy" foods as provocative agents. Rather, they note that sensitivities tend to occur as reactions to commonly eaten foods. These include many nutritious foods such as milk, wheat, corn, and eggs, as well as food additives and sweeteners (Egger et al., 1985).

A recent study by Egger, Carter, Graham, Gumley, and Soothill (1985) presented a model for work in this area. Subjects for this study included 76 children ranging in age from 2 to 15 years who were diagnosed as hyperkinetic or as demonstrating overactivity as a prominent feature of a more widespread behavioral disturbance. For the first phase of the study the children were placed on individually designed elimination diets in which all foods suspected of provoking a behavioral or allergic reaction in the child were eliminated. Sixty-two of the children (82%) showed improved behavior when placed on these individualized diets.

A second phase of the study involved 28 of the children who had shown improvement during the first phase. Each child was observed for a period of 7 to 14 days during which his or her diet included a food that had been identified as provoking unwanted behaviors, and for a similar period of time during which a placebo was used. As with the studies of food dyes and sugar, the placebo and challenge foods were prepared so that it was not possible to distinguish between them. Throughout the study, behaviors of the children were assessed by their parents and by members of the research team. Both sets of ratings indicated that behaviors of the children were considerably improved during the placebo phase of the study.

In addition to documenting a relationship between food sensitivities and behavior, results of the Egger et al. study also demonstrate the wide range of foods to which individual children may display a sensitivity. The foods most often found to provoke allergic reactions included cows milk, wheat, eggs, and oranges, as well as tartrazine (food coloring), benzoic acid (preservative), and chocolate. In all, 47 provocative foods were identified and most children reacted to more than one food.

Results of the Egger et al. study, along with the results of related investigations (Egger et al., 1985; King, 1981) provide a clear indication that food sensitivities can be involved in provoking problem behaviors. At the moment, however, there is a great deal of controversy regarding food sensitivities (Kniker & Rodriguez, 1986; National Dairy Council, 1983, 1985) and much more research is needed. Investigators working in this area are faced with a number of difficult problems. For example, because food sensitivities are individualized in terms of both the foods that stimulate reactions (independent variables) and the behavioral responses that are provoked (dependent variables), many of the procedures that are "musts" in terms of traditional experimental design, such as random selection of subjects, random assignment of subjects to groups, and identical treatment procedures, can not be applied to research in this area. Rather, more innovative research designs, including designs that include aspects of "N of one" studies (Weiss et al., 1980) are needed, as are more innovative approaches to data analysis (Cox, 1981; King, 1981).

Research in this area also is complicated by the fact that there are no simple procedures for evaluating food sensitivities. The most effective procedure appears to be the elimination diet. However, implementation of an elimination diet involves a major restructuring of the eating habits of a child—a very difficult task to accomplish (Egger et al., 1985).

In summary, although there still is a good deal of controversy regarding the phenomena of food sensitivities, and although this is a difficult area in which to conduct research, both clinical reports and research findings have documented instances in which behavioral problems have been provoked by food sensitivities. Thus, it is important that clinicians and researchers who work with children with behavior problems keep in mind the possibility that in some cases the "unwanted" behaviors with which they are dealing *might* be related to food sensitivities (Ilg, Ames, & Baker, 1981).

CONCLUSIONS

In conclusion, it is evident that there are links between dietary factors and child behavior. One of the most important aspects of research in this area concerns identification of the relationship between malnutrition and deficits in social responsiveness. As well as helping us to understand the role of nutritional status in social and personality development, identification of these relationships also will help us to understand the role played by social factors, such as reduced responsiveness to others, in the development of the cognitive deficits associated with malnutrition. From a public policy perspective, research findings in this area highlight the need for all of us concerned with the welfare of children to campaign for the development of comprehensive and effective policies to fight world hunger—including working to insure the allocation of sufficient resources to provide adequate nutrition for all children in the United States.

Recent research also has begun to identify instances in which individual children show adverse behavioral reactions to the ingestion of specific foods. Although there is a great deal of controversy in this area, and although it appears that for a majority of children with behavioral problems these problems cannot be linked to ingestion of a specific food or food additive, evidence is accumulating that there are *some* children for whom behavioral problems clearly are linked to food sensitivities. It is time for questions regarding food sensitivities to change from those asking if such sensitivities exist to those exploring the conditions under which they occur. Interdisciplinary research identifying the mechanisms behind these reactions also is necessary. In addition, because food sensitivities are individualized in terms of the foods that stimulate reactions and the behavioral reactions that are provoked, more innovative research designs and approaches to data analysis are needed.

ACKNOWLEDGMENTS

The author would like to acknowledge, with many thanks, the assistance and encouragement of Ruth W. Crocker, M.Ed., R.D., and Robert H. Lerman, M.D. PhD. who served as nutritional consultants in the preparation of this manuscript.

REFERENCES

Barrett, D. E. (1984). Malnutrition and child behavior: Conceptualization, assessment and an empirical study of social-emotional functioning. In J. Brozek & B. Schurch (Eds.), *Malnutrition and behavior: Critical assessment of key issues* (pp. 280–306). Lausanne, Switzerland: Nestle Foundation.

Barrett, D. E., Radke-Yarrow, M., & Klein, R. E. (1982). Chronic malnutrition and child behavior: Effects of early caloric supplementation on social and emotional functioning at school age. *Developmental Psychology, 18,* 541–556.

Behar, D., Rapoport, J. L., Adams, A. J., Berg, C. J., & Cornblath, M. (1984). Sugar challenge testing with children considered behaviorally "sugar reactive." *Nutrition and Behavior, 1,* 227–288.

Belsky, J. (1981). Early human experience: A family perspective. *Developmental Psychology, 17,* 3–23.

Bronfenbrenner, U. (1979). *The ecology of human development.* Cambridge, MA: Harvard University Press.

Brozek, J., & Schurch, B. (Eds.). (1984). *Malnutrition and behavior: Critical assessment of key issues.* Lausanne, Switzerland: Nestle Foundation.

Chavez, A., & Martinez, C. (1982). *Growing up in a developing community: A bio-ecologic study of the development of children from poor peasant families in Mexico.* Mexico: Institute of Nutrition of Central America and Panama.

Conners, C. K. (1980). *Food additives and hyperactive children.* New York: Plenum.

Conners, C. K. (1984). Nutritional therapy in children. In J. R. Galler (Ed.), *Nutrition and behavior* (pp. 159–192). New York: Plenum.

Conners, C. K., Goyette, C. H., Southwick, D. A., Lees, J. M., & Andrulonis, P. A. (1976). Food additives and hyperkinesis: A controlled double-blind experiment. *Pediatrics, 58,* 154–166.

Conners, C. K., Wells, K. C., Horn, W. F.. Blouin, A. G., Beerbohm, E. K., O'Donnell, D. J., Seidel, W. T., & Shaw, D. S. (in press). The effects of sucrose and fructose on classroom behavior of child psychiatric patients. *Nutrition and Behavior.*

Cox, C. (1981). Detection of treatment effects when only a portion of subjects respond. In S. A. Miller (Ed.), *Nutrition & behavior* (pp. 285–289). Philadelphia: The Franklin Institute Press.

Crook, W. G. (1975). Food allergy—the great masquerader. *Pediatric Clinics of North America, 22,* 227–238.

Egger, J., Carter, C. M., Graham, P. J., Gumley, D., & Soothill, J. F. (March 9, 1985). Controlled trials of oligoantigenic treatment in the hyperkinetic syndrome. *The Lancet* (No. 8428) 540–545.

Egger, J., Carter, C. M., Wilson, J., Turner, M. W., & Soothill, J. F. (October 15, 1983). Is migrane food allergy? A double-blind controlled trial of oligoantigenic diet treatment. *The Lancet* (No. 8355) 865–869.

Feingold, B. F. (1975a). Hyperkinesis and learning disabilities linked to artificial food flavors and colors. *American Journal of Nursing, 75,* 797–803.

Feingold, B. F. (1975b). *Why your child is hyperactive.* New York: Random House.

Galler, J. R. (Ed.). (1984). *Nutrition and behavior.* New York: Plenum.

Goldenring, J. R., Wool, R. S., Shaywitz, B. A., Batter, D. K., Cohen, D. J., Young, G., & Teicher, M. H. (1980). Effects of continuous gastric infusion of food dyes on developing rat pups. *Life Sciences, 27,* 1897–1904.

Goldman, J. A., Lerman, R. H., Contois, J. H. & Udall, J. N. (1984). Sucrose ingestion, activity and task orientation. *Journal of Pediatric Research, 18*(4) 104A (Abstract).

Goldman, J. A., Lerman, R. H., Contois, J. H., & Udall, J. N. Jr. (1986). Behavioral effects of sucrose on preschool children. *Journal of Abnormal Child Psychology, 14,* 565–577.

Goyette, C. H., Conners, C. K., Petti, T. A., & Curtis, L. E. (1978). Effects of artificial colors on hyperkinetic children: A double-blind challenge study. *Psychopharmacology Bulletin, 14,* 39–40.

Harley, J. P., Matthews, C. G., & Eichman, P. (1978). Synthetic food colors and hyperactivity in children: A double-blind challenge experiment. *Pediatrics, 62,* 975–983.

Harley, J. P., Ray, R. S., Tomasi, L., Eichman, P. L., Matthews, C. G., Chun, R., Cleeland, C. S., & Traisman, E. (1978). Hyperkinesis and food additives: Testing the Feingold hypothesis. *Pediatrics, 61,* 818–828.

Hartup, W. W. (1983). Peer relations. In P. H. Mussen (Ed.), *Handbook of child psychology: Vol. 4. Socialization, personality and social development* (pp. 103–197). New York: Wiley.

Ilg, F. L., Ames, L. B., & Baker, S. M. (1981). *Child behavior: Specific advice on problems of child behavior* (rev. ed.). New York: Harper & Row.

King, D. S. (1981). Can allergic exposure provoke psychological symptoms? A double-blind test. *Biological Psychiatry, 16,* 3–19.

Klein, R. E., Irwin, M., Engle, P. L., & Yarbrough, C. (1977). Malnutrition and mental development in rural Guatemala. In N. Warren (Ed.), *Studies in cross-cultural psychology* (pp. 92–119). New York: Academic Press.

Kniker, W. T., & Rodriguez, M. R. (1986). Non-IgE mediated and delayed adverse reactions to foods or additives. In J. C. Brereman (Ed.), *Handbook on food allergies* (pp. 125–161). New York: Marcel Dekker.

Lester, B. M. (1979). A synergistic process approach to the study of prenatal malnutrition. *International Journal of Behavioral Development, 2,* 377–394.

Lester, M. L., Thatcher, R. W., & Monroe-Lord, L. (1982). Refined carbohydrate intake, hair cadmium levels and cognitive functioning in children. *Nutrition and Behavior, 1,* 3–13.

Levitsky, D. A. (Ed. (1979). *Malnutrition, environment and behavior: New perspectives.* Ithaca NY: Cornell University Press.

Lipton, M. A., Nemeroff, C. B., & Mailman, R. B. (1979). Hyperkinesis and food additives. In R. J. Wurtman & J. J. Wurtman (Eds.), *Nutrition and the brain: Vol. 4. Toxic effects of food constituents on the brain* (pp. 1–27). New York: Raven Press.

Logan, W. J., & Swanson, J. (1979). Erythrosin B inhibition of neutrotransmitter accumulation by rat brain homogenate. *Science, 206,* 363–364.

Margen, S. (1984). Energy-protein malnutrition: The web of causes and consequences. In J. Brozek & B. Schurch (Eds.), *Malnutrition and behavior: Critical assessment of key issues* (pp. 20–31). Lausanne, Switzerland: Nestle Foundation.

May, C. D. (1984). Food sensitivity: Facts and fancies. *Nutrition Reviews, 42,* 72–78.

McLaren, D. S. (1984). Forms and degrees of energy-protien deficits. In J. Brozek & B. Schurch (Eds.), *Malnutrition and behavior: Critical assessment of key issues* (pp. 42–50). Lausanne, Switzerland: Nestle Foundation.

Miller, S. A. (Ed.). (1981). *Nutrition & behavior.* Philadelphia: The Franklin Institute Press.

Morgan, K. I., & Zabik, M. E. (1981). Amount and food sources of total sugar intake by children ages 5 to 12 years. *American Journal of Clinical Nutrition, 34,* 404–413.

National Diary Council (1983, March/April). Food sensitivity. *Dairy Council Digest, 54,* 7–11.

National Dairy Council (1985, July/August). Diet and behavior. *Dairy Council Digest, 56,* 19–24.

O'Banion, D., Armstrong, B., Cummings, R. A., & Stange, J. (1978). Disruptive behavior: A dietary approach. *Journal of Autism and Childhood Schizophrenia, 8,* 325–337.

Phlegar, F. L., & Phlegar, B. (1979, September). Diet and schoolchildren. *Phi Delta Kappan,* 162–165.

Pollitt, E., Garza, C., & Leibel, R. L. (1984). Nutrition and public policy. In H. W. Stevenson & A. E. Siegel (Eds.), *Child development research and social policy* (Vol. 1, pp. 421–470). Chicago: University of Chicago Press.

Pollitt, E., & Thomson, C. (1977). Protein–calorie malnutrition and behavior. A view from psychology. In R. J. Wurtman & J. J. Wurtman (Eds.), *Nutrition and the brain: Vol. 2. Control of behavior and biology of the brain in protein-calorie malnutrition* (pp. 1–27). New York: Raven Press.

Prinz, R. J., Roberts, W. A., & Hantman, E. (1980). Dietary correlates of hyperactive behavior in children. *Journal of Consulting and Clinical Psychology, 48,* 760–769.

Randolph, T. G. (1947). Allergy as a causative factor of fatigue, irritability and behavior problems of children. *Journal of Pediatrics, 31,* 560–572.

Rapp, D. (1978). Does diet affect hyperactivity? *Journal of Learning Disabilities, 11,* 56–62.

Riddle, D. B., & Prinz, R. (1984, August). *Sugar consumption in young children.* Paper presented at the Annual Convention of the American Psychological Association, Toronto.

Rimland, B. (1983). The Feingold diet: An assessment of the reviews by Mattes, by Kavale and Forness, and others. *Journal of Learning Disabilities, 16,* 331–333.

Rossetti-Ferreira, M. C. (1978). Malnutrition and mother–infant asynchrony: Slow mental development. *International Journal of Behavioral Development, 1,* 207–219.

Rubin, K. H., & Ross, H. S. (Eds.). (1982). *Peer relationships and social skills in children.* New York: Springer-Verlag.

Shantz, C. U. (1983). Social cognition. In P. H. Mussen (Ed.), *Handbook of child psychology: Vol. 3. Cognitive development* (pp. 495–556). New York: Wiley.

Silbergeld, E. K. (1981). Erythrosin B is a specific inhibitor of high affinity 3H-ouabain binding and ion transport in rat brain. *Neuropharmacology, 20,* 87–90.

Stare, F. J., Whelan, E. M., & Sheridan, M. (1980). Diet and hyperactivity: Is there a relationship? *Pediatrics, 66,* 521–525.

Stevenson, H. W., & Siegel, A. E. (Eds.). (1984). *Child development research and social policy* (Vol. 1). Chicago: University of Chicago Press.

Swanson, J. M., & Kinsbourne, M. (1979). Artificial color and hyperactive behavior. In R. M. Knights & D. J. Bakker (Eds.), *Treatment of hyperactive and learning disabled children* (pp. 131–149). Baltimore: University Park Press.

Swanson, J. M., & Kinsbourne, M. (1980). Food dyes impair performance of hyperactive children on a laboratory learning task. *Science, 207,* 1485–1487.

U.S. Senate Select Committee on Nutrition and Human Needs (1977). *Dietary Goals for the United States* (2nd. ed.). Washington, DC: U.S. Government Printing Office.

Walsh, F. (Ed.). (1982). *Normal Family Processes.* New York: Guilford Press.

Warren, J. V. (1975). Medical and toxicological issues. In *Sweeteners—Issues and uncertainties.* National Academy of Sciences Academy Forum, Fourth of a Series (pp. 36–40). Washington DC: National Academy of Sciences.

Weiss, B., Williams, J. H., Margen, S., Abrams, B., Caan, B., Citron, L. J., Cox, C., McKibben, J., Ogar, D., & Schultz, S. (1980). Behavioral responses to artificial food colors. *Science, 207,* 1487–1489.

Wender, E. H. (1980). New evidence on food additives and hyperkinesis: A critical analysis. *American Journal of Diseases of Childhood, 134,* 1122–1124.

Williams, J. I., Cram, D. M., Tausig, F. T., & Webster, E. (1978). Relative effects of drugs and diet on hyperactive behaviors: An experimental study. *Pediatrics, 61,* 811–817.

Wolraich, M., Milich, R., Stumbo, P., & Schultz, F. (1985). Effects of sucrose ingestion on the behavior of hyperactive boys. *Journal of Pediatrics, 106,* 675–682.

Wurtman, R. J. (1982). Nutrients that modify brain function. *Scientific American, 246,* 50–59.

Zeskind, P. S., Goff, D. M., & Huntington, L. (1984). Models of development. In J. Brozek & B. Schurch (Eds.), *Malnutrition and behavior: Critical assessment of key issues* (pp. 428–440). Lausanne, Switzerland: Nestle Foundation.

Communication

Karen Levine
Edward Mueller
Boston University

INTRODUCTION

In the course of becoming a communicative being, the infant–child undergoes dramatic changes. In fact, when observing a 3- month-old smiling at her mother and a 7-year-old arguing with her peers about how to be a good friend, it is difficult to imagine how the infant will ever become such a 7-year-old, or even that the 7-year-old was once such an infant. The purpose of this chapter is to discuss theory and research suggesting routes from the minimal communicativeness of infancy to the sophisticated communicative competence of middle childhood.

Intra and Interpersonal Theories of Communication

Chomsky (1965), Skinner (1957), Bruner (1983b), Snow and Gilbreath (1983), and Holzman (1984) have proposed different theories of initial communicative endowment, with different degrees of "preprogrammedness" for language. Chomsky (1965) proposed the Language Acquisition Device (LAD), an innate language-specific potential. Skinner, at the other pole, proposed no innate language-related ability. He believed language, like everything else, was learned through conditioning, with the infant's language environment as the stimulus (Skinner, 1957). Bruner, offering a kind of compromise between Skinner and Chomsky, suggests that language emerges out of the interaction between the language acquisition support system (the LASS), that is, the language and social environment created by the caregiver, and the LAD, or whatever kind of innate language potential infants may have. Snow and Gilbreath (1983), too, focused

207

on the language-acquisition support system, adding that there are many different and adequate support systems in different cultures, but that they are all able to combine with developing cognitive structures in the infant to stimulate language development. Both Bruner and Snow proposed that contingency searching (i.e., searching for responses in the environment that are contingent on the infant's action) is a vital innate cognitive structure. Holzman (1984) suggested that infants arrive with a readiness to acquire a communication system. She suggests that this readiness is another system equivalent to the innate readiness for attachment suggested by Bowlby (1969).

This question can be approached both theoretically and empirically. Theoretically, the question is what is the smallest necessary set of inborn equipment for the construction of communication? At least three innate qualities seem necessary: (1) spontaneous activity, (2) sustained attention, and (3) a tendency to repeat that which "works" (contingent repetition). The first two hypothesized innate tendencies are straightforward and clearly present and necessary; that is, the infant is attentive and active from birth as reflected in movement, visual fixation, and the like.

The third hypothesized innate quality, the infant's tendency to repeat what works, is a little more complicated. "Works" refers to that which has an effect, i.e., appears to cause change. Several studies have shown that infants do tend to repeat what causes change (Papousek, 1969 cited in Bruner, 1983a; Rovee & Rovee, 1969; Uzgiris & Hunt, 1975; Watson & Ramey, 1969), particularly if the change is very consistently contingent on the infant's actions (Watson, 1972). This third tendency is similar to Snow's (1984) and Bruner's (1983a) postulate of an innate search for contingencies.

Combining the three hypothesized givens, a typical scenario has the infant flailing his arms, watching, say, his hand, which accidently bumps a mobile that moves. As this action "worked," or caused a change, the infant will then flail again (Piaget, 1963).

Infants appear to get pleasure from effecting change. They seem to get more pleasure as they become more familiar with the element they are effecting, as evidenced by increasingly vigorous smiling and cooing after several days of experience for 10 minutes each day with a head movement contingent mobile (Watson, 1972). Whether early effective behaviors are centered around people or objects may be partly dependent on the infant's environment (interpersonal) and on his or her internal physical and psychological (intrapersonal) makeup, and on a fit between the two (Sameroff, 1975). Children with autism, for example, because of their unique intrapersonal makeup, are often more attached to objects than to people. Severely abused children, because of their unfortunate interpersonal experiences, can withdraw completely from people and become more attached to the object world.

Infants have innate physical qualities that are fundamentally socially communicative. Their relatively large eyes and forehead are thought to trigger caretaking responses in adults (Lorenz, 1943). The neonate's cry and smile are also interpreted as communicative (Harding, 1983). Thus, physically and behaviorally, the infant is incidently communicative in uniquely human ways long before he or she is intentionally communicative. Again, because infants with distorting facial deformities can learn to be competent communicators, these innate physical features do not seem to be essential to the development of communication. Infants born with severe cleft palettes seem to engage in less preverbal communicative interaction with their mothers in the first few months of life, but this may be due to maternal depression about the infants' condition (Field & Vega-Lahr, 1984).

Infants also seem to have innate or very early developing perceptual abilities that are biased towards qualities important in interaction with people. Neonates at 18 hours can distinguish tape recordings of their own cry from the cries of other infants (Martin & Clark, 1982), suggesting an innate sensitivity to subtle qualities of voice tone. Three-day-olds can distinguish their mothers' voices from voices of strangers (DeCasper & Fifer, 1980). From about 3 weeks, infants prefer to look at pictures of correctly constructed rather than scrambled faces (Fantz, 1961).

Findings from two areas of research suggest, however, that these innate perceptual skills are of less importance to the infant's communicative potential than the aforementioned three postulated innate tendencies: (a) Deaf and blind children can learn to communicate at about the same rate as normal children if their caregivers are knowledgeable about and sensitive to their handicap from early infancy (Fraiberg, 1974; McIntire, 1977; Rowland, 1984); (b) there is a great deal of evidence that infants initially percieve amodally (Stern, 1985), that is, that they do not distinguish between modes of perception. This research is based on ingenious experiments that capitialize on the fact that infants habituate to familiar stimuli. When given a choice between two stimuli, they will prefer to look at the one perceived as novel. Infants from as young as 3 weeks seem to perceive a cross-modal equivalence between corresponding stimuli in the modes of touch and sight (Meltzoff & Borton, 1979) and sight and sound (Lewcowicz & Turkewitz, 1980).

Thus, whereas infants have an innate special attunemen: to perception related to human communication, they do also initially perceive other, nonperson-produced modes of stimuli and appear to translate all modes into a general perceptual experience possessing certain flavors or rhythms that can be applied cross modally.

It seems likely, however, that innate incidently communicative qualities and person-oriented perceptual skills allow the process of communicative development to advance more quickly and under less than optimal circumstances.

Social Prototype Model

The very term *model* suggests something structural and inaccessible. Yet by "social prototypes" we mean something *meaningful and substantive*. They always consist of meanings for action with an "other." Initially, these meanings are extremely concrete and are little more than assemblies (see Stern, 1985) of the concrete commonalities of interactions, such as "When I vocalize, Mommy vocalizes." But across the first year they become increasingly general understandings of meaningful interactions. They include extractions like "If I cry, mother is likely to attend to me and comfort me" or "If I vocalize mother is likely to start a joyful tickling exchange." By 10 or 12 months, the model may be "abstract" in the sense of being composed of meanings that are by then quite "general." However out of awareness this process may be (see Bretherton, in press), the child has "concluded" that other is "good," "responsive," "entertaining," "intrusive," "ignoring," and the like. This is a major generalization by the infant from models limited to specific shared topics with their associated emotions.

The developing infant thus forms evolving prototypes of meaning based on the patterning of the common affective dimensions of his or her discrete interactive experiences with "other." This prototype is the basis for his or her motivations for and expectations of subsequent interactions with future "others."

There are three points that must be supported for this hypothesis to have validity:

1. The infant is cognitively capable of establishing something as seemingly abstract as a prototype.
2. The social prototype has an intense affective component.
3. The infant utilizes this prototype in subsequent interaction and across all domains of interaction and with a variety of partners.

There is empirical evidence that the infant does, at least at some point in the first year, develop prototypes of experience. Amodal perception as just described necessarily invokes some kind of generalized representation of perceptual experience that is a prerequisite to the formation of prototypes in memory. Kagan (1984) argues that biological maturation resulting in memory- and cognitive-capacity development renders the infant increasingly able to monitor continually incoming experience in terms of current prototypes or representations of averages of previous experience over the first year. There is empirical evidence that infants as young as 10 months at least perceive faces in terms of prototypes (Strauss, 1979).

The strong affective component of a social prototype of early interaction may develop through two related processes. The first has to do with more traditional explanations of attachment (Ainsworth, 1969; Bowlby, 1969). The caregiver is repeatedly involved in caregiving acts, such as holding and feeding, that soothe the infant and restore physiological homeostasis; and so the caregiver, through conditioning, may become associated with intense positive or negative feelings, depending on the infant–caregiver relationship.

The other source of strong affect has to do with Watson's (1972) finding that repeated interaction over many days with the same contingently responding stimulus produces increasingly vigorous smiling and cooing in the infant. As Watson pointed out, the infant's response to consistently contingent behaviors, i.e., increased smiling and cooing, is one that brings on further contingent responding in adults. Responsive adults, then, are ideal perpetuators of infants' emerging interactive tendencies. Both caregiving and repeated contingent responding probably contribute to the affective component of the social prototype.

A social prototype model is based on the premise that the developing infant continually tries to recall the prototype in subsequent interactions. Freud (1933) proposed that subsequent to the initial satisfaction of an instinct the original source of this satisfaction becomes a motivator that is henceforth incorporated into that instinct; that is, because the infant initially had his or her instinct of "making it work" satisfied interpersonally, with the caregiver he or she will attempt to recreate those interactions with subsequent environmental "interactibles," including people and things.

The healthy caregiver, too, is motivated to share meaning with the infant, for the social prototype persists throughout life. How any specific caregiver does this will likely be effected by the shape of his or her own social interactive prototype, i.e., by his or her own earliest caregiver–infant interactions, and by prototype modifications resulting from subsequent interactions, a familiar notion to both psychoanalytic theory and, more recently, to family systems theory (Framo, 1972). Intergenerational interaction prototype theory is beyond the scope of this chapter but is dealt with elsewhere (Framo, 1972; Stern, 1985).

To summarize, for the infant, the subjective experience of being understood, or sharing meaning, can be conceptualized as a locus of predictable contingency responses with a familiar other. Early interaction results in the development of a repetoire of meaning sharing that may be much of the basis for attachment. The situations in which meaning sharing takes place become increasingly complex as the infant develops physically and cognitively and his or her world expands to include elements other than the caregiver, including objects, other adults, peers, groups of peers, and people from other cultures with other "codes" for representing meaning. It seems possible that the development of more elaborate communication may be motivated by an attempt to recreate the state of sharing meaning with another person in increasingly complex situations (Dore, 1983; Stern, 1985).

INITIAL OVERVIEW OF STAGES
OF COMMUNICATIVE DEVELOPMENT

The development of communication can be viewed as a continuum from incidental communication to interaction to communication. Throughout this continuum, as the need for explicitness or concrete enactment of attachment decreases, communication becomes more symbolic. For example, a warm responsive physical environment in infancy, a blown kiss in toddlerhood, a phone call in childhood, and a letter in adulthood can potentially all serve the same communicative function. We use the word "stage" loosely, to refer to a phase in which a certain interactive or communicative style is predominant. A sketch of the stages of this continuum is given next.

1. For about the first 2 months of life, the interactive "frame" between caregiver and infant develops. This frame consists of mutual regulation of the infant's physiological homeostasis, rhythmic synchrony, and periods of joint attention in which the infant engages in spontaneous activity and the caregiver responds contingently.

2. Between about 2 and 10 months the infant's social prototype emerges and develops. This prototype is first based on the early interaction from the primitive frame and gradually develops an affective component. In this period the child normally becomes aware of self–other boundaries. In this model, the infant initially perceives in terms of discrete experiences and gradually deduces separateness of self (Stern, 1985), rather than initially perceiving the self as fused with the caregiver as in traditional psychoanalytic theory.

Extensive caregiver–infant communication in the form of "protoconversations," or alternating turns of smiling, moving, and vocalizing in periods of joint attention occurs in this period. (Bateson, 1975; Brazelton, Koslowski, & Main, 1974; Stern, 1974; Trevarthen, 1977). Caregivers also play or begin to "teach" their infants by creating repetitive predictable topics and means of communication around such activities as peekaboo (Bruner, 1983a).

Around the middle of the first year, the infant becomes very interested in the object world (Als, 1982; Trevarthen, 1977) and assimilates it to the social prototype, thus perceiving it as animistic. In this sense a social-prototype approach understands the child in normal development as having a social bias in their interaction with physical objects. In other words, they are hypothesized to treat physical objects as social more often than they treat social objects as physical.

At about 10 months clear indications of intentional communication in the form of gesture to the primary caregiver about the world become apparent (Murphy & Messer, 1977).

Toward the end of the first year infants seem to see themselves as omniscient, perhaps as a product of the social prototype; that is, they have learned that they can generally effect the social world and the object world, but they are not fully aware of the limits of their powers.

3. Around the beginning of the second year, communication in the form of words becomes possible, but the meanings of these words are somewhat idiosyn-

cratic and context based, a problem in group day care (Cazden, 1981). Peer interaction generally occurs within pairs rather than in larger groups, supporting the idea that the toddler assimilates peers to the caregiver infant social prototype. Peer communication is frequently in the semistructured form of "shared meaning" (Brenner & Mueller, 1982), which are interactions in which toddler peers create a microcosm of predictable contingent and mutually understood actions that do not rely on verbal communication.

Well-adjusted toddlers seem to be struggling with their subjective learned feelings of omniscience based on the social prototype, and objective evidence of their relative powerlessness in many domains of their daily life, including their interactions with peers, with adults who have increasingly high expectations of them, and with the powerful machine world of, for example, cars and trucks. In the first year of the toddler's life, with a responsive caregiver, most of their communicative initiations were responded to in a satsifactory and predictable way, perhaps "teaching them" that they were King or Queen in their world. The clash of the learned truth with the real world may be an important dimension of toddlerhood and an important impetus for further communicative development.

Through repeated experience of noneffectance with objects, particularly in the peer world where object possession struggle is one of the most frequent interactions (Brenner & Mueller, 1982), at some point during the second year objects may become deanimated.

In the preschool years, verbal communication with a group is possible, for language is standardized enough to be understood by old and new acquaintances within the culture of the language learned. The child is no longer limited to a familiar peer who understands a certain "shared meaning." This may again be both exciting and threatening, for the intimacy of the private communication world is lost. It is interesting that preschoolers often set up group microcosms of play from which they exclude others (Garvey, 1984), thus maintaining a version of the prototype, now extended through culturally standardized communication to a group of peers.

In the elementary school years, language becomes an objective reality separate from communication. Other communicative symbol systems such as written language and foreign languages tend to be learned in this period.

Teachers in classrooms sometimes continue to use the method of creating a communicative microcosm and teaching students through scaffolding within this microcosm.

Intergroup cross-cultural communication theoretically becomes possible as the arbitrariness of the specific language learned is realized. In fact, though, this can be quite problematic (Hartrup, 1983; Michaels, 1981).

The desire to establish and maintain close relationships within the social order of a group, in the face of increasing autonomy, continues to play an important motivating role for and function of communication.

Integration of Self–Other World:
Intentional Communication

According to most theories of communicative development, after the infant develops interactive schemata with a caregiver and with objects, he or she then becomes able to integrate the two, sometime towards the end of the first year, just before speech (Bates et al., 1977; Bruner, 1983a; Sugarman, 1984). According to Sugarman (1984), this integration is the hallmark of the most stringent definition of intentional communication, which is "actions directed toward an external object combined with actions directed toward a person" (p.28). Infants combine these actions with glances, gestures, and what Dore calls "indexicals," which are meaningful, relatively consistent vocal nonword utterances. The functions of these forms of intentional communication are many and varied and include what Bates et al. (1977) called *protoimperitives* (i.e., gesturing to an adult to do something with an object such as open a jar or bring it to the child), and *protodeclaritives* (i.e., showing an object to an adult as indicated by alternating eye contact with the adult with looking at or pointing to an object).

There is evidence that this step of integration of object and socially directed acts, with eye contact, is a genuine prerequisite to communication to speech for both normally developing children (Bates et al., 1977; Sugarman, 1984) and autistic children (Curcio, 1978; Sugarman, 1984).

Communicative Speech
and Peer Communications (the Second Year)

Communicative Speech. Around the beginning of the second year as symbolic thought becomes possible, the toddler begins to develop speech. The processes involved in this transition from preverbal to linguistic communication is currently the focus of a great deal of research (cf. Bruner, 1983a; Golinkoff & Gordon, 1983; Snow, 1984; Sugarman, 1984).

Both Dore (1983) and Stern (1985) conceived of language as initially a transitional object in Winnicott's (1965) sense of the word.

Stern (1985) portrayed the emergence of speech as both a blessing and a curse. It is a blessing in that it adds a new medium that greatly expands the range of topic through which the toddler can share meaning and thus maintain harmony with a caregiver. It is a curse in that it forces an intermediary onto all subsequent experience including social interaction. The toddler is "at the risk of losing the force and wholeness of original experience" (p. 177). This sad theory is reminiscent of the loss of a harmonious magical quality of experience in early childhood such as is portrayed for example in Peter Pan and Mary Poppins. Stern adds the hopeful note that adults can still recapture the wholeness of experience through art and poetry, immediate forms of communication outside the realm of standard language. Perhaps adults can also recapture it interpersonally when communicating intensely and nonverbally with infants, toddlers, and lovers, for example, in physical play.

Toddler Peer Communication.   A series of studies on peer relations of toddlers in groups has revealed a great deal about infant and toddler peer communication including a special communication system between peers in the second year of life (Bragg, 1983; Brenner & Mueller, 1982; Mueller & Brenner, 1977; Mueller & Lucas, 1975; Vandell, Wilson, & Buchanan, 1980). Infants and very young toddlers communicate with peers through socially directed behaviors (SDBs) (Mueller & Brenner, 1977). An SDB is a potentially social act such as a vocalization or a point, accompanied by looking at another person. From at least 12 months, toddlers who are exposed to peers on a regular basis will engage in what has been called "shared meanings" (Brenner & Mueller, 1982). These are social games made up of chains of SDBs, in which both peers show evidence of having the same "theme" in mind.

Brenner and Mueller studied peer interaction in two toddler playgroups. They observed 12 themes that were used as topics for shared meanings. Many of these themes were shared frequently and were employed by a majority of the children. Although their list of repeated shared meanings was developed from an all male playgroup, subsequent research has revealed a similar list in a female playgroup (Bragg, 1983). Indeed, the same themes appear in all studies to date, but so far all work is limited to American children. The three most common themes were "motor copy," "object exchange," and "object possession struggle."

In Brenner and Mueller's study, one playgroup began when the toddlers were 12 months old, and the other when the toddlers were 16½ months old. Effects of age and peer experience on play and communication style could thus be kept somewhat separate. In the older group, 56% of observed social interactions were in the form of shared meaning, whereas in the younger group only 36% were in the form of shared meaning. Because of the different playgroup matriculation ages, the children in both the playgroups had the same amount of peer experience. The younger group showed an increase in the amount of shared meaning interactions over the 7-month period of observation, whereas the older group had a steady amount, the same amount as the highest amount reached by the younger group. Thus, there is some evidence that communication in the form of shared meaning is not just a function of peer experience but may be a developmental phenomenon. Of course, interactions with the caregiver as well as development may be what cause this seemingly age-related qualitative change in communication style.

Formats Versus Shared Meanings.   The set of shared-meaning interactions intersects with but is not synonomous with what Bruner calls *formats* (the repeated mother–infant games discussed previously). The main difference is that in a format the adult has a sophisticated form of the game in mind, whereas the infant only needs to have a very simplified conceptualization of it. In a shared meaning both partners must have much the same understanding of the game, thus seemingly giving us an accurate appraisal of toddlers' social-representational capabilities. Another related difference is that formats generally proceed through a predictable evolution as the infant develops cognitively (Bruner, 1983a), through the clever scaffolding of the adult. A peer-shared meaning may well begin as a finished product. A well-developed caregiver–infant format, that is, one in which the child has the same conceptualization of the game as the mother, may be identical to a peer-shared meaning interaction.

A quality shared by all formats, including those in which the mother must do most of the "work," and peer-shared meanings is that they are self-contained, predictable, and repeated communication events that share many features with conversation. These features include back and forth turn taking, a relationship of each act to the previous act, and a topic that defines some acts as relevant and others as not (Bruner, 1983a). Whether formats, shared meanings, and conversation are homologous or analogous remains to be studied through longitudinal work.

The first toddler social communications generally center around objects. Object-free communication develops later (Hartup, 1983; Mueller & Lucas, 1975). This is the opposite sequence of mother–infant communicative development. There are two related plausible explanations for this difference: (1) The youngest playgroups in which toddler communication was studied were formed when the toddlers were 12 months. By that time they had all had a great deal of experience with objects and little with peers. Maybe infants reared together would develop nonobject shared meanings first; (2) the early object-free interactions with the mother may be possible because of facilitative work done by the mother that is beyond the capability of a toddler, i.e., the scaffolding. Again, it could be that children together from infancy would be so familiar with each other's communication methods that the developmental route to peer-shared meaning would be abbreviated. This issue is currently being explored by Vandell (personal communication, December, 1985) through observations of infant twins.

Why does toddler peer communication take the form of these shared meanings? This includes at least two questions: (1) What is the motivational basis of their engaging a peer in this kind of back and forth repetitive play; (2) what determines the set of specific themes that do emerge among toddlers? Only the first question will be discussed as the second is outside the scope of this chapter.

Viewed through the social-prototype model, toddlers are motivated to engage in, and clearly enjoy engaging in, positive-affect shared meanings, because through these interactions they recreate the emotionally gratifying state of sharing meaning with the caregiver; for example, in formats and in the earlier protoconversations. After repeated shared-meaning interactions with the same partner, only a slight signal on the part of either toddler can instigate the shared meaning, for the other quickly recognizes the referent (Musatti & Mueller, 1985). Giving that signal to a toddler who does not know that particular shared meaning will not result in a shared meaning. Thus, it is to the toddler's advantage to seek out the same peer with whom he or she has shared the meaning on previous occasions.

A repetoire of several mutually familiar shared meanings between two toddlers begins to look very much like friendship. In a sense the toddler has come full circle: Seeking to recreate the interactions of his or her initial attachment relationship, the toddler engages in attachment like interactions, i.e., shared meanings with a peer. Through the building blocks of these shared meanings, he or she may develop a new friendship at least for the duration of the encounter, and sometimes a new long-term attachment like relationship.

The work to date (Howes, 1983; Mueller & Lucas, 1975), however, suggests that only in some cases do the fleeting interactions develop into stable peer attachments. Toddler playgroup friendships, when they do occur, tend to be more stable than the playgroup friendships of infants or preschool children (Howes, 1983).

The Preschool Years

By the time children are of preschool age, they communicate with one another quite effectively. Mueller (1972) found that in one preschool group of 3½- to 5½-year-olds, 62% of the children's utterances were "successful," meaning that they resulted in an appropriate verbal response from the listener. Factors that determined communicative success included clarity of the utterance, clarity of reference, syntactic form of the utterance, and interspeaker distance, factors that also clearly influence communicative effectiveness in older children and adults. Thus, preschool children are generally able to adapt their communication to the listener in these important ways. Even mildly developmentally delayed preschool children adjust their message, both syntactically and semantically, according to the verbal level of their listener (Guralnick & Paul-Brown, 1986).

Between 3 and 5 years children become increasingly able to incorporate the perspective of their listener into their communications. Young 3-year-olds are able to spontaneously realize that a child who has been out of the room during a toy demonstration will not have information about that toy, and they will provide some of that information (Perner & Leekam, 1986). By the time children are almost 4 years they provide much more complete information to the child who was out of the room. In a study exploring developmental sensitivity to topic in a conversational context, children were shown pictures of people performing simple actions after an experimenter talked with them about actions or objects or people (Luszcz & Bacharach, 1983). Three-year-olds tended to speak about objects no matter what the experimenter had previously talked about with them, whereas 5-year olds' utterances about the pictures tended to be in the same domain as the experimenter's, suggesting that by 5 years children are sensitive to implicit topic cues in conversation. Whether these kinds of increases in communicative competence are due to a generally increased cognitive information-processing capacity or specific communicative development is a matter of debate (Menyuk, 1977).

Garvey (1984) found that older preschool children frequently use language with peers to distinguish the "in-group" from the "out-group" by communicating about the game to its participants. Thus, they establish and maintain solidarity with peers who are playing the game of the moment while excluding those who are not. This is reminiscent of what we hypothesized as the primary use of beginning language as it emerges out of the social prototype, i.e., to confirm attachment by sharing of meaning. One wonders if the exclusion is present in the older children's peer play as an attempt to recapture the element of complete harmony of the infant–caregiver dyadic world, which may be a part of the early social-interaction prototype.

Brown (1980) analyzed conversations between preschool children and adults. He found a continuation of the creation of microcosms of predictable conversational elements, which he calls *games* and which are reminiscent of protoconversations, formats, and shared meanings. In these games both adult and preschooler use their knowledge of the predictable structure and content of the game as an aid to understanding the other.

Elementary School Years

Structured and predictable microcosms for communication persist in teacher–child communication in the classroom in the elementary school years. Cazden (1983) reviews several studies of communication in elementary classrooms. In many of these studies (e.g., Mehan, 1979; Wertsch, 1979, all cited in Cazden, 1983), the teacher uses a "scaffolding" style of communication; that is, the teacher creates a predictable structured communicative microcosm within which the student learns to respond in a specific standard communication style. As Cazden discusses, this style is clearly reminiscent of early caregiver–infant interaction, as discussed by Snow (1977) and also by Kaye and Wells (1980), in which the caregiver leaves a placeholder in his or her monologue and interprets any infant behavior as meaningful, and then gradually "ups the ante." It is also reminiscent of Bruner's formats (Cazden, 1983) and of Brown's communication games. Thus, adult scaffolding of child communication seems to be one communication style through which information is imparted, both about the world and about communication itself, throughout early and middle childhood. In the school setting though, the scaffold may be more rigid and less dynamically fine tuned to the children's development.

Structured communication systems work only when participants have similar or potentially similar notions of what that structure is. Michaels and Cook-Gumperz (1979) did an ethnography of a racially integrated first-grade classroom with a white teacher during "sharing time" or "circle time." The white children all had a very specific style of sharing their stories of what important events had happened to them at home, and a similar notion of what constituted "an important event." The teacher had the same implicit communication structure as these white children and was thus able to understand them and to help them communicate even more effectively, through scaffolding techniques. Their shared communication style rendered this a generally sucessful and happy experience for the white children.

The black children, on the other hand, communicated within a very different although equally formulaic and predictable structure. Michaels and Cook-Gumperz provide detailed analyses of both black and white sharing-time communication structures. The white teacher was generally unable to assimilate the black children's communication structure to her schema of sharing time, nor did she accommodate her schema to their style. She seemed to believe that her role was to both teach the black children the white communication style, and to genuinely not understand the black communication style. This resulted in the black children's sharing turns becoming a frustrating experience for all concerned. Both the teacher and the black children expressed negative feelings toward the other regarding sharing time, in private interviews with Michaels and Cook-Gumperz. Thus, this study is another illustration of the relationship between interpersonal affect and communicative success.

Cazden (1983) discussed a study by a researcher who taught elementary school teachers in a black town what she had learned from observing the black children's communication styles (Heath, 1982, cited in Cazden 1983). She then suggested how the teachers could accommodate their communication schemata to the black children's styles. Once the teachers changed their communication style appropriately, the children participated much more actively in the classroom discussions than they had previously, suggesting the importance of shared communication structures within a group of diverse people.

Conflict continues to be an important function of and impetus for communication among peers at the elementary school level. Maynard (1985), in a contextualist ethnography of episodes of conflict among first graders in unsupervised reading groups, found that through communication around conflict the sociopolitical structure of the class was continually reworked. Social alliances were formed and broken and reformed, and in general seemed fluid and also varied by issue. Maynard points out that through these fluid alliances, more stable relationships may be forming. In a more experimental study, Nelson and Aboud (1985) studied conflict resolution among third- and fourth-grade friend and nonfriend pairs. In one part of the study, the children were told to discuss a social question for which they had earlier separately given conflicting responses. Friend pairs provided each other with more explanations of their own opinions than did nonfriend pairs, and they were also more critical of each other. Further, friend pairs were more likely to change their responses to more socially sophisticated levels than were nonfriend pairs, suggesting that their explanations and critisisms were productive. Thus, conflict within a friendship leads to communication around that conflict that seems to be conducive to social growth. Perhaps friend pairs were motivated to engage in more self-explanation than were nonfriend pairs, because of their desire to create a state of shared understanding and thus maintain the harmony of their friendship. Thus the tight weave of communicative development and affective elements of relationship persists.

CONCLUSION

Elementary schoolchildren have come a long way communicatively since their neonate days of synchronous head movements with adults, and nursing "diaglogues." We end with an anecdote that illustrates how the sophisticated communication system of the older child can operate as his or her attachment medium.

The second author was in an airplane seated behind a 7-year-old boy and his father. Before take off the boy was playing happily with his airplane toys. When the plane began to taxi forward the boy broke into a shower of questions: "Daddy, how high are we going? How are the wings attached? Where do they put the gas in?" The father responded calmly and informatively to each question, which seemed to calm his son. As the plane settled at its steady flying altitude and the seatbelt sign went off, the boy returned to his play. When the plane began its landing the questions resumed: "Daddy, How high are we now? How are the wings attached? Where will they put the gas in?"

The 7-year-old at a time of stress seemed to be reassured through this predictable communicative interaction, much as the infant would be reassured with hugs.

ACKNOWLEDGMENT

The preparation of this chapter was supported by the John D. and Catherine T. MacArthur Foundation.

REFERENCES

Ainsworth, M. D. S. (1969). Object relations, dependency and attachment: A theoretical review of the infant–mother relationship. *Child Development, 40,* 969–1026.

Als, H. (1982). The unfolding of behavioral organization. In E. Tronick (Ed.), *Social interchange in infancy* (pp. 125–160). Baltimore: University Park Press.

Bates, E., Benigni, L., Bretherton, I., Camaioni, L., & Volterra, V. (1977). From gesture to the first word: On cognitive and social prerequisites. In M. Lewis & L. A. Rosenblum (Eds.), *Interaction, conversation and the development of language* (pp. 247–307). New York: Wiley.

Bateson, M. C. (1975). Mother–infant exchanges: The epigenesis of conversation interaction. *Annals of the New York Academy of Science,* 101–113.

Bowlby, J. (1969). *Attachment and loss: Vol. 3. Loss: Sadness and depression.* New York: Basic Books.

Bragg, C. F. (1983, April). *Before "shared meaning": The elicitation and maintenance of social themes among toddlers.* Paper presented at the 50th Biennial Meeting of the Society for Research in Child Development, Detroit.

Brazelton, T. B., Koslowski, B., & Main, M. (1974). The origins of reciprocity: The early mother–infant interaction. In M. Lewis & L. A. Rosen (Eds.), *The effect of the infant on its caregiver* (pp. 49–76). New York: Wiley.

Brenner, J., & Mueller, E. (1982). Shared meaning in boy toddlers' peer relations. *Child Development, 53,* 380–391.

Bretherton, I. (in press). New perspectives on attachment relations in infancy: Security, communication and internal working models. In J. Osofsky (Ed.), *Handbook of infant relations* (2nd ed.). New York: Wiley.

Brown, R. (1980). The maintenance of conversation. In D. R. Olson (Ed.), *The social foundations of language and thought: Essays in honor of Jerome S. Bruner* (pp. 187–210). New York: W. W. Norton.

Bruner, J. S. (1983a). *Child's talk: Learning to use language.* New York: W. W. Norton.

Bruner, J. S. (1983b). The acquisition of pragmatic commitments. In R. M. Golinkoff (Ed.), *The transition from prelinguistic to linguistic communication* (pp. 27–42). Hillsdale, NJ: Lawrence Earlbaum Associates.

Cazden, C. B. (Ed.). (1981). *Language in early childhood education (rev. ed.).* Washington, DC: National Association for the Education of Young Children.

Cazden, C. B. (1983). Peekaboo as an instructional model: Discourse development at home and at school. In B. Bain (Ed.), *The sociogenesis of language and human conduct* (pp. 33–58). New York: Plenum.

Chomsky, N. (1965). *Aspects of a theory of syntax.* Cambridge, MA: MIT Press.

Curcio, F. (1978). Sensorimotor functioning and communication in mute autistic children. *Journal of Autism and Childhood Schizophrenia, 8,* 281–293.

DeCasper, A. J., & Fifer, W. P. (1980). Of human bonding: Newborns prefer their mothers' voices. *Science, 208,* 1174–1176.

Dore, J. (1983). Feeling, form, and intention in the baby's transition to language. In R. M. Golinkoff (Ed.), *The transition from prelinguistic to linguistic communication* (pp. 167–190). Hillsdale, NJ: Lawrence Erlbaum Associates.

Fantz, R. L. (1961). The origin of form perception. *Scientific American, 204,* 66–73.

Field, T. M., & Vega-Lahr, N. (1984). Early Interactions between infants with cranio-facial anomalies and their mothers. *Infant Behavior and Development, 7,* 527–530.

Fraiberg, S. (1974). Blind infants and their mothers: An examination of the sign system. In M. Lewis & L. A. Rosen (Eds.), *The effect of the infant on its caregiver* (pp. 215–232). New York: Wiley.

Framo, J. (1972). Symptoms from a family transactional viewpoint. In C. Saper & H. S. Kaplan (Eds.), *Progress in group and family therapy.* New York: Brunner Mazel.

Freud, S. (1933). *New introductory lectures on psychoanalysis.* New York: Wiley.

Garvey, C. (1984). *Children's talk.* Cambridge, MA: Harvard University Press.

Golinkoff, R. M., & Gordon, L. (1983). In the beginning was the word: A history of the study of language acquisition. In R. M. Golinkoff (Ed.), *The transition from prelinguistic to linguistic communication* (pp. 1–25). Hillsdale, NJ: Lawrence Erlbaum Associates.

Guralnick, M. J., & Paul-Brown, D. (1986). Communicative interactions of mildly delayed and normally developing preschool children—effects of listener's developmental level. *Journal of Speech and Hearing Research, 29,* 2–10.

Harding, C. G. (1983). Setting the stage for language acquisition: Communication development in the first year. In R. M. Golinkoff (Ed.), *The transition from prelinguistic to linguistic communication* (pp. 93–113). Hillsdale, NJ: Lawrence Erlbaum Associates.

Hartup, W. W. (1983). Peer relations. In E. M. Hetherington (Ed.), P. H. Mussen (series Ed.), *Handbook of child psychology: Vol. 4. Socialization, personality and social development* (pp. 103–196). New York: Wiley.

Heath, S. B. (1982). Questioning at home and at school. In G. Spindler (Ed.), *The ethnography of schooling: Educational anthropology in action* (pp. 102–131). New York: Holt, Rinehart, & Winston.

Holzman, M. (1984). Evidence for a reciprocal model of language development. *Journal of Psycholinguistic Research, 13*(2), 119–146.

Howes, C. (1983). Patterns of friendship. *Child Development, 54*, 1041–1053.

Kagan, J. (1984). *The nature of the child.* New York: Basic Books.

Kaye, K., & Wells, A. J. (1980). Mothers juggling and the burst–pause pattern in neonatal feeding. *Infant Behavior and Development, 3*, 29–46.

Lewcowicz, D. J., & Turkewitz, G. (1980). Crossmodal equivalence in early infancy: Audio-visual intensity matching. *Developmental Psychology, 16*, 597–607.

Lorenz, (1943). Die angebornen Formen moglicher Erfahrung. *Zeitschrift fur Tierpsychologie, 5*, 233–409.

Luszcz, M. A., & Bacharach, V. R. (1983). The emergence of communicative competence: Detection of conversational topics. *Journal of Child Language, 10*, 623–637.

Martin, G. B., & Clark, R. D., (1982). Distress crying in neonates: Species and peer specificity. *Developmental Psychology, 18*, 3–9.

Maynard, D. W. (1985). On the functions of social conflict among children. *American Sociological Review, 50*, 207–223.

McIntire M., (1977). The acquisition of A.S.L. hand configurations. *Sign Language Studies, 16*, 247–266.

Mehan, H. (1979). *Learning lessons.* Cambridge, MA: Harvard University Press.

Meltzoff, A. N., & Borton, W. (1979). Intermodal matching by human neonates. *Nature, 282*, 403–404.

Menyuk, P. (1977). *Language and maturation.* Cambridge, MA: MIT Press.

Michaels, S. (1981). "Sharing time": Children's narrative styles and differential access to literacy. *Language in Society, 10*, 423–442.

Michaels, S., & Cook-Gumperz, J. (1979). *A study of sharing time with first grade students: Discourse narratives in the classroom.* Berkely, CA: Berkeley Linguistics Society.

Mueller, E. (1972). The maintenance of verbal exchanges between young children. *Child Development, 43*, 930–938.

Mueller, E., & Brenner, J. (1977). The growth of social interaction in a toddler playgroup: The role of peer experience. *Child Development, 48*, 854–861.

Mueller, E., & Lucas, T. (1975). A developmental analysis of peer interaction among toddlers. In M. Lewis & L. A. Rosenblum (Eds.), *Friendship and peer relations* (pp. 223–257). New York: Wiley.

Murphy, C. M., & Messer, D. J. (1977). Mothers, infants and pointing: A study of gesture. In H. R. Schaffer (Ed.), *Studies in mother–infant interaction* (pp. 325–354). London: Academic Press.

Musatti T., & Mueller E. (1985). Expressions of representational growth in toddlers' peer communication. *Social Cognition, 3*, 383–399.

Nelson, K., & Aboud, F. E. (1985). The resolution of social conflict between friends. *Child Development, 56*, 1009–1017.

Papousek, H. (1969). *Elaborations of conditioned head-turning.* Paper presented at the symposium on Learning of Human Infants, London.

Perner, J., & Leekam, S. R. (1986). Belief and quantity: Three-year olds' adaption to listener's knowledge. *Journal of Child Language, 13*, 305–315.

Piaget, J. (1963). *The origins of intelligence in children.* New York: W. W. Norton.

Rovee, K., & Rovee, D. (1969). Conjugate reinforcement of infant exploratory behavior. *Journal of Experimental Child Psychology, 8*, 33–39.

Rowland, C. (1984). Preverbal communication of blind infants and their mothers. *Journal of Visual Impairment and Blindness, 78*(7), 296–302.

Sameroff, A. (1975). Early influences on development: Fact or fancy? *Merrill–Palmer Quarterly,* 267–294.

Skinner, B. F. (1957). *Verbal behavior.* Englewood Cliffs, NJ: Prentice–Hall.

Snow, C. E. (1977). The development of conversation between mothers and babies. *Journal of Child Language, 4*, 1–22.

Snow, C. E. (1984). Parent–child interaction and the development of communicative ability. In R. L. Schiefelbusch & J. Pickar (Eds.), *The acquisition of communicative competence* (pp. 70–107). Baltimore: University Park Press.

Snow, C. E., & Gilbreath, B. J. (1983). Explaining transitions. In R. M. Golinkoff (Ed.), *The transition from prelinguistic to linguistic communication* (pp. 281–296). Hillsdale, NJ: Lawrence Erlbaum Associates.

Stern, D. N. (1974). The goal and structure of mother–infant play. *Journal of American Academy of Child Psychiatry, 13*, 402–421.

Stern, D. N. (1985). *The interpersonal world of the infant: A view from psychoanalysis and developmental psychology.* New York: Basic Books.

Strauss, M. S. (1979). Abstraction of prototypical information by adults in ten-month-old infants. *Journal of Experimental Psychology: Human Learning and Memory, 5*, 618–632.

Sugarman, S. (1984). Parent–child interaction and the development of communicative ability. In R. Scheifelbush & J. Pickar (Eds.), *The acquisition of communicative competence* (pp. 23–67). Baltimore: University Park Press.

Trevarthen, C. (1977). Descriptive analyses of infant communicative behavior. In H. R. Schaffer (Ed.), *Studies in mother–infant interaction* (pp. 227–270). New York: Academic Press.

Uzgiris, I. C., & Hunt, J. M. V. (1975). *Assessment in infancy: Ordinal scales of psychological development.* Urbana: University of Illinois Press.

Vandell, D., Wilson, K., & Buchanan, N. (1980). Peer interaction in the first year of life: An examination of its structure, content, and sensitivity to toys. *Child Development, 51*, 481–488.

Watson, J. (1972). Smiling, cooing, and "The Game." *Merrill–Palmer Quarterly,* 323–340.

Watson, J., & Ramey, C. (1969, March). *Reactions to response-contingent stimulation in early infancy.* Revision of paper presented at biennial meeting of the Society for Research in Child Development, Santa Monica, CA.

Wertsch, J. V. (1979). From social interaction to higher psychological processes: A clarification and application of Vygotsky's theory. *Human Development, 22*, 1–22.

Winnicott, D. W. (1965). *The maturational processes and the facilitating environment.* New York: International Universities Press.

Individual Differences and Socialization

11

Walter Emmerich
Educational Testing Service

INTRODUCTION

Background

How does the study of individual differences among children contribute to an understanding of the socialization process? The standard answer of a generation ago went something like this: "The young child's behaviors are largely unformed and malleable, and behavioral variations among socializing agents, especially parents, result in behavioral differences among children, say, in aggression or sex typing. The tasks of research are to identify the patterns or dimensions of socializing behaviors and to establish and explain their relationships with individual differences among children." This treatment of individual differences, as the "dependent variable," came under increased criticism during the late 1960s (e.g., Bell, 1968; Kohlberg, 1969), and to this day there remains a lively interest in redefining the role of individual differences in socialization (Maccoby, 1984).

An unmistakable trend has been the emphasis on behavioral differences among children as dynamic influences on the socialization process. An important implication is that the efforts of socializing agents are elicited, organized, and guided by existing or emerging behavioral tendencies that vary from child to child. Stating the matter in this way may still jar a bit because of the reversal of figure and ground: Features of the child's behavior that might be the products of experience are taken as givens, to be built on or otherwise reckoned with by socializing agents.

For this idea to work, individual differences in behavior cannot disappear in

225

the flux of situational variations. Mischel (1968) has raised our consciousness of the power of situational factors in behavior, although he does not appear to have called for abandoning the analysis of individual differences (Mischel, 1984). Nevertheless, radical situationism has been a definite undercurrent that has led some to doubt any but the weakest stance on the role of individual differences in socialization. In contrast, we present concepts and some of the evidence suggesting that individual differences among children markedly influence socialization. Some of the material covered in this chapter suggests that socialization is influenced by individual differences in behavior rooted in constitutional or maturational factors. In an equally important sense, however, social cognition, social interaction, and social control are seen as central to the socialization process, especially with regard to how socializing agents (and the child) perceive the child's behavioral attributes and respond to them.

Aims

Two major stances on the role of individual differences in socialization are examined in this chapter. The first is cognitive developmental, and the discussion of this position draws on Kohlberg's (1969) formulation. For reasons that become apparent, this position is referred to as the moderate stance on the role of individual differences in socialization, a characterization that also seems to fit much of the recent literature on the development of social cognition (Shantz, 1983). The second position is in the tradition of differential psychology and is referred to as the strong stance. Bell's (1968) reinterpretation of the direction of effects in socialization provided a major impetus for recent thinking about individual differences in the strong sense, and we consider some of its implications, giving special attention to the concept of adaptivity. In addition to examining the two positions in their own terms, a framework that articulates the two stances (McCall, 1981) is discussed and used to outline possible integrative processes in socialization during early and middle childhood.

Regarding the scope of the presentation, we refer primarily to individual differences within a population rather than to group or population differences. Although reciprocal influences are considered, relatively little attention is given to the study of evolving interaction patterns in the context of the family (e.g., Lerner & Spanier, 1978; Patterson, 1982). These dynamics are highly relevant for the socialization process (Maccoby, 1984), but extracting individual-difference measures from them poses issues not addressed here. The discussion of integrative processes emphasizes relationships between children and socializing agents as well as the child's coordinating capacities, whereas little attention is given here to relationships between the individual and the group. Finally, the presentation moves rather freely among different behavioral domains, such as social cognition, intelligence, and personality, and does so without qualifying the argument in relation to the behavior domain.

THE MODERATE STANCE

Universals

In this view (Kohlberg, 1969), socialization is marked by sequential progressions through developmentally ordered milestones or steps. The steps are defined in terms of the ways that children understand and structure their social experiences. These structures are related to broader (Piagetian) constructions, and they are said to arise from the child's interactions with the environment. Each step is believed to channel the child's competency motives, behavioral proclivities (e.g., imitation), and affective-evaluational processes. The steps that occur during infancy and childhood are universal in the sense that, sooner or later, most children will attain all of them. Moreover, an attainment is likely to have dynamic influences on socializing agents (Maccoby, 1984). The question addressed here is whether the same can be said regarding individual differences in the rates of attainment.

Individual Differences

At those ages when some but not most children have attained a particular step, it is meaningful to consider individual differences in terms of rate of movement in attaining that step. But at the age when most children have attained the step, individual differences related to that step have largely disappeared, and individual differences pertaining to the qualitatively distinct features of the next step in the sequence begin to emerge. Thus, for any step in a socialization sequence, there is a delimited age range within which the step-related array of individual differences in rate-of-attainment can be of significance for the socialization process.

Interaction

If individual differences in rate are primarily maturational; socializing agents need only ensure that the quality of the child's social environment does not fall below some minimum level. However, Kohlberg's emphasis on interaction suggests that individual differences in rate are influenced by variations in environmental quality above the minimum. Environmental quality is signified by the degree of match between the child's emerging step within a sequence and the agent's socializing efforts. If the socializing agent is in tune with the child's emerging construction of the social world, it becomes possible to accelerate the child's socialization by stimulating the child to think in terms of that emerging construction. On the other hand, less than fine tuning should slow the rate, and gross mismatches should further depress the rate.

An element of reciprocity is involved. In order to provide an optimal match, the socializing agent would need to understand the child's current developmental status (rate and breadth) in relation to the next step in the sequence and skillfully translate such understandings into stimulating efforts. However, the reciprocal relationship does not influence the direction of the child's behavioral development, and it is for this reason that a cognitive-developmental formulation takes only a moderate stance on the role of individual differences. Specifically, according to this view, the step-related individual differences eventually disappear rather than becoming fixed as differential traits. Also, the child's passage through the socialization sequence is assured as long as mismatching is not overly severe or prolonged.

When a socialization sequence involves multiple steps, parents and other socializing agents must somehow recalibrate in relation to each successive step. We know rather little about how such processes operate, in part because of ambiguities that remain in pinning down the sequences. Students of social cognition and its development have been caught up in the search for universal steps rather than tracking individual differences in rate. This is understandable, but we lack tests of the conjecture, arising from the interaction assumption, that the quality of the matches provided by socializing agents influence individual differences in rates of passage through socialization sequences.

Under certain conditions it might be possible to test this conjecture. Subjects would be selected so that the matches of socializing agents generally meet at least minimum quality levels. (This restriction is required to eliminate the possibility that the slowest observed rates are due to environmentally induced disruptions of maturational timetables.) Measures would need to be carefully constructed to gauge match–mismatch between the agent's responses to the child and the child's social understandings. Independent assessments would measure individual differences among the children in their rates of change toward the common step, perhaps using an age-of-attainment index. Given these conditions, the interaction position predicts that quality of match and rate of development will be positively correlated, and it becomes plausible to infer that the direction of influence is from the former to the latter.

Maturation

In the event that naturalistic studies were to provide little support for the cognitive-developmental assumption on interaction, attention would probably shift to the biological underpinnings of individual differences in rates of passage through socialization sequences. The cognitive-developmental approach would adopt a maturationist stance on the role of individual differences, and the prescription for optimal socialization would be something like the following: "Yes, by all means ensure that the child's environment meets at least minimum quality standards, but beyond that, learn to live with the child's particular rates of development and be wary of acceleration programs." Research on individual differences would concentrate on establishing more precisely what is meant by minimum environmental quality for each step, tracking the possible psychopathological consequences of environmental failures in meeting the minimum quality criteria, and perhaps designing therapies to ameliorate such consequences.

Of course, unresolved questions regarding interaction and maturation within the cognitive-developmental approach bear only on that type of individual-difference variability that emerges during a certain age period, rises to a maximum over time, and then diminishes as most children attain the developmental step. Unresolved questions regarding the influences of environmental and biological factors on the development of enduring individual differences lie outside the purview of the cognitive-developmental approach to socialization, at least in its present form.

THE STRONG STANCE

The strong stance emphasizes the development of individual differences in enduring (stable) behavioral traits, although no broad consensus has emerged regarding the nature and number of fundamental traits. What we do have are criteria for establishing the existence of individual differences in the strong sense: whether the age of origin can be pinned down; whether the attribute does in fact stabilize, and when; whether stability increases with age; and, whether the attribute's pattern of correlations with independent measures provide evidence for construct validity. In the discussion that follows, we consider some ramifications of these and related criteria.

Quantitative Measurement

Whatever its content, a behavioral attribute is conceptualized in quantitative terms, such as frequency, intensity, or extensity. Measurement operations assign quantitative values to individuals, rather than using qualitative or semiquantitative indexes to locate individuals within a developmental sequence. Absolute measurement serves as an ideal even though, for a variety of reasons, actual measurement operations and data analyses rarely meet the requirements of absolute measurement.

Tracing Origins

A sample's mean on the attribute typically serves as the reference norm for considering the array of individual differences. Because an initial period of rapid growth is likely, the reference norm (mean) is ordinarily expected to shift developmentally to some limit defined by the relatively flat curve after the major period of growth. Indeed, it is important to know the particular developmental function form for an attribute (Wohlwill, 1973) prior to beginning the search for that age when stable individual differences begin to emerge. At the very least, the age of origin (in the individual-difference sense) will be somewhat later than that age when the attribute first becomes detectable in the population. This restriction occurs because near-zero base rates generally are too low to yield reliable measurement (internal consistency).

The traditional expectation is that the ordering of individual differences on the attribute will begin to stabilize at that age when reliable measurement becomes possible. However, cumulating evidence for the instability of intelligence prior to early childhood has cast doubt on the traditional assumption that individual differences begin to stabilize at the youngest age that reliable measurement is possible (McCall, 1981).

McCall has offered a plausible explanation for this state of affairs. A distinction is drawn between two broad phases in the growth of intelligence (McCall, 1981; Scarr-Salapatek, 1976). During the first phase, canalization ensures that most children will proceed along a common (species-typical) developmental pathway. The canalization process is sufficiently powerful to rapidly correct individual fluctuations from the developmental trajectory, resulting in successions of different rank orderings of individuals on the attribute (instability). During the second phase, however, after most children have attained the rudimentary species-typical forms of intelligence, the canalization process loses its grip, and individual differences in intelligence begin to stabilize. Consequently, the search for the origins of individual differences in the strong sense needs to be shifted well beyond the youngest age that reliable measurement becomes possible.

One counterargument is as follows. McCall has applied his two-phase scheme not to the development of a single quantifiable attribute or component of intelligence, but rather to a broad construct, that of general intelligence. Indeed, his distinction between the two phases is grounded in strong evidence for progressions through qualitatively distinct organizations of intelligence during the first phase (McCall, 1981). Such reorganizations of the meaning of intelligence signify discontinuity in the attributes being measured, and it is reasonable to suppose that sharp developmental discontinuities will be accompanied by instability of individual differences. However, if we were to determine the separate developmental function form for each of the attributes contained in measures of general intelligence, thereby eliminating discontinuities in measurement, the origins of stable individual differences on the separate components could be "moved back" to the youngest age for which measurement is reliable.

This counterargument is instructive because it illustrates the extent to which the strong stance ultimately depends on quantitative measurement. And yet the reduction strategy that it suggests may not actually enable the investigator to circumvent McCall's central point. Canalization may occur quite generally during the period of rapid attribute growth. If so, then even a component of intelligence (and perhaps of any behavioral construct) that is measured similarly at each age would yield stability patterns that conform to the two-phase scheme. We return to this point later in the discussion.

Influences on Stability

The first phase in McCall's scheme is primarily under the control of species-typical genetic programs. During the second phase, however, the emergence and stabilization of individual differences may be controlled by biological or by environmental influences, or, as seems likely, by some combination. As just one example, a different kind of genetic program, one that varies among individuals, might get switched on at the beginning of the second phase (Plomin, 1983). Then, as the child develops increasing awareness of the self's needs, abilities, interests, and vulnerabilities, the child would increasingly select those environments (niches) that are most suitable (Scarr & McCartney, 1983). As a result, individual differences on a given attribute should stabilize increasingly with age during the second phase.

This example illustrates how the strong stance on individual differences can generate hypotheses on intraindividual integrative processes. Specifically, the child would develop knowledge regarding the self's traits, come to understand the opportunity structure in the environment, and coordinate these kinds of information when evaluating and making environmental selections. Whether and when children make these coordinations remains to be determined, but the research evidence suggests that the process may be under way by middle childhood (Shantz, 1983).

A related possibility is that individual differences tend to become magnified over time through differential positive feedback (Wohlwill, 1980). To illustrate, in exercising his or her intellectual ability, a child of relatively high ability would be in a better position to exploit opportunities for further intellectual stimulation and growth than would a child of relatively low ability. Increases in stability with age would occur even when the environment remains reasonably constant over time. On the other hand, compensatory feedback could also operate to elevate the ability levels of children of relatively low ability. This might occur, for example, as the result of a successful intervention program. Individual-difference variability in the overall population would be reduced, perhaps thereby attenuating the stability correlations, although the positive differential feedback process would still be expected to be the more pervasive influence in the general population (Wohlwill, 1980).

Dimensionality

The strong stance has also emphasized the formation and development of individual differences on broad dimensions, often defined by patterns of covariation among conceptually related attributes (Baltes, Reese, & Nesselroade, 1977; Emmerich, 1968; Moss & Susman, 1980; Wohlwill, 1973). Several recent trends in this tradition are of special relevance for socialization. First, there has been a tendency to move the search for coherent personality structures down the age scale, illustrated by recent work on the attachment construct (Sroufe & Waters, 1977) and on temperament (Buss & Plomin, 1984; Laosa, 1985; Matheny, Wilson, & Nuss, 1984; Rothbart & Derryberry, 1981). We already have a reasonably good understanding of the dimensionality of the child's social behavior during the preschool period, and the new work on the earlier age periods offers the promise of making it possible to trace the dimensionality of social behavior from infancy through the preschool period.

There has also been a revitalization of interest in viewing early-formed dispositional tendencies as master traits, such as ego control, that influence the subsequent course of the child's development and socialization experiences (Block, 1982; Block & Block, 1980; Lerner & Lerner, 1983; Sroufe, 1983). Because this approach uses measurement operations that take account of variations in the behavioral manifestations of master traits, it can provide continuity of measurement across contexts and developmental periods, consistent with the basic assumptions of the strong stance.

A third trend has been to consider how early-formed individual differences influence the developmental pathway taken by the child (Block, 1971; Fischer & Silvern, 1985; Maccoby, 1984). The nature and number of potential developmental pathways will depend on the nature and number of postulated dimensions as well as how (and when) the dimensions are said to intersect to define personality classifications (Emmerich, 1968).

The concept of alternative pathways has been worked out in some detail for the preschool years (Emmerich, 1971, 1977a, b; Emmerich, Cocking, & Sigel, 1979). In this approach, the child's behaviors are comprehensively measured within one or more natural settings, such as free play. The measured attributes are then composited to form a number of social-emotional constructs such as Cooperative, Withdrawn, and Hostile–Defiant, and a number of task-oriented constructs such as Gross Motor Activity, Cognitive Activity, and Autonomous Achievement. Each of the behavioral constructs has a certain location within a three-dimensional superstructure, defined by Introversion–Extroversion, Love–Hostility, and Task orientation (Schaefer, 1971). Using a spherical model, the behavioral constructs can be mapped onto the sphere's surface. When that is done, the social-emotional constructs are ordered as a circumplex around the sphere's equator, and the task-oriented constructs are located closer to one of the poles.

The concept of differential pathways is introduced as follows (Emmerich, 1971, 1977a). By determining a child's scores on the various behavioral constructs, it becomes possible to "locate" the child's current position on the sphere's surface. From that position, the child's baseline, it is possible for the child to remain at about the same location (behavioral consistency) or for the child to "move" away from the baseline position in any of a number of directions on the surface of the sphere (behavioral change). Each direction away from the child's current baseline defines a potential gradient for behavioral change (Foa, 1968), and the actual gradient followed by a particular child describes that child's developmental pathway. For example, a child (or subgroup) might "move" along the circumplex-ordered constructs, say from Withdrawn to Submissive to Cooperative, whereas another child (or subgroup) might "move" in the reverse direction, as has been found for a sample of at-risk children between early and middle childhood (Kohn, 1977).

ADAPTIVITY

Given that individual differences (in the strong sense) emerge, stabilize, and become organized as structures, the question of their significance for socializing agents remains to be considered. An important bridging concept has been that of adaptivity. In general, socializing agents attempt to engage the child's adaptive responses and to ameliorate the child's maladaptive responses. However, this broad prescription can mean different things on different occasions. There are times when socializing agents attempt to induce children to adapt to situational requirements without giving special attention to individual differences. At other times the situational requirements are salient, but the socializing agent will also take account of individual differences, say, in adaptational style (temperament). On still other occasions the agent will attend primarily to the child's individuality, perhaps even modifying situational requirements in response to individual differences. The discussion that follows illustrates how individual differences bear on these distinctive socialization tasks during early childhood.

Adapting to the Situation

When situational requirements predominate, socializing agents attempt to elicit child behaviors that are "adaptive" in the sense that they are situationally relevant and fitting. Nevertheless, the strong stance implies that, within rather broad limits, consistent individual differences will be manifested even when children are adapting to situation-specific demands (Scarr & McCartney, 1983).

The point is illustrated by certain results from a study of nursery school children's behaviors in each of two contexts (Emmerich, 1977b). One of the contexts was the usual unstructured classroom free-play situation. The other was a teacher-directed small group session, held outside of the regular classroom, typically in groups of four children. During the small-group sessions teachers carried out lesson plans designed to engage a variety of cognitive processes. Throughout a semester, eight boys and eight girls from working-class and middle-class backgrounds were observed and rated repeatedly in the two settings. The data were reduced to the social-emotional and task-oriented constructs mentioned earlier. Behavioral changes during the semester were determined by deriving separate scores on each construct for the first and second halves of the semester.

The children generally exhibited more positive social behaviors during free play than during the small-group sessions. For example, they were significantly more affiliative with peers during free play than in the small groups. This and related situational differences in social behavior were not surprising in view of the fact that the small-group sessions were relatively formal instructional contexts. Nevertheless, the mean of the six individual consistency correlations among the two contexts and the two age periods was .56 on the measure of affiliation with peers, and comparable consistency correlations were found on a number of related social-emotional measures.

With regard to task orientation, during the course of the semester Cognitive Activity increased significantly more rapidly within the small-group context than within the free-play context. For a variety of other activity measures, however, there were decreases over time within small groups but not within free play. Here we see evidence for increased adaptation over time in relation to the specific situational demands of the small-group sessions. And yet the mean individual consistency correlation among the contexts and age periods for Cognitive Activity was .71.

Mutual Adaptation

When socializing agents attend simultaneously to situational requirements and to the child's adaptive style (temperament), "adaptivity" takes on a different meaning, that of "goodness-of-fit" between socializing efforts and individual differences (Lerner & Lerner, 1983; Thomas & Chess, 1977, 1980). Adaptation is said to occur when the child's temperamental characteristics match situational demands, whereas adaptation is said to be jeopardized to the extent that mismatches occur. For example, if the mother expects rhythmicity in biological functioning, or low distractibility, but the child's temperamental tendencies are otherwise, a situation arises that can readily evolve maladaptively. Because temperamental characteristics are multidimensional, multivariate goodness-of-fit scores would be derived within each socializing context. And because the child will encounter situations that do not match with the child's temperamental profile, all children can be expected to experience mismatches in the course of development.

This approach suggests that the child's adaptations, measured contextually in terms of goodness-of-fit, can be composited to form a master trait measure of "adaptability." The individual's match–mismatch experiences may accumulate across contexts and developmental periods, producing stable individual differences in adaptability. However, this formulation also emphasizes the potential for raising an individual's level of adaptability by means of interventions designed to enhance self-regulatory processes (Bandura, 1982; Lerner & Lerner, 1983). This possible link between the development of self-regulation and the master trait of adaptability illustrates once again how the strong stance can generate hypotheses on intraindividual integrative processes in socialization.

Note that this particular approach does not (and perhaps cannot) take a strong stance on the direct role of temperament in socialization. Lerner & Lerner (1983) themselves mention that temperament by situation interactions may call for modifying the usual reliability criteria when measuring temperament. But there are problems in supposing that both the temperament measures and the composite measure of adaptability stabilize in the course of development. Because goodness-of-fit is said to be situation specific, the stable temperament measures would be expected to be uncorrelated with the stable measure of adaptability. But if that were the case, temperament might directly influence socialization, independent of goodness-of-fit. Alternatively, if the multiple correlation between the measures of temperament and the composite measure of adaptability were to be moderate to high, we would begin to wonder whether the latter measure has discriminant validity when compared to the temperament measures, scored as "main effects" across situations.

Here we face a basic conceptual dilemma. Because adaptability is conceptualized as an immediately occurring derivative of any temperament by situation transaction, it becomes unlikely that the adaptability measure, on the one hand, and the underlying temperament measures, on the other, can *both* be individual-difference traits in the strong sense, at least at the same point in time. Although Lerner and Lerner (1983) appeared to be placing their bets on the master trait of adaptability, the possibility that temperament stabilizes in the course of development is also receiving increased research attention (Buss & Plomin, 1984; Laosa, 1985; Matheny, Wilson, & Nuss, 1984). Resolution of this dilemma will depend on which type of construct best meets the usual criteria for establishing the existence of individual differences in the strong sense.

Adapting to the Child

The child's individuality can also alter the situational demands that the child experiences. For example, Buss and Plomin (1984) suggest that temperamental differences with regard to activity, sociality, and emotionality can influence the child's selections among alternative environments, change the course of a social interaction, and/or modify an environment's impact on the child's behavior. Because children are limited in their resources and capacities to modify their environments, socializing agents who are sensitive, say, to the child's temperament, may attempt to alter the child's environment accordingly. In the extreme, of course, such efforts could be maladaptive (e.g., overprotective). And yet there is evidence that socializing agents (parents) tend to believe that their active

efforts to modify the child's situation, when successful, do have adaptive consequences (Emmerich, 1969).

The influence of the child's individuality on socializing agents can be quite
striking. As a case in point, we consider selected findings from a study of the
influences of individual differences among preschool children on their teachers'
beliefs regarding effective teaching techniques (Emmerich, 1973). Thirty-five
teachers, most from Head Start programs, rated each child in their respective
classrooms on the efficacy of each of 15 different teaching techniques in fostering the child's learning (4-point scales). A question posed by the study was
whether individual differences in cognitive functioning, measured prior to the
beginning of the school year, would subsequently influence the teachers' judgments on the differential effectiveness of the various teaching techniques. One of
the instruments used was the Caldwell Preschool Inventory (Shipman, 1971), a
broad-based test of perceptual-motor, verbal, and quantitative skills. It was
presumed that individual differences on these skills would be quite stable
throughout the preschool year, providing the teacher with a steady stream of
reliable information as the children's differential cognitive skills became apparent in the classroom context. (In support of this presumption, the Preschool
Inventory measure correlated .63 with the same measure taken about a year
later.)

Based on composite scores on the Preschool Inventory prior to school entry,
the children were classified into one of three levels of cognitive functioning:
High ($N = 122$); Medium ($N = 118$); Low ($N = 123$). After correcting the
teachers' efficacy ratings for individual differences among the teachers, mean
teacher ratings for each of the 15 teaching techniques were determined for the
High, Medium, and Low child groups, and the means were compared.

There were positive relationships ($ps < .001$) between the child's cognitive
level and the mean efficacy judgments of the teachers on such teaching techniques as: "Increase the difficulty or complexity of a learning task"; "Instruct
by explaining a task's requirements to the child verbally before or while the child
does the task;" and "Give the child considerable freedom to choose and carry
out learning tasks on his own." On the other hand, no relationship was apparent
for "Take initiative in planning and setting up learning experiences for the
child," or "Inform the child when he makes a correct response." There was also
a negative but nonsignificant relationship for "Give the child individual instruction."

These and other findings suggest not only that the teachers had assimilated
information on the children's differential cognitive skills, but that they could
translate such information into differential prescriptions for effective teaching.
We did not determine whether the teachers actually implemented these prescriptions in their classrooms. Nevertheless, the contents of the differentiating technique statements, and of the statements that were not differentiating, suggest that
the teachers were in tune with the controlling individual-difference dimension.

At the very least, then, the teachers were prepared to alter situational demands in response to the child's individuality.

ARTICULATING THE STANCES

The Two-Phase Scheme

McCall's (1981) two-phase scheme, discussed earlier, provides a framework for joining the moderate and strong stances on the role of individual differences in socialization. We suggest that, for at least some behavioral attributes, and perhaps generally, the moderate stance applies to the first phase in McCall's scheme, whereas the strong stance applies to the second phase. The discussion that follows considers the major assumptions and implications of this interpretation.

The species-typical pathways noted by McCall would be directed toward sequential steps, such as those postulated by the cognitive-developmental approach. With one possible exception, this view is consistent with McCall's characterization of the first phase. The possible exception is that we have reserved judgment on the validity of the interaction assumption, whereas McCall suggests that the first phase is influenced primarily by individual maturational timetables, at least in the case of general intelligence.

The major problem in joining the two stances is that they deal with different phenomena. The moderate stance emphasizes qualitative reorganization at each developmental step in the series. This means that measurement operations applied during the first phase would have to be discontinuous and refer to individual differences in rates-of-attainment. By contrast, the strong stance emphasizes the quantitative properties of attributes. This means that measurement operations applied during the second phase would have to be continuous and refer to individual differences in levels-of-attainment. From the standpoint of the moderate stance, there would be a disjunction between the transient individual differences and the emerging stable traits. From the standpoint of the strong stance, there would be a disjunction in moving from discontinuous measurement to continuous measurement.

The second of these disjunctions might be resolved in the manner suggested earlier. Discontinuity of measurement could be avoided by decomposing an individual-difference construct, such as general intelligence, into its separate attributes. The procedure would be to establish the developmental function form for each attribute and then to determine the age of transition from phase one to phase two by pinpointing when, during the period of major growth, the attribute begins to stabilize. When the developmental function forms of conceptually related attributes are shown to run in parallel, their respective ages of transition are likely to be close to one another, in which case higher order (second phase) constructs could safely by derived without violating the assumption of continuity of measurement.

Assuming that this resolution would be acceptable to the strong stance, consider next how it might be brought to bear in resolving the disjunction created for the moderate stance. Let us grant that the sequential steps cannot be reduced to collections of quantitative attributes. Nevertheless, it is still the case that a qualitative step has a quantitative aspect, though that aspect has not been of primary interest to cognitive-developmental theory (Flavell & Wohlwill, 1969). Consider the familiar example of Piagetian conservation. From a cognitive-developmental perspective, attainment of the ability to conserve can mean that the child has reached a threshold criterion (consolidation) that enables the child to move on to a higher level of cognitive development. And yet the ability to conserve is not an all-or-none matter, but rather a distinct kind of ability that can vary quantitatively. Furthermore, the threshold criterion need not represent "high ability" to conserve. We can imagine designing conservation tasks that most people cannot solve, even though those who cannot solve the difficult tasks would not thereby be unable to perform formal operations. At the same time, those who can solve difficult conservation problems could be said to have "high ability" to conserve.

To summarize the argument thus far, attaining a particular step in a socialization sequence might entail reaching a threshold quantity on a behavioral attribute. Attainment of the threshold value (quantity) would be species typical, making it possible for the child to progress to the next species-typical step in the sequence. At the same time, the child who has just attained the threshold value would have thereby attained only a moderate amount of the behavioral attribute. The amount would be expected to continue to increase in the reference population (mean) and eventually become an individual-difference trait in the strong sense.

The disjunctions under consideration would not occur if the suggested threshold value on the attribute were to be reached at the same time that the attribute begins to stabilize. Figure 11.1 illustrates how this might happen. The period of major growth ends at Age B, when the population mean is b. The strong stance implies that stabilization will begin to occur prior to Age B, but after that age period during which canalization predominates. The moderate stance implies that some threshold value on the attribute, say, a, enables the child to progress toward the next step in the sequence (which would be represented by a different developmental function form). If Age A, the age when the population mean reaches the threshold value, a, were also the age when stabilization begins, Age A would define the transition point between phases one and two, and the two stances would be joined.[1]

---

[1]In this particular illustration the inflection point on the growth curve has been selected to determine the threshold value, a. This device seems plausible though not critical for the argument.

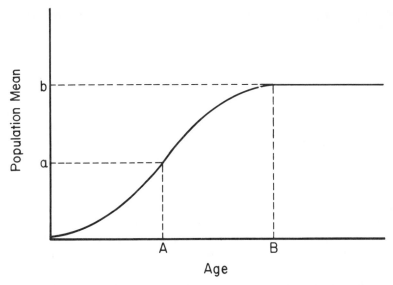

FIG. 11.1. Hypothetical developmental function form for a behavioral attribute.

Although this way of articulating the two stances involves a reduction strategy, it does not altogether substitute quantitative measurement for qualitative measurement, a procedure that would blur important qualitative changes in behavioral development (Wohlwill, 1973). Rather, below-threshold values on continuous behavioral attributes are seen as possible candidates for characterizing one or another step in a developmental sequence (first phase), whereas above-threshold values on continuous behavioral attributes are seen as possible candidates for deriving individual-difference constructs in the strong sense (second phase).

When this dual approach is applied to sets of conceptually related attributes, it may even be possible to broaden the range of continuous attributes under consideration without violating cognitive-developmental assumptions regarding qualitative change. For example, suppose that we knew the developmental function form for each attribute representing a structural underpinning for attaining the threshold value for conservation, the latter signified by a in Fig. 11.1. Suppose further that the population means for all these underpinnings were also to reach their respective threshold values by Age A (Fig. 11.1). We might then be in a position to claim that attainment of the threshold value for conservation depends on threshold attainments of all the conceptually related underpinnings. Note that such a claim does not imply that "conservation" is merely an arbitrary term standing for the collection of underpinnings (reductionism). Moreover, when guided by the two-phase scheme, our attention would be directed to the other (qualitative) steps in the sequence, each of which would be based on a different attribute having its own developmental function form, threshold value, characteristic age of (threshold) attainment in the population, and set of underpinnings.

Integrative Processes

Let us now take stock on several ways that individual differences can bear on intraindividual integrative processes in socialization. We have just suggested one kind of integration that may occur during the first phase: The component attributes underlying a qualitative organization may all reach their respective threshold values by a certain age, enabling the child to integrate them in a new way. If such integrations were to extend across comparably timed steps within different socialization sequences, they would perhaps constitute stage-like integrations.

Another type of integration is that which occurs *across* the two phases. Two examples have already been mentioned. One was the suggested coordination of knowledge about the self's emerging traits with developing understandings of environmental opportunities. The other was the potential for altering the child's adaptability through the development of self-regulatory skills. In these cases the child's location within a developmental sequence (phase one) can be said to be coordinated with the child's location on a stable trait (phase two). (As long as phase-appropriate measurement operations are used within the respective domains, such crossovers between the two phases do not constitute unwarranted paradigm mixing.) These examples serve to illustrate why the study of individual differences that stabilize during early childhood may be very important for understanding integrative processes in socialization that arise during middle childhood.

More commonly, cross-domain relationships have been sought between measures known (or presumed) to be in the second phase. Because in this case all the variables entering into cross-domain relationships would be at least moderately stable, the nexus connecting the two domains also would be expected to be reasonably stable. To illustrate, stable individual differences in preschool children's understandings of word meanings and syntax, measured by test instruments, have been found to correlate positively with at least moderately stable measures of the children's adaptations to free play, with the cross-domain correlations reaching as high as .60 (Emmerich, Cocking, & Sigel, 1979). The evidence also suggests that the stability of verbal intelligence during this age period probably mediates this linkage between cognitive functioning and social functioning.

Finally, from the perspective of the socializing agent, we have seen how individual differences among children call for a variety of balancing acts. When situational requirements are pressing, robust features of the child's individuality will sometimes facilitate and sometimes clash with the immediate demands. When the situational demands are important, but less pressing, socializing agents may attempt to coordinate their efforts in relation to the child's social understandings or adaptational style. And when the socializing agent seizes an opportunity to modify the situation in terms of the child's individuality, care is required so as not to overshoot the mark. Deciding which of these tacks to follow can itself be a complex judgment, and carrying out a chosen course of action in an optimal way will draw on the socializing agent's own integrative skills.

REFERENCES

Baltes, P. B., Reese, H. W., & Nesselroade, J. R. (1977). *Life-span developmental psychology: Introduction to research methods*. Monterey, CA: Brooks/Cole.
Bandura, A. (1982). Self-efficacy mechanism in human agency. *American Psychologist, 37*, 122–147.
Bell, R. Q. (1968). A reinterpretation of the direction of effects in studies of socialization. *Psychological Review, 75*, 81–95.
Block, J. (1971). *Lives through time*. Berkeley, CA: Bancroft Books.
Block, J. (1982). Assimilation, accommodation, and the dynamics of personality development. *Child Development, 53*, 281–95.
Block, J. H., & Block, J. (1980). The role of ego-control and ego-resiliency in the organization of behavior. In W. A. Collins (Ed.), *Minnesota symposia on child psychology* (Vol. 13, pp. 39–101). Hillsdale, NJ: Lawrence Erlbaum Associates.
Buss, A. H., & Plomin, R. (1984). *Temperament: Early developing personality traits*. Hillsdale, NJ: Lawrence Erlbaum Associates.
Emmerich, W. (1968). Personality development and concepts of structure. *Child Development, 39*, 671–690.
Emmerich, W. (1969). The parental role: A cognitive-functional approach. *Monographs of the Society for Research in Child Development, 34*, No. 8.
Emmerich, W. (1971). *Disadvantaged children and their first school experiences: ETS-Head Start longitudinal study. Structure and development of personal-social behaviors in preschool settings* (ETS PR-71-20). Princeton, NJ: Educational Testing Service.
Emmerich, W. (1973). *Disadvantaged children and their first school experiences: ETS-Head Start longitudinal study. Preschool teachers' beliefs on effective teaching techniques and their relationships to pupil characteristics* (ETS PR-73-12). Princeton, NJ: Educational Testing Service.
Emmerich, W. (1977a). Structure and development of personal-social behaviors in economically disadvantaged children. *Genetic Psychology Monographs, 95*, 191–245.
Emmerich, W. (1977b). Evaluating alternative models of development: An illustrative study of preschool personal-social behaviors. *Child Development, 48*, 1401–1410.
Emmerich, W., Cocking, R. R., & Sigel, I. E. (1979). Relationships between cognitive and social functioning in preschool children. *Developmental Psychology, 15*, 495–504.
Fischer, K. W., & Silvern, L. (1985) Stages and individual differences in cognitive development. *Annual Review of Psychology, 36*, 613–648.
Flavell, J. H., & Wohlwill, J. F. (1969). Formal and functional aspects of cognitive development. In D. Elkind & J. H. Flavell (Eds.), *Studies in cognitive development: Essays in honor of Jean Piaget* (pp. 67–127). London and New York: Oxford University Press.
Foa, U. (1968). Three kinds of behavioral changes. *Psychological Bulletin, 70*, 460–473.
Kohlberg, L. (1969). Stage and sequence: The cognitive-developmental approach to socialization. In D. A. Goslin (Ed.), *Handbook of socialization theory and research* (pp. 347–480). Chicago: Rand McNally.

Kohn, M. (1977). *Social competence, symptoms and under-achievement in childhood: A longitudinal perspective.* New York: Wiley.

Laosa, L. M. (1985). Temperament, performance, and culture: Dimensions of early behavioral style in Chicano families. In M. C. Wang (Ed.), *Temperament and school learning* (pp. 19–56). Learning Research and Development Center, University of Pittsburgh: Pittsburgh, PA.

Lerner, J. V., & Lerner, R. M. (1983). Temperament and adaptation across life: Theoretical and empirical issues. In P. B. Baltes & O. G. Brim (Eds.), *Life-span development and behavior* (Vol. 5, pp. 197–228). New York: Academic Press.

Lerner, R. M., & Spanier, G. B. (1978). *Child influences on marital and family interaction: A life-span perspective.* New York: Academic Press.

Maccoby, E. E. (1984). Socialization and developmental change. *Child Development, 55,* 317–328.

Matheny, A. P., Wilson, R. S., & Nuss, S. M. (1984). Toddler temperament: Stability across settings and over ages. *Child Development, 55,* 1200–1211.

McCall, R. (1981). Nature–nurture and the two realms of development. *Child Development, 52,* 1–12.

Mischel, W. (1968). *Personality and assessment.* New York: Wiley.

Mischel, W. (1984). Convergences and challenges in the search for consistency. *American Psychologist, 39,* 351–364.

Moss, H. A., & Susman, E. J. (1980). Longitudinal study of personality development. In O. G. Brim, Jr. & J. Kagan (Eds.), *Constancy and change in human development* (pp. 530–595). Cambridge, MA: Harvard University Press.

Patterson, G. R. (1982). *Coercive family process.* Eugene, OR: Castalia.

Plomin, R. (1983). Developmental behavioral genetics. *Child Development, 54,* 253–259.

Rothbart, M. K., & Derryberry, D. (1981). Development of individual differences in temperament. In M. E. Lamb & A. L. Brown (Eds.), *Advances in developmental psychology* (Vol. 1, pp. 37–86). Hillsdale, NJ: Lawrence Erlbaum Associates.

Scarr, S., & McCartney, K. (1983). How people make their own environments: A theory of genotype-environment correlations. *Child Development, 54,* 424–435.

Scarr-Salapatek, S. (1976). An evoluationary perspective on infant intelligence: Species patterns and individual variations. In M. Lewis (Ed.), *Origins of intelligence: Infancy and childhood* (pp. 165–197). New York: Plenum.

Schaefer, E. S. (1971). Development of hierarchical, configurational models for parent behavior and child behavior. In J. P. Hill (Ed.), *Minnesota symposia on child psychology* (Vol. 5, pp. 130–161). Minneapolis: University of Minnesota Press.

Shantz, C. U. (1983). Social cognition. In J. Flavell & E. Markman (Eds.), *Handbook of child psychology: Vol. 3. Cognitive development* (4th ed., pp. 495–555). New York: Wiley.

Shipman, V. C. (1971). *Disadvantaged children and their first school experiences: Structure and development of cognitive competencies and styles prior to school entry.* (PR-71-19) Princeton, NJ: Educational Testing Service.

Sroufe, L. A. (1983). Infant–caregiver attachment and patterns of adaptation in preschool: The roots of maladaptation and competence. In M. Perlmutter (Ed.), *Minnesota symposia in child psychology* (Vol. 16, pp. 41–83). Hillsdale, NJ: Lawrence Erlbaum Associates.

Sroufe, L. A., & Waters, E. (1977). Attachment as an organizational construct. *Child Development, 48,* 1184–1199.

Thomas, A., & Chess, S. (1977). *Temperament and development.* New York: Brunner/Mazel.

Thomas, A., & Chess, S. (1980). *The dynamics of psychological development,* New York: Brunner/Mazel.

Wohlwill, J. F. (1973). *The Study of Behavioral Development.* New York: Academic Press.

Wohlwill, J. F. (1980). Cognitive development in childhood. In O. G. Brim, Jr. & J. Kagan (Eds.), *Constancy and change in human development* (pp. 359–444). Cambridge, MA: Harvard University Press.

Author Index

Subject Index

A

Academic culture, 172, 173
Acceptance, 67–69
Acculturation, 168
Achievement ethic, 179
Acquaintances, 142
Adaptations, 13, 14, 233–235
  behavioral, 16–18
  mutual, 234, 235
Adaptivity, 226, 233–237
Adolescent Egocentrism, 58
Alternative pathways, 232
Amodal perception, 209, 210
Anal stage, 6
Applied developmental psychology, 24–37, 34
Applied research, 24–37
Assimilation, 109
Attachment theory, 11, 12
Autonomy, 7, 8

B

Behavior
  Diet and, 189–201
  effective, 208
  individual differences and, 225, 226, 232, 233
  intelligent, 13, 14
  situational factors and, 226
  social, 10, 81, 160
Behavior change, 16–19, 233
  asynchronous, 16, 17

effects of ICPS training, 25, 37
synchronous, 16

C

Caldwell Preschool Inventory, 236
Canalization, 230
Child rearing
  deliberate, 132, 133
  nondeliberate, 132, 133
  procedures, 128–130
  propositions, 133–136
Cognitive development, 12–15, 53, 55, 56, 59, 107, 108
  causal factors, 14
  effects of malnutrition on, 190
Cognitive-developmental theory, 53
Cognitive limitations, 48
Cognitive processes, 14
Cognitive skills, 24–25
Cognitive social functioning, 13–15
Communication, 104, 207–220
  affective component. 210–212
  elementary school age, 218–220
  incidental, 209, 211, 212
  innate abilities, 209
  intentional, 209, 211, 212, 214
  interpersonal, 207–209
  intrapersonal, 207–209
  linguistic, 214
  parent–child, 209
  preschool, 217, 218
  preverbal, 214